D0163442

WITHDRAWN

The Mirror

C.W. Eckersberg, *Woman before a Mirror* (1841). Hirschsprung Collection, Copenhagen, Denmark.

THE MIRROR

A History

Sabine Melchior-Bonnet

Translated by

Katharine H. Jewett

with a preface by

Jean Delumeau

Routledge

New York London

The Mirror: A History was originally published in French in 1994
under the title *Histoire du Miroir*

Assistance for the translation was provided by the French
Ministry of Culture.

Published in 2001 by
Routledge
29 West 35th Street
New York, NY 10001

Published in Great Britain by
Routledge
11 New Fetter Lane
London EC4P 4EE

Routledge is an imprint of the Taylor & Francis Group.

Printed in the United States of America on acid-free paper.

10 9 8 7 6 5 4 3 2 1

Library of Congress Cataloging-in-Publication Data
Melchior-Bonnet, Sabine.
[Histoire du miroir. English]
The mirror : a history / Sabine Melchior-Bonnet; translated by Katherine H. Jewett; with a preface by Jean Delumeau.
p. cm.
Includes bibliographical references and index.
ISBN 0-415-92447-2
1. Mirrors—History. I. Title.

QC385 .M4513 2000
155.9'1—dc21 00-042204

Contents

Translator's Note

In French there are two words that are most often used to denote what we know in English as "mirror": *glace* and *miroir*; today they are used almost interchangeably. A *miroir* is a reflective, generally silvery surface of metal, stone, or glass. In earlier times, however, *glace* often meant "glass," mirrored or not. To indicate the technical difference between *glace* and *miroir* in this text, I have translated "miroir" as "mirror" and used "piece of glass," "pane of glass," "looking glass," and simply "glass" to stand for the French "glace." When no technical difference is involved, I have used "mirror" to replace either French term.

The technical detail of Sabine Melchior-Bonnet's history of mirror-making posed a challenge with regard to the French word *étain*, which in English can mean either "tin" or "pewter." In consulting glassmaking manuals that have been translated from French to English, most notably, Alfred Sauzay's *Wonders of Glass-Making in All Ages* (1870), I found that *étain* is translated as "tin" and have used that translation here.

Certain "loaded" terms, such as the French *précieuse*, used to describe a seventeenth-century French woman who puts on airs of nobility and learnedness, appear in the original French. The same is true for the titles of the many untranslated texts cited by the author.

Madame Melchior-Bonnet also uses the term *italien* to refer to inhabitants of Venice in the seventeenth and eighteenth centuries, when there was no Italian nation; the Venetian Republic was its own country. Despite the incorrectness of the term, I have translated her *italien* as "Italian" so that the English translation might be as close as possible to the original French.

In the parts of this text that deal with psychoanalysis, my initial attempts to translate the gender neutrality of reflexive French verbs in phrases like *le sujet peut se dire* ("the subject can say to himself or herself"), proved too cumbersome in English. In the end I chose to revert to a masculine "subject" that represents both genders.

Finally, I would like to acknowledge the indispensable aid of Dr. Kathleen Mulkern Smail in completing this project.

—Katharine H. Jewett, Ph.D.

Preface

As the reader will quickly become aware, this is a dazzling book. In it, Sabine Melchior-Bonnet marries science and art, literature and philosophy, and history and meditation with a mastery and a quality of writing that is, at times, dizzying. Many of us would like to write as she does, or better yet, to know how to find *the* brilliant, exact phrasing that enlightens her reader.

The very idea of a historical essay on the mirror is remarkable. How could we not have thought of it earlier? The development of this now ordinary object, once rare and expensive, has marked out the course of our civilization. To guide us in this voyage through time, Sabine Melchior-Bonnet first recalls the primitive techniques of mirror making: the initial use of metal, the slow perfecting of the process of glassmaking, the difficulties of silvering, the passage from blown glass to cast glass, and the major role in the manufacture of mirrors played first by Murano, Italy, then by the Saint-Gobain Company in France.

In the sixteenth century, both steel and glass mirrors were used. But glass triumphed in the seventeenth century, most notably at Versailles, where 306 panes gave the illusion of eighteen huge, solid mirrors. At the end of the century, two-thirds of Parisian households owned a mirror. In the eighteenth century, the object invaded household decor, encroaching on the domain of tapestries. The *psyché*, or free-standing, full-length mirror on a pivoting frame, became popular in the early nineteenth century, a period that later witnessed the success of the mirrored armoire. Today, of course, we see mirrors everywhere without even taking notice of them.

After offering a thorough and precise history of mirror making, Sabine Melchior-Bonnet changes register (without fully departing from the domain of history) in order to examine the changing significance of the mirror in human society, including the many philosophical, psychological, and moral associations that have developed around it over time, like its relationship to good and evil, God and the devil, man and woman, the self and its reflection, the self-portrait and confession. With so many different leads to follow, the author proves a skillful navigator through fascinating terrain, not allowing us to stray off course.

I believe I can summarize her intent, rich as it is, by using the two categories of positive and negative, the mirror itself being in essence ambivalent. To whomever knew how to look into it, the mirror once offered an untainted image of divinity. Many painters represented Mary and the baby Jesus holding a mirror. One also said in the Middle Ages that God is the perfect mirror because "he is a shining mirror unto himself." Furthermore, Plato affirmed that the soul is the reflection of the divine. Later, Saint Augustine expressed this idea more precisely, in a more tragic mode, suggesting that the man who sees himself in the mirror of the Bible sees both the splendor of God and his own wretchedness. For Dürer, who represented himself as the Suffering Christ, man is the self-portrait of God, and God's face authenticates man's. Yet another aspect of the mirror's meaning was the medieval *speculum*, such as the one compiled by the thirteenth-century Dominican monk Vincent de Beauvais, a vast encyclopedia attempting to catalog all knowledge. Finally, the numerous metaphorical "mirrors" of medieval literature, notably the "mirrors of princes," constituted a moralistic genre in which readers were invited to look upon an ideal model for their behavior.

Despite these divine associations, the mirror's lure was not to be trusted. Narcissus allowed himself to be captivated by his own reflection. Although the mirror could be a trap, it could also—and this was particularly true in the seventeenth and eighteenth centuries—teach manipulation of appearances, of transforming oneself into "an eager sycophant, a rival in love and a counselor to the coquettes." It thus became an indispensable object in a "society of reflections" where "the self needs, in order to exist, to be repeated in visual echos." But what was the mirror if not a trickster? Moralists denounced it vehemently. To them, the mirror attracted "crazed stares," ignited lust, and hid—or unveiled, depending on the circumstances—both demon and death. In their discourse, "vanities," mirrors, and skeletons were all interrelated. The mirror was a dangerous and deceptive tool: "In duplication, dissimilarities creep in." The right hand in the mirror is the left hand of the one who is reflected. Moreover, using technical knowledge one could exploit the mystifying powers of the mirror to produce calculated deformations, induce delirium, and indeed depict a decomposition of the self.

The mirror was and is particularly ambiguous for women. It is true that woman "awakens to life when she has access to her own image" and the mirror will always be "the privileged and vulnerable province of femininity." But Cervantes warned: "Woman is a brilliant crystal mirror that the slightest breath dulls and obscures." And Simone Weil observed, "A beautiful woman, looking at herself in the mirror, might believe she is only that. But an ugly woman knows she is not only that."

These few extracts from the brilliant work of Sabine Melchior-Bonnet constitute but a brief sampling. The entire book should be quoted—and therefore must be read. For it bears witness to a vast body of knowledge and reveals a true writer who addresses a great and beautiful subject with flair.

—Jean Delumeau

Introduction

Small, rare, expensive, valuable—for centuries such were the only mirrors in existence until the Royal Saint-Gobain Company in Paris perfected a manufacturing process that expanded its production and thereby enlarged its clientele. At the end of the seventeenth century, the philosopher Saint-Simon recorded the exorbitant price paid for a mirror by the countess de Fiesque: "I had," she said, "a nasty piece of land that brought in nothing but wheat; I sold it and in return I got this beautiful mirror. Did I not work wonders—some wheat for this beautiful mirror?"[1] And Gédéon Tallemant des Réaux, a chronicler of seventeenth-century France, reported the following ordeal of one Monsieur d'Orgeval: "Our large mirror is broken. Five hundred écus up the ass!"[2]

Ardently coveted, but no larger than a dinner plate, the mirror was for a long time a symbol of aristocratic luxury, a means of maintaining appearance. Situated at the crossroads of nature and culture, it educated the eye and assisted in relaying lessons in civility. From a glance in the mirror flowed not only a taste for ornament and an attention to social display and hierarchy, but also a new geography of the body, which made visible previously unfamiliar images (one's back and profile) and stirred up sensations of modesty and self-consciousness. At the time of the

French Revolution, a great noblewoman, arrested in her home, thought to take only two objects with her to prison: "I took for myself, without even thinking, a small mirror in a cardboard frame and a pair of new slippers."[3] Her own image was all she possessed; even while destitute in prison, this supreme concern with appearance for her signaled a mastery over the self.

Estate inventories and illustrated documents allow us to date the first appearance of the pure and flat "crystal" mirror, and to trace the spread of its use. The mirror's transformation from luxury object to everyday trinket, so well integrated into our daily life today, developed slowly, impeded not only by technical and economic obstacles, but also by psychological and moral misgivings. We are now so accustomed to encountering our image at every turn in mirrors, photographs, and on videotape that it is difficult to measure the extraordinary impact on human sensibilities brought about by the possibility of seeing oneself from head to toe in a mirror, not to mention the upheaval in the perception of space caused by the invention of mirrored panels between doors and windows. How did one live with a face or clothe a body that, without the aid of the mirror, one knew only through the gaze of others? Imagine the astonishment of meeting one's mirror image for the first time? How was the mirror's upsetting of equilibrium, its emptiness and fullness, and its sense of being outside and inside first experienced?

It is difficult in the course of historical inquiry to recapture emotions, perceptions, and nuances of past sentiment and sensibilities, to fully absorb what historian Alain Corbin calls a "measure of meanings," whose fleeting traces are revealed only incidentally.[4] Locating and interpreting these traces must take place within a system of perception and representation that changes according to each era. An initial difficulty facing us lies in the fact that all "objective" data—royal accounts, estate inventories, treatises on manners, correspondence, memoirs—favor court society and city life over rural life. The second difficulty can be found in the multiple meanings of the word *mirror:* the semantic range of the term extends to extreme poles, from that of myth to the literature of the self, and from the symbolic to the literal. Moreover, these meanings sometimes blur together. The mirror makes an early appearance in the vocabulary of the theologian, where it gives rise to a moral—and enduring—discourse that charts out the capacity for self-examination and develops the dialectic of essence and appearance. On the other hand, the mirror image as an element of identity in autobiographical accounts comes about much later and much less frequently.

A third challenge stems from the notion that historical study should include literary observation—the insight of the writer comes in the firsthand grappling with problems of perception. The scope of this study was thus enlarged to include fictional narratives when they converged with scientific observation, nonetheless taking into account in these sources the personal sensitivities of an author, the rhetoric of an era, and just how far the symbolic vicissitudes of a word can stray from the reality of practice. Finally, the mirror shares, with the art of painting, an emphasis on the worth of the image, resemblance, and simulation, all of which are intertwined with the theme of looking at one's self. The visual arts are thus inseparable from any study of the mirror.

The importance of the mirror image to the organization of personality was underscored a century ago by psychologists such as Henri Wallon, Paul Schilder, and Jean Lhermitte, who recognized that the construction of the subject was progressive and implied the conscious differentiation between the exterior world and other people. The subject, capable of objectivizing himself and of coordinating exterior perceptions with interior sensations, can then progress from the consciousness of the body to the consciousness of the self. This notion of "bodily projection," the representation that each person makes of his or her body in space which culminates in its recognition in the mirror, was revisited by psychoanalysis, which instead prefers the idea of a "libidinal structure" of the image of the body. Psychoanalysts believe that it is desire that gives shape to the disparate details of the senses. This structure is incorporated into the famous "mirror stage in the developing function of the I," described by Jacques Lacan in 1949.[5] To Lacan, the image of the body is integral to the development of symbolic activity: the child in front of the mirror progresses from perceiving piecemeal images of his body to recognizing its unity. The child takes pleasure in the spectacle of himself and, at the same time he understands the difference between the image and its model; standing before the mirror he acquires a new capacity for mental projection. As an enlargement of mental space, the specular image is not a fixed unity, but rather a constructed one requiring concentration to maintain it. One's own mirror image is never so internalized as to make the mirror a primary means of identification and self-representation; but failure to recognize it can indicate the onset of serious psychological problems.

The mirror, "matrix of the symbolic," accompanies the human quest for identity. In order to grasp the magical, miraculous quality of the first face-to-face encounter with the mirror, one must turn to narratives rich in mythic imagery. Narcissus is the first hero of this troubling encounter with the self, but an eighteenth-century Korean tale breathes new life into his experience.[6] It is the story of a poor pottery merchant, Pak, whose wife has but one dream—to possess a bronze mirror. When her husband returns with the coveted object, she discovers with stupefaction an unknown face. Pak appeared to have come back to her alone, but now as she gazes upon his image she sees a woman standing next to him and wonders, "Who is that tramp?" For the first time Madame Pak sees herself, and she fails to understand that the woman next to her husband is herself. Pak then grabs the mirror and sees in it a man whom he takes to be his wife's lover. Arguments, screams, and insults ensue. The couple heads to the prefect in order to settle the dispute, bringing with them their apple of discord. It is then the prefect's turn to gaze at the magical object and see a civil servant dressed in uniform. Could this be his newly arrived successor, now come to replace him . . .

As contrived as it may seem, this story nonetheless remains significant. The tale has counterparts in many cultures.[7] To see oneself in the mirror, to identify oneself, requires a mental operation by which the subject is capable of objectivizing himself, of separating what is outside from what is inside. This operation can be successful if the subject recognizes the reflection as his own likeness and can say, "I am the other of that other." The relationship of self to self and the familiarity of the self cannot be directly established and remains trapped in the reciprocity of seeing and being seen. The particularity of human conduct in front of the mirror—the symbolic inscription of the subject—has been established in a series of experiments that examined animals' reactions when placed before a mirror.[8] Only mature chimpanzees were able to identify themselves; however, even then their recognition does not appear to develop into the process of psychic structuring found in humans.

There are many ways to look at oneself in the mirror: with fear, modesty, joy, complacency, or defiance. One can look for resemblance or difference, kinship or foreignness. The mirror image can be remarkably accurate but can also be distorted and imperfect. Men of the eighteenth century, by then familiar with household mirrors, did not look at themselves in the same manner as men of the twelfth century, for whom the reflected image went hand in hand with the devil. More profoundly, the representation of the self depended on a complex idea of humankind, at one time both being and appearing. This sense was elaborated at the same time as relations of the soul to the body developed and as the individual became defined according to his ties to God, to others and to himself. As long as the body was excluded from the subjective, true self, the mirror returned only a mere semblance, open to manipulation and lies. But it is also this semblance, in its continuity, that proves to man that he really exists, just as he did the day before. In his novel *Les Jeunes-France* (1833), Théophile Gautier's hero, Rodolphe, assures himself before the mirror each morning that "he had not grown horns in his sleep." While seeming a frivolous gesture, the gaze in the mirror nonetheless confirms the subject's integrity in the face of concerns about mutilation and dismemberment.

Lacan's mirror stage, whereby the individual discovers himself "within" and "without" through the gaze of an other, has operated throughout centuries of history. The notions of subjectivity and identity were first established within religious and social realms, where self-portraiture and autobiography, the habitual practices of reflection and of introspection, are first played out. Against this backdrop, one who gazes at himself in the mirror strives to regain the resemblance that unites man with his creator and the solidarity that links him to his peers. His singularity and diversity are less important than his universality. But in his self-study, he may also leave the reassuring boundaries of known models and discover a strange and troubling representation of himself in which he perceives traces of the radical other, and where his awareness of himself becomes troubled and alienated. The mirror thus underscores the hazy, inverted, and intentionally distorted nature of any self-portrait.

Such is the ambiguity and richness of the reflection, at once identical to and different from the original. These two sides of the mirror, opposed here for the sake of analysis, are in day-to-day reality fused into a complex alloy—a person is always both the same and otherwise, similar and different, with countless faces. The problem of the mirror as an instrument of self-knowledge has been transformed over the centuries and has not been exhausted by the object's lowly status today. Although it has become entirely commonplace, the mirror retains its magical, mystifying, and creative power. "What secret do you seek in your cracked mirror?" wonders the narrator of Georges Perec's 1967 novel, *A Man Asleep*, his doleful eye riveted to the mirror.[9]

Part One

THE ORIGIN OF THE MIRROR

I will have a magnificent drawing room. . . . I shall have three mirrors in there, each seven feet high. I have always liked that kind of somber, magnificent decoration. "I wonder what the measurements are of the largest mirror they make at Saint-Gobain?" And the man who had just spent three-quarters of an hour thinking of taking his own life promptly climbed on to a chair to hunt in his bookshelves for the Saint-Gobain mirror catalogue.

—Stendhal, *Armance*

1

The Secret of Venice

Metal Mirrors and Glass Mirrors

The First Mirrors

Even though the mirror was for centuries a rare object endowed with magical and often disturbing powers, it would be wrong to speak of a pre-mirror and a post-mirror schism. Man has been interested in his own image since prehistoric times, using all sorts of expedients—from dark and shiny stones to pools of water—in order to catch his reflection. The myths of Narcissus, who is enchanted by his own image, and Perseus, who makes Medusa see herself in his shield, bear witness to this early curiosity toward reflecting surfaces. Indeed, even in his own shadow, man had already found his double. He had to wait centuries, however, before he could obtain a bright, clear, and true image of himself. The metaphorical distance from the polished surface of a small lead mirror to the great mirrors manufactured by the Saint-Gobain Company is about the same as that between oilpaper panes and the glass display windows of department stores. The act of seeing oneself between two mirrors—whether in profile or from behind—is, in proportion to the scale of history, very recent.

Greek mirror carried by a slave (c. 440 B.C.). Cambridge.

Ancient Mediterranean civilizations were obsessed with beauty. Mycenea, Greece, Etruria, Rome and, before them, Egypt, made mirrors of metal, most often by mixing an alloy of copper and tin.[1] Bronze was also used, but in very thin sheets to minimize rusting. Appropriately, the invention of the mirror was attributed to Hephaistos, the Greek god of fire and metal. Scenes of elegant Corinthians gazing at themselves in small disks of polished metal attached to handles or footstands and sometimes decorated on the back with mythological scenes can be seen on antique pottery from the fifth century B.C. More refined mirrors were made of silver, or more rarely, of gold; silvering and gilding were applied with heat. Nearly always rounded, these mirrors were either concave or convex, the former enlarging the size of the reflected object, the latter reducing it. Ancient mirrors were generally very small—roughly five to eight inches in diameter—and were used primarily in three ways: as pocket mirrors enclosed in cases; as grooming mirrors equipped with a welded handle and a ring so they could be held before a master's face by his slave while he went about his daily grooming and then hung on the wall; and finally, as stationary mirrors propped on a three-legged stand, which often depicted a feminine or masculine silhouette. Scrolls, palms, and crowns decorated the metal or wood frames of the polished disk. Their owners took great care of them and protected them from rust, stains, and scratches with fabric coverings, remnants of which are still visible in the specimens that exist today.

Mirrors similar to Greek ones with handles, footstands, and cases have been found in the tombs of Etruscan women. As for wealthy Roman women, their inability to deprive themselves of such objects merited this reprimand by Seneca, "For a single one of these mirrors of chiseled silver or gold, inlaid with gems, women are capable of spending an amount equal to the dowry the State once offered to poor generals' daughters!"[2] Romans later invented new shapes, producing square or rectangular mirrors, perhaps borrowed from the Etruscans, with ivory handles. Fine sponges were attached to the frames and were used to clean the metal, which needed to be polished before each use. Eventually servants themselves acquired mirrors, and silver surpassed bronze as the preferred metal. Under the Roman Empire, mirrors were also used by men. Lucius Apuleius, the philosopher and writer, owned one, and satirical poet Juvenal mocked the emperor Otho, who counted his mirror among the principal pieces of his military equipment! Among the most wealthy, mirrors reached such large proportions that one's entire body could be viewed in them: *Specula totis paria corporibus* [Mirrors equal to the whole of the body], said Seneca. In exceptional cases, even the walls of apartments were sometimes inlaid with mirrors.[3]

Besides metal, Romans also valued obsidian, a very black and transparent volcanic rock, for its reflective powers, even though, as Pliny the Elder, author of *Natural History*, noted, this stone "reveals the shadows of objects much more than the objects themselves."[4] Pieces of polished obsidian more than six thousand years old have been found in Anatolia. Pliny, who collected abundant documentation on the different materials used in his time, also mentions mirrors of black carbuncle, and emerald mirrors that belonged to the emperor Nero. Some of these mirrors were used to adorn palaces. Nero covered his Domus Auria ("golden house") with reflective phengite (a type of mica) that "gave off such a dazzling glow that they overpowered the natural light of day."[5] Seneca remarked, "He is truly poor whose room is not lined with a few panes of glass."[6] Pliny recorded that the emperor Domitian, susceptible to great anxieties, had the walls of his porticos covered with squares of phengite, so that he could view what was going on behind him as he strolled, and thus was able to arm himself in advance against the dangers that he believed threatened his life.[7]

Whether the ancients were familiar with glass mirrors is a matter of debate.[8] Only two written references have been found; the first by a commentator on Aristotle, Alexander of Aphrodisias, in the third century A.D., and the second is found in the work of Pliny the Elder, who attributes the invention of glass mirrors to the inhabitants of Sidon (now Saida in Lebanon), "makers of glass." Glass mirrors that have been found in archaeological digs date back no further than the third century A.D. Dozens have been inventoried, primarily from Egypt, Gaul, Asia Minor, and Germany. They are extremely small (from roughly under one to three inches in diameter), and their usefulness was limited; indeed, they make one think of amulets or jewelry rather than of objects for grooming. The 1895 digs at Antinoë in Egypt uncovered some small, well-preserved convex mirrors, roughly carved and backed with lead: one was set in a frame of plaster, the other, in a small metal crown, between the hands of a young girl. Slightly colored, the glass capsule was made with a blowing rod, and in the convex curve behind the lens there is a layer of melted lead, on which a coating of gold or of tin was applied. Variations on this mirror-making process prevailed for centuries. Given the difficulty of the procedure and the poor quality of the results, metallic mirrors were preferred over glass for many years to come.

The Arrival of Glass Mirrors

As long as a technique for producing flat, thin, and clear glass remained elusive, and as long as it was impossible to spread a hot layer of metal onto glass without causing breakage induced by thermal shock, the glass mirror could never exceed a small tea saucer in size. Progress was slow and benefited from all sorts of indirect contributions. The first obstacle to overcome was the opaque quality of glass. Composed of sand containing iron oxide, early glass gave off a blue-green hue that diminished its transparency. Attempts at decoloration through the addition of manganese oxide resulted in glass of a dirty yellow or gray color and produced air bubbles. Results were somewhat improved when the proportions of ingredients in the glass itself were modified: repeated attempts at adding a mixture of soda, potash, and fern ashes to limestone and manganese eventually produced the desired colorlessness. Still, glassmakers during the Middle Ages were, for a long time, more successful at producing colored glass and jewelry stones than clear glass.

A second difficulty consisted in making glass regular and flat enough to serve as plate or stained glass windows. Théophile the monk, a twelfth-century scribe, made numerous references in his writings to contemporary glassmaking techniques. French glassmakers were considered masters of the art, and in his writings, Théophile revealed their formula—two parts beech tree ashes to one part washed sand—and their method, glassblowing procedures inherited from the ancients.[9] This technique was perfected throughout the Middle Ages: while the ball of glass was attached to a stem and blown, it was rotated rapidly; the glass flared out into a sort of tray from which very small irregular squares were cut and then set in lead to serve as windowpanes.

The technique of cylindrical glassworking—the only process that permitted the manufacture of mirrors—was the next step. A regular, cylindrical "sleeve" was blown through a straw; the two ends were cut off and the whole piece was spliced lengthwise and spread over a flat hearth. Glass produced in this way had a natural shine and was of a fairly uniform thickness. But there was much breakage before the technique was mastered, and for a long time oiled paper was preferred for windows over expensive glass panes. In a famous story, the duke of Northumberland, upon leaving his castle, had all of the glass panes in his windows removed to ensure their safety during his absence![10] When Marie de Médicis replaced her stained-glass windows with clear glass, it was regarded as an unprecedented luxury. In 1674, during Louis XIV's siege of Dôle, La Grande Mademoiselle (Anne-Marie-Louise d'Orléans, duchess of Montpensier) decamped to a country house where, she remarked disparagingly, all the window frames were made of paper except one, fitted with glass panes and "even then the middle of the glass was a lamp bottom!"[11] In short, the glass window was rare and small in the early years of the eighteenth century and alongside clear glass, oiled paper was still much in use: Didérot's 1781 *Encyclopédie* describes the work of *chassissiers*, professionals who covered windows with paper.

To the general difficulties of glass manufacture, mirror making adds the complication of reflective silvering. As mentioned previously, one ancient technique, used by the Romans, consisted in applying hot lead to a layer of glass, but the glass layer that served as a support had to be fairly thin and regular to resist the heat. After the ball of glass was blown, melted lead was poured into a concave bowl and was then removed. The mirror was never larger than what could be cut from the glass ball, and

Quentin Metsys, *The Moneychanger and His Wife* (1514). Louvre, Paris, France.

the curvature gave it a bulging shape that can be found in Flemish paintings and German engravings of the fifteenth and sixteenth centuries. This is the mirror on the table in Quentin Metsys's *Moneychanger and His Wife* and on the bedroom wall in Van Eyck's *Arnolfini Portrait;* no larger than a tea saucer and reflecting a distorted image. One hundred fifty years later, Velásquez's *Las Meninas*, and De Witte's *Woman at the Keyboard* present perfectly flat mirrors of larger dimensions.

Many ancient texts mention mirrors silvered with lead and boast of the clarity of their reflections, but clarity is relative. In his *Speculum majus* (c. 1250), Vincent de Beauvais judged glass mirrors "silvered" with lead to be superior to those of polished metal because "glass is a better receptor of light rays due to its transparency." Soon thereafter, John Peckham, a Franciscan from Oxford, wrote a treatise on optics that mentioned glass mirrors covered in lead along with mirrors of steel, copper, and polished marble. He noted that if the lead was scraped away from glass mirrors, no image could be reflected.[12]

The technique of silvering mirrors made rather slow progress. In the thirteenth century, small, rounded mirrors were made in Basel and exported to Genoa.[13] In the fourteenth century, Florentine artisans learned how to apply lead without heat and soon lead was being replaced with tin or pewter. The Venetian alchemist Fioravanti speaks of German mirror makers who applied a "mixture of lead, tin, silver and wine sediment to the globe of the glass. They brush it on and the mixture attaches itself to the glass; then, they cut the globes into round pieces that become the aforementioned mirrors."[14] Traffic in quicksilver through Anvers at the beginning of the sixteenth century indicates that mirror makers were then using mercury for silvering. This technique circulated throughout northern Europe. As luxury objects, mirrors became widespread in châteaux, then in bourgeois homes in the cities, and eventually were sold at major fairs. But they did not replace the larger and more easily handled steel mirrors that were used for daily grooming.

The silvered glass mirror produced only a very imperfect image and the curious enjoyed them especially for their optical distortions: in the château of Hesdin, in the fifteenth century, the accounts of the financial manager of the duke of Burgundy reveal that at the door of the entrance gallery there was a "mirror with several visible stains" in which visitors who looked at themselves appeared disfigured. Moreover, notes a contemporary, "one sees someone else there rather more than oneself."[15] Of modest dimensions, these mirrors served mostly as architectural and personal decoration. They were sometimes attached to clothing and can be found, rather surprisingly, in religious ceremonies. Early in his career as a metallurgist, after having succeeded in making metal and then glass mirrors, Johannes Gutenberg sold them to pilgrims traveling to Aix-la-Chapelle (now Aachen in Germany, the site of Charlemagne's shrine), so they could attach them to their hats. Pilgrims believed that mirrors were able to attract and capture the grace emanating from holy relics, despite the crowds that prevented them from getting close to the altars and relics themselves.[16] The prodigious properties of mirrors, studied by scholars from the Middle Ages, and in particular by the famous Oxford school, did not fail to interest literary writers as well. Jean de Meung, the thirteenth-century poet, dedicates two hundred and fifty lines of the *Roman de la Rose* to the "marvelous powers of the mirror."[17] At the time, most commentators viewed science and the supernatural as intimately linked, and as an art of fire, the manufacture of glass shored the prestige of the alchemist's quest for the philosopher's stone. The transformation of half-solid, half-liquid molten glass into a transparent and rigid substance indeed seemed like alchemy.

Thanks to a valuable witness, Volcyr de Sérouville, secretary to the duke of Lorraine, we have a methodical study of the techniques and centers of mirror production in the duchy in the early sixteenth century. A curious and precise observer, he admits a fascination for "this marvelous artifice."[18] Thanks to him we know how the worker pierced the molten glass with "an iron attached to the end of a stick," how he pulled out "the glowing timber which, once blown and rolled out on a plank became so round and swollen that it took the form and size of large, average and small mirrors, as needed." The worker then applied lead "with great skill in order to reveal the luster and reverberation of those things placed in front of said mirrors." In elaborating at length on the properties of the mirror and the reproduction of the image, "a process in which clarity [is] distilled from matter," the author seeks to share his admiration with an ignorant reader to whom he can explain at once both the causes and the effects of the reflection.

Volcyr lists next the great glass-producing centers of Lorraine of his era: Banville-aux-miroirs, Saint-Quirin, Raon, Nicolas-Blamontois. Their reputation extended "far beyond Christianity," affirms another chronicler, who proudly concludes: "there are no people as ingenious as the Lorrains, who have invented a way to make mirrors of glass."[19] Mirror manufacture in Lorraine eventually declined under the weight of wars and Venetian competition.

The Venetians still challenge the Lorraines over who was the first to perfect glass making. In fact, from the second half of the fifteenth century, glassmakers from Murano knew how to make a glass so pure, white, and fine that they called it "crystalline" because of its similarities to rock crystal, whose transparency and shine it resembled. Thus it was distinguished from "common glass." The historian Vincenzo Lazari attributes this innovation to a family of master glassmakers, the Berovieris, in 1463, but artisans from other regions also claimed a share of credit for the success. There were glassworks at Verona from 1402, and also in Padua, Bologna, Ravenna, and Ferrara. At this time, the Azémar family also claimed that it had been producing crystal for two hundred years in Languedoc. The glassworks of Bohemia were also famous in the sixteenth century. Indeed, Germans figure among the possible inventors of the modern glassmaking process, as two glassmakers from Murano, the Del Gallos, seemed to confirm in 1503. They declared that they were the only ones to know "the secret of making mirrors of crystalline glass, a most valuable and singular thing . . . unknown throughout the world, except for one house in Germany and one in Flanders, who sell their mirrors at excessive prices." In order to upstage competitors, the Del Gallos asked the Venetian Republic to grant a period of twenty-five years during which they would have the exclusive right to practice and perfect their technique in complete tranquility.[20]

The Venetian reputation was established enough to attract workers from northern Europe and to overtake its competition. François du Tisal, a master glassmaker, obtained authorization from the Duke of Lorraine to leave the region in order to study the Venetian process on site. Although the Italian doge recoiled at the idea of hosting foreign craftsmen, du Tisal received permission to establish himself in Venice and to build a furnace there, as long as he agreed to share his own vast knowledge of making "tablets and plates of glass for windows." After two years of training, du Tisal returned to Lorraine in 1505 and obtained authorization from the duke to create a new glassworks for "the manufacture of said crystalline" in the Darney forest. Soon thereafter, however, the Venetian glassmaking industry expanded and wiped out all competitive initiatives from abroad.

What exactly was their secret, the source of so much wealth for the republic of Venice? Thomaso Garzoni de Bagnacavallo, in his *Piazza universale*, offers three explanations for the superiority of Murano mirrors: the salinity of the sea water, the beauty and the clarity of the flame (due to the woods used in the firing process), and the quantities of salt and soda.[21] What brought about these results, in fact, was the quality and proportion of the components, combined with the artisans' experience accumulated over hundreds of years. From 1255 on, artisans, makers of flasks or pearls of glass, settled at Murano, and Venetian glassmakers didn't waste any time in joining them there, either because they believed themselves to be more sheltered from fires that ravaged Venice, or because they sought to protect their secrets from the curious. Moreover, the Venetian Republic nurtured them and treated them more like artists than artisans. It protected and monitored them, and granted them many privileges, such as the right to marry daughters of nobles.

Some of these families even became celebrities. The Berovieris, the Briatis, the Bertolinis, the Mottas, and the Del Gallos were all great masters who relentlessly pursued the perfection of their craft. Their efforts bore fruit: they realized that the ashes of kali, an herb that they brought back from Egypt by boat, when mixed with a certain quantity of sand, acted as a bleaching agent because of its low phosphorous content and richness in manganese. Thus, they obtained a molten glass that was especially white. By randomly modifying the proportions, they found the formula for silicate of potash and lime, whose properties would not be surpassed until the nineteenth century with the manufacture of a glass made from silicate of potash and lead—crystal, in the modern sense of the word. As they were perfecting the technique of cylindrical blowing, the Venetians improved silvering by combining tin and mercury. With this they arrived at this "divinely beautiful, pure and incorruptible object, the mirror." It was "certainly a beautiful and useful invention, among all other things," stated Vannuci Beringaccio (d. 1539), "even if the price is excessive."[22] But soon these costly efforts would pay off and make Venice rich for two centuries.

The alchemist Fioravanti, who in 1564 published his *Miroir des arts et des sciences*, a work translated into French in 1584 and republished several times, echoes the story of this work of wonder and details the firing process, without offering precise details regarding the relative quantities of the components: "In the furnace they form a ball of glass, and trim it to make square pieces of the size that pleases them. They put them on an iron palette and turn them in the furnace until they spread across the palette," and, he added, "such mirrors are also made in Germany." Even so, Fioravanti doesn't neglect the production of steel mirrors, which had recently achieved a remarkable quality. He also offers the recipe for various alloys: for a pound of one made from bronze and tin, add "one ounce of crystalline arsenic, one half-ounce of silver antimony, and a half ounce of charred wine sediment; mix everything together and let it melt and liquify for at least four hours." These processes, notes the alchemist, "seem miraculous even though they are natural."

Although the Venetian monopoly was jealously guarded, the city was unable to prevent the emigration of some workers to northern countries. Mirrors from Venice were exported not only to the rest of Europe, but to the East as well. The Isfahan palace (located in modern Iran) had its room of mirrors, while at the Lahore palace, the walls of the royal apartments were covered in pure gold with beautiful Venetian mirrors hung at eye level around the entire perimeter.[23] And yet, due to its lack of innovation, this marvelous industry faltered and submitted to assaults from powerful rivals. Certainly Venice produced the purest mirrors in the world, set in precious frames made of beveled glass borders and skillfully adjusted with metal screws. However, despite its efforts and the beauty of these frames that prolonged the mirror's usefulness, for a lengthy period Venice could not find a way to enlarge the format and dimensions of its tray-sized mirrors. They hardly surpassed forty square inches in the eighteenth century since glass blowing techniques were incapable of creating larger surfaces.[24] According to several accounts, the Italian industry collapsed in about 1685, when confronted with competition from France and Bohemia.

A Costly Luxury

The Mirror in the Sixteenth Century

Beware of being cuckolded
By a woman painting her face
Whose thoughts are far from her marriage
Carrying a crystalline mirror.[25]

The woman at her toilette has always attracted the wrath of censors and the scorn of misogynists. To them her polished beauty hides a heart of stone and her flirtatiousness inevitably leads to her husband's ruin. The young couple in Claude Mermet's *Farce Joyeuse et Récréative* must have paid dearly for the small "crystalline mirror" the author describes! But was it really made of crystal or was it more likely a counterfeit? Throughout the entire sixteenth century the glassworks of Lorraine strove to sell mirrors "with a crystalline appearance" to compete with those from Venice, without ever reaching the same degree of perfection. Many of the great centers of Lorraine, mentioned by Volcyr de Sérouville, ended up stagnating and disappearing completely. The real Venetian mirror remained a rare object in the sixteenth century, and for two more centuries, polished metal mirrors remained the most widespread.

The small steel mirror was an everyday object that could be bought at the fair or at the clothier's. Street vendors passing through town recruited clients with the well-known, rhyming cry of "Little mirrors shiny and snug / Ready to reflect your ugly mug!" The ambulatory merchant in another contemporary account sang "I sell purses, belts and laces / I know how to tie-up your shoes / and have mirrors for the sweetest faces."[26]

Common mirrors made of tin did not cost too much if they were small—10 or 15 sols at the beginning of the sixteenth century, and 20 or 30 by the end.[27] When compared with other objects appraised in estate inventories, they are equivalent to the price of a wool sweater, five pairs of gloves, or a small oak chair. A haberdasher from Auxerre, Julien Delaforge, left "eight illuminated mirrors" at a value of 70 sols in his inventory of 1586.[28] In Marseille, the merchant Jean-Baptiste Munitian had nine mirrors in stock, alongside gloves and hats, indicating an active trade.

Venetian mirrors, or at least "Venetian style" mirrors, could also be purchased, but only from well-stocked, high-end haberdashers who specialized in valuable objects. One such merchant,

André Clément, kept a boutique called the "Fleur de Lys" in the rue Saint-Jacques in Paris. His 1520 inventory mentions "two mirrors from Venice," in a sizable stock of merchandise valued at 5,530 pounds.[29] Indeed, the beautiful Venetian mirror could not be found just anywhere, and was even more difficult to find outside the city of Paris. Black, polished jet stone often replaced crystal. Philippe Duplessis-Mornay, Henri IV's superintendent general of mines, was lucky to find a stock of "five beautiful mirrors of jet" on a trip, which he quickly bought for his wife so that she might distribute them as she pleased, but he added, "I want you to keep the big mirror that I bought for you as it is extremely rare and its like has not been seen."[30] This rare object is perhaps a Venetian mirror with a crystal border.

From this point on, mirrors could be had at any price and of any quality. An indispensable tool for grooming, the mirror (along with a "case" and a "comb") was part of the trousseau of young urbanites. The pocket mirror was as big as a modern powder compact, enclosed in a round or square box made of ivory, ebony or, more modestly, of the wood of a pear tree. It was worn at the belt; thus, at any time of day a lady could reapply rouge to her cheeks or adjust the position of her bonnet.[31] It was this mirror that the woman in a ballad by Eugène Deschamps demands from her fiancé, creating a bone of contention between them:

> A mirror so I can admire myself
> You must give me one of the ivory ones
> And the case that is noble and genteel
> Hung from silver chains.[32]

These mirrors sometimes served as jewelry, like those in the inventory of the treasury of Charles V, with their silver- or gold-enameled cases, decorated with sapphires and pearls (1380). The mirrors themselves have for the most part disappeared, but their cases, engraved with scenes of hunting or of love, have survived.[33]

Larger than the pocket mirror, the *miroir de toilette*, or grooming mirror, recalled the mirrors of the ancients. It was fitted with a sleeve of wood, carved ivory, or engraved silver according to its price, and a small shutter, or piece of fabric, protected the polished surface from rust or scratches. These hand-held mirrors are visible in the many reproductions found in etchings in miniature from the Renaissance. They were occasionally mounted on a sculpted stand called a *demoiselle* or a "valet," which allowed the mirror to stand upright on furniture, and even to be inclined if equipped with a stem. The stand was sometimes as tall as a human being. Jeanne d'Evreux's 1372 last will and testament mentions a "demoiselle of gilded silver in the shape of a siren holding a mirror." The panel from the famed tapestry *The Lady and the Unicorn* entitled "Sight" gives an indication of the mirror's modest dimensions, which at the time did not surpass sixteen inches, including the frame.

An Irresistible Infatuation

Throughout the sixteenth century, steel and glass mirrors were used jointly. In his *Blasons domestiques contenant la décoration d'une maison honnête* [*Domestic Heraldry Borne by Respected Houses,* 1539], Gilles Corrozet admires both his "very clear steel mirror" and "the rather darkened glass mirror." Valuable auxiliary of light and beauty, the mirror held a choice position among household furnishings and lent its brilliance to meagerly lighted households. "It should be a mirror of good size," insists Corrozet. The engraving that accompanies his first edition displays a mirror about the size of a human head mounted on a stand that is fairly high and very ornate. François I did not neglect to order four or five steel mirrors of large dimension from his jewelers, Guillaume Hotman and Allard Plommyer, in 1533 and 1534.[34] More frequently, royal or princely mirrors were made of silver and gold and were set in rare and expensive frames, like that of Gabrielle d'Estrée, which was garnished with diamonds

LES BLASONS

Le blaſon du

MIROIR.

Iroir cler & reſplendiſ ſant,
Miroir plaiſant, reſiouyſ ſant,
Miroir ardant de grand ſplendeur,

From Gilles Corrozet, *Blasons Domestiques* (1539).

and rubies and valued at 750 pounds in 1599. Within the aristocracy, the crystal mirror only gradually replaced the metal mirror which almost completely disappeared from estate inventories in the last third of the seventeenth century. In about 1650, in his *Perspective curieuse* (1638), Jean-François Niceron offers yet another recipe for making concave steel mirrors for experimental purposes. A century later, a cutler, Jean-Jacques Perret, received a certificate from the *Académie royale des Sciences* because "he was able to endow steel with a polish as beautiful as that of silver." His invention was suggested for those who wanted to learn how to shave their own faces.[35]

But for one who had gazed upon himself in a Venetian mirror, there was no comparison. François I, fond of all novelties and a lover of luxury and Italian art, hastened to order such Venetian mirrors from his goldsmiths. In 1532 Allard Plommyer delivered one to him that was decorated with gold and precious stones. The following year, Jehan Grain furnished him with thirteen, and in 1538 Plommyer and Pouchet brought him yet eleven more. Just one of these small mirrors with its expensive frame cost 360 ecus of gold. A new fashion was started, a need created that would eventually cost France fabulous sums because her royal courtiers could not resist the seduction of these novelties. They followed an example that came from above: Catherine de Médicis, as an Italian woman already well familiar with these treasures, had a famous *cabinet de miroirs* (chamber of mirrors) installed after the death of Henri II. Above the fireplace, "a portrait of the fire king could indeed be seen represented in a mirror" and on the surfaces of the walls, "one hundred and nineteen Venetian mirrors were set into the panelling of the chamber."[36] In the 1615 estate inventory of Marguerite de Valois, in her home on the rue Seine, "four mirrors of rock crystal" decorated with gold, embellished with lapis lazulis and diamonds, can be found. Just one of these mirrors was worth 1,500 pounds. Queen Anne of Austria had her own "chamber of mirrors" at the Louvre, where her maidservants groomed her hair.

As all of the nobility demanded them, a mirror craze had begun. In 1633 a ball was given at the hôtel de Chevreuse in the queen's presence, and the room was decorated with alternating mirrors and tapestries. In 1651, when the archbishop of Sens gave a party in honor of the duchess of Longueville, fifty mirrors from Venice adorned the room. They were worth a few ironic lines in Jean Loret's *Muse historique*, which told of

> faces, grimaces and postures
> laughter, favors, charms
> the breasts, the hands, the arms
> of the beautiful group of conspirators
> that we celebrate in this room

all multiplying before the mirror. The chamber of mirrors became the height of fashion, and a young *précieuse* could not be imagined without one of her own. The duchess de La Vallière's *cabinet de miroirs* contained fourteen mirrors and surpassed that of the duchess de Bouillon. The Grande Mademoiselle in exile at Saint-Fargeau had miniature chambers and wardrobes installed, and mirrors soon followed. "In their enchanted chambers, fabric no longer has a place/On all the walls on all four sides / Encrusted mirrors, show their face" remarked one observer.[37]

The inventory of Nicolas Fouquet, finance minister to Louis XIV, contains an impressive collection of mirrors with varying frames of gold, silver, vermeil, ivory, and tortoise shell. Cardinal Mazarin, who also had many, offered them as raffle prizes. The chamber of the Dauphin, described by the art historian André Félibien, contained "on all sides and on the ceiling, mirrors with compartments and golden borders on a background of ebony marquetry." In the chamber of the marshal of Lorges, Saint-Simon's father-in-law, the countryside of the Montmartre butte is reflected on the walls by means of "two pairs of mirrors."[38] The furniture inventories of the crown, drawn up under Louis XIV, counted 563 mirrors.

Fortunes were depleted not only on wall mirrors, but also on mirrored jewelry, valued in inventories along with rings and necklaces and often offered as among the most sumptuous wedding gifts. Mirrored jewelry given to Isabelle de Saint-Chamond in 1610 by her father was "crystal encased in gold, decorated with eight ruby roses," and the rich bride in the following poem wears: "Mirrors made of Venetian glass / The laced fan, the flaps *à la Guise* / So many chains of jet and so many bracelets."[39] Mirrors attached to the belt and set on a little silver chain were also a fashion trend. The dramatist Pierre Corneille decorates his beautiful Angélique with one (*La Place royal*, 1635) and Pascal writes of a "pretty girl covered with mirrors and necklaces." The poet Jean de La Fontaine sees mirrors everywhere "on the pockets of gentlemen" and "on the belts of women."[40] These objects are undoubtedly not all made of crystal, but they were expensive nonetheless because of their decoration.

The nobility's infatuation with such mirrors quickly spread to notable members of the administration and to the Parisian bourgeoisie, and estate inventories inform us of the mirror's widespread use. Take Marguerite Mercier, for example, the wife of one of Louis XIV's butlers, M. d'Espesse, whose income was relatively high. At their marriage in 1654, the couple had 1,750 pounds of income per trimester. They owned no property and rented an apartment. The mistress of the household, worried about finances, regularly repaired, cleaned, and dyed her trousseau. In 1655, when she gave birth to a daughter, her husband offered her "her first mirror with ribbons and iron hooks." Its cost: 165 pounds.[41]

In most cases, the presence of a mirror in the home indicates that its occupant worked in commerce or as a representative, in contact with the court. These were families of magistrates, advisers to the king, ambassadors, and officers of justice. The mercantile bourgeoisie followed suit, but contented itself with mirrors of small dimensions—less than twelve inches—and modest borders, in frames of pear tree wood. Jean-Pierre Camus, bishop of Belley and moralist storyteller, noted that the rich watched solar eclipses with the aid of a mirror while the poor made do with a basin of water (*La Tour des miroirs,* 1631). Charles Sorel, in his *Histoire comique de Francion*, writes of a school regent who had seen his reflection only in a bucket of water and who, in love with one of his pupils, spent all his savings on a mirror in order to see how he would look in her eyes!

Before 1630, mirrors were still rare. In two hundred forty-eight estate inventories drawn up in Paris between 1581 and 1622, only thirty-seven mirrors are inventoried, nine of Venetian glass and the twenty-eight others of "bronze," "copper," "steel," and "azure glass": two mirrors belonging to the nobility (from eighteen inventories), fifteen belonging to magistrates and advisers to the king (forty inventories), two belonging to auxiliaries of justice and doctors (sixteen inventories), ten belonging to bourgeois of Paris (fifty inventories), and one in a group of journeymen workers (thirty inventories).[42] In twenty cases, these mirrors were used in the main bedroom, and in only five cases were they found in the common room of the house. Five homes of the 248 possessed two mirrors. Alongside this general accounting, a few special cases can be noted: an advisor to the court of the Parliament had three mirrors in his home; a stableman of the king, man-at-arms of the company, owned "six large Venetian mirrors encased in ebony, valued at seven pounds." The homes in which mirrors were absent were not necessarily devoid of material possessions: sixty percent of the homes studied contained several paintings and 16 percent had tapestries. The presence of mirrors could not therefore be linked only to one's level of resources, but rather to one's lifestyle and to the pull of attraction to aristocratic models.

In the twenty years that followed, attitudes clearly changed, and the mirror appeared twice as often: fifty-five mirrors were tallied out of 160 inventories drawn up between 1638 and 1648, or one mirror in every three households. From then on the popularity of mirrors would reach all social classes: from low-wage earners (such as vinegar makers and carriage makers) to bourgeois tailors, furniture salespeople, and advisors to the king. In twenty-two cases, the families possessed inherited income worth more than 600 pounds, and in twenty cases, of more than 1,000 pounds. But in some ten cases, the inventories listed goods worth less than 500 pounds. Along with mirrors hung on walls, the inventories mention small mirrors used for grooming and also "mirrors of broken glass."

After 1650, the mirror was even more widespread and could be found in two out of three Parisian inventories.[43] A single family often owned several: an actor for the king, for example, possessed six, but they were perhaps tools, used to study the gestures of his craft. The absence of a mirror thus became significant.

Curiously, there were some distinguished Parisian bourgeois families—the parliamentary prosecutor, the general inspector, the king's stableman, and a master tailor—who did not possess any mirrors even though they had high incomes and possessed other luxury items like tapestries and silver. One possible explanation may be a preference for paintings; mirrors were still quite small in comparison. "This precious miracle," notes one Parisian observer at the end of the seventeenth century, "is found today as often in the hands of the great as in those of the small."[44]

Toward a French Industry

In the early sixteenth century, French spending on mirrored glass grew to meet an increased desire for material goods and a rise in standards of living. A Venetian mirror, framed in a rich border of silver, was worth more than a painting by Raphael: the mirror cost 8,000 pounds, the painting only 3,000.[45] What is more, because an economic depression had stripped Italy of numerous potential customers, Venice increased its initiatives toward foreign markets and focused these efforts on France, one of its best customers. It thus became urgent that the French kingdom limit imports by creating its own mirror industry.

Beginning in 1530, François I made decrees aimed at protecting the gentry glassmakers already numerous in the kingdom (in Normandy, for example) who produced both hollow and flat glass. Some of these factories were already employing a sizable foreign work force, as the promise of good wages enticed many to cross the border. The duke de Nevers, of the Gonzaga family in Mantua, was easily able to attract experienced Italian teams to establish factories that produced Venetian-style mirrors in France. The most well known of these Italian families transplanted to France were the Sarrodes, who did not produce mirrors at first.

In 1551, King Henri II, continuing his father's policies, offered Theseo Mutio, an Italian man from Bologna, the ten-year sole privilege to produce "glass, mirrors, enamelled tubes and other sorts of Venetian style glass." Theseo accepted on the condition that the king protect his art from the many imitators tempted to "counterfeit his work and by these means obstruct the repayment of his loans." Seven years later, his brother Ludovic came to join him at Saint-Germain-en-Laye, where he had settled, but like Theseo, he was unable to smuggle "tools and other necessary instruments" out of Venice, whose leaders strenuously opposed their working abroad. In December 1561, the two Mutio brothers received letters of nobility as French glassmakers, and they signed a new lease for their Saint-Germain priory, indicating the permanence of their settlement and their confidence in their own success. Hopes were high when the first products of their manufacture were judged "of the same beauty and excellence" as work bought in Murano. But at this point, sadly, the records of the Mutios' efforts come to an abrupt end. Why didn't they succeed in breaking into the new market despite the support and protection bestowed on them by Catherine de Médicis? One reason is certainly that the civil wars that were ruining France did not favor luxuries. The Mutio factory faltered and no mention of them can be found in the last third of the century; it is unclear how long their experiment lasted.

Henri IV also took a turn at encouraging glassmakers by granting them titles of nobility, whether they were French or foreigners. He gave licenses to the two Sarrode brothers, Jacques and Vincent, from the Italian glass center of Altare, and to their nephew Horace Ponte, making them responsible for creating a Venetian-style crystal glass factory in Melun. The Sarrodes, originally from the duchy of Mantua, had begun by building their ovens near Nevers, but the geographical location of Melun, on a large body of water and near Paris, offered many more advantages. To their aid, Henri IV forbade the installation of all other glassmakers within a radius of less than approximately forty leagues. These privileges gave way to bitter disputes and jealousies, and once again the results of the enterprise were disappointing. Ultimately, the Sarrodes refused to introduce French workers to the crystal manufacturing process, claiming that they were not permitted to do so and that, if the art was passed on, "all their workers would leave them." They bequeathed their ovens to a nephew, Castellano, a remarkable glassmaker who gallicized his name, established himself on the banks of the Loire, and maintained a thirty-year monopoly. Castellan then hired a family member, Bernard Perrot, and both men were often mentioned for their groundbreaking experiments. They may have been the inventors of the technique of casting glass, but their innovation, although well known, was never officially rewarded.[46] There were many other Italian experiments on French soil (the Ferros worked in Dauphiné, the Salviatis in Charente, the Bornioles in Provence), but none of them ever achieved the desired results. In any case, they all jealously guarded their techniques and refused to speak about their work. French artisans continued to produce mirrors of "common" (that is to say irregular and colored) glass. A breakthrough was believed to have been reached when a glassworker from Udine, Bastian de Nadal, arrived in Paris in 1632 with an express offer to make Venetian-style mirrors. Caught up in a brawl, he had been forced to flee his native city in haste to avoid problems with the police, but his stay in France was short: when informed of his whereabouts, the Venetian ambassador went to work making promises and threats in order to dissuade him from establishing himself abroad, and in a matter of weeks, Nadal, armed with a safe-conduct pass, returned to the Italian fold. Other attempts to establish a mirror industry under the reign of Louis XIII were recorded, but they each came to a sudden end from a lack of support or of skill.

Venice kept itself regularly informed of the efforts and progress achieved on the other side of the Alps through its ambassador Sagredo: he pointed out, for example, that a certain

Bon, or Dabon, had installed two ovens that allowed the manufacture of glass jewelry and small mirrors. The knight of Hennezel, a gentleman from Lorraine who settled in the faubourg Saint-Michel, seemed to have the best glassmaking reputation among the French, and it was not long before the king's minister Colbert allocated him a subsidy of 50,000 ecus.[47] But he never received the money and was forced to abandon the industry. Several establishments in Normandy, in Lorraine, in Picardy, and near Lyon and Limoges, where wood was abundant, produced glass without successfully making mirrors. The Tourlaville factory near Cherbourg, however, in the capable hands of Lucas de Nehou, produced an excellent white glass for the windows of the Val de Grâce church in Paris and was even able to manufacture several mirrored glasses. In the end none of these scattered efforts was conclusive, despite the king's wishes, and French dealers who supplied mirrors to private individuals continued to import their wares from Venice, and in larger and larger quantities as the century advanced.

Louis XIV's powerful finance minister, Colbert, therefore decided to concentrate his efforts. Instead of continuing to support the small noncompetitive and unstable glassmakers indefinitely, he canceled all manufacturing privileges hitherto granted and ordered the establishment of a state enterprise. By 1662 the Royal Company of Furniture and Tapestries of the Crown was already thriving, and it was according to this model that Colbert decided to create a royal manufacture of mirrors with Italian artisans laboring alongside French workers. The French ambassador to Venice was secretly made responsible for the recruitment of artisans and master Venetian glassmakers, using emissaries sent to the Venetian Republic. Colbert also chose a competent financier, Sir Nicolas Dunoyer, the son of one of the king's butlers and a tax collector in Orléans, to establish the policies and procedures of the new company. In October 1665, Louis XIV was persuaded by Colbert to grant Dunoyer a privilege that began: "Because the great calm that peace has brought to our kingdom obliges us to turn our efforts to seeking those things that can be produced not only in abundance, but also to serve as decoration and embellishment, we have generously invited foreigners . . ."[48]

Dunoyer established himself near the abbey of Saint-Antoine on the rue de Reuilly, where he was joined by several associates close to Colbert—able financiers, secretary-advisors to the king and general tax collectors—in a complex financial arrangement. Dunoyer himself did not delay in stepping back and ceding his position to his brother Claude. A painting of the royal arms was hung on the door of their offices, and the doormen wore the king's livery. Hopes were high. It would be nearly a quarter of a century, however, before significant results were achieved.[49]

2

The Royal Glass and Mirror Company

An Affair of Industrial Espionage

Colbert's Plan

Two corpses in three weeks: strange things were happening in the workshops on the rue de Reuilly. First, in January 1667, a Venetian metal polisher died after several days of a violent fever. Next, a glassblower, also a Venetian who was particularly skilled in preparing molten glass, died after experiencing sharp stomach pains. The young Royal Company of Glass and Mirrors, founded by Colbert, thus lost two of its best artisans, and their deaths paralyzed the factory. An autopsy was requested, and Dunoyer, the head of the factory, wasted no time in voicing his suspicion of the Venetian Republic's hand behind these sudden deaths. This story attracted nineteenth-century archivist Elphège Frémy, who closely studied Venetian diplomatic documents ("Archivo di Stato—Inquisitori in Francia," the "Dispacci dagli ambasciatori in Francia," and the "Lettore agli ambasciatori in Francia"), some sixty dispatches in all, and recounted the stages of this veritable industrial spy novel that pitted the nascent Royal Company against the master glassmakers of Murano. One cannot resist recounting the fantastic events he uncovered.[1]

What is certain is that France, through its embassy in Venice, sought the aid of the Murano workers while Venice did all it could to block the progress of French competition. After twenty months of existence, the French company, plagued by strikes and the mysterious deaths and defections of foreign workers, had not yet produced any notable results. Frémy undoubtedly overestimated the significance of Dunoyer's efforts at the expense of other less well-known experiments carried out on French soil. This colorful episode in the history of Saint-Gobain emphasizes the ultimate uselessness of help from Venetians and sheds light on the difficult beginnings of the Royal Company of Glass and Mirrors.

Between 1665 and 1670, mirror imports increased massively in France as demand continued to grow. In 1665, 216 cases of Venetian mirrors entered France on the accounts of nine merchants, according to the records of one tax bureau. This mirror craze brought with it a catastrophic financial drain at a time of monetary penury. The French spent at least 100,000 ecus on mirrors from Venice each year (and three times that amount for Venetian lace). The king was the first of these insatiable clients. He bought thousands of pounds worth of mirrors from the Venetians in 1665.

Venice had carefully protected a monopoly that had made her very wealthy. She had long ago installed a ring of defenses around her workers by reserving precious benefits for them—rights of citizenship, tax exemptions, the right to marry daughters of nobles—and also by making a few preventive threats. Murano was sheltered from the curious gaze of outsiders and its workers were forbidden to emigrate or even to communicate with foreigners. If they were caught fleeing or even accused of wanting to flee, the "terrible tribunal" considered them a threat to the security of the state and prosecuted them as "traitors to the fatherland"; their goods were confiscated and reprisals extended to their entire families, who served as hostages. The laws, dating back several centuries, allowed the following stringent measures:

> If any worker or artist should transport his talents to a foreign country and if he doesn't obey the order to return, all of his closest relatives will be put in prison and if, in spite of the imprisonment of his relatives, he stubbornly insists on remaining in the foreign country, an emissary will be sent to kill him and, after his death, his family will be set free.[2]

Any aspiring deserter was thus forewarned. The decrees were undoubtedly not always applied, far from it, for a strong emigration ensued to Anvers, Hainaut, and Liège (all cities in modern Belgium) in the sixteenth century. But precedents did exist: two Venetian workers, called to Germany by Leopold I, were assassinated in 1547. In 1589, a certain Antonio Obizzo was condemned, by proxy, to four years in the galleys for having joined a master glassmaker in Anvers. A reward of 100 pounds, to be taken from the goods of the guilty man, was offered to anyone who could capture him. Colbert was aware of these facts, and French overtures to Venetian workers were accordingly prudent and clandestine. According to the secret correspondence that Colbert exchanged with his ambassadors and that his ambassadors exchanged with their emissaries, the latter were under orders to hire Italian workers by making them fabulous promises. The initial efforts would take two years and entail a great deal of money and maneuvering.[3]

Their first steps date back to 1664. Pierre de Bonzi, bishop of Béziers, was serving as France's ambassador to Venice, despite being from an old Florentine family, when he was given the added mission of recruiting Murano mirror workers who would agree to settle in France and help launch the company. The ambassador's response on November 8 was hardly encouraging. He recounted in detail the difficulties of such an operation on account of the draconian regulation discouraging the Venetian workers' emigration, stating that "whoever might suggest that they go to France would run the risk of being thrown into the sea." For the good of the kingdom, however, Bonzi agreed to take on such risks. His mission took place in two stages: first, skillful workers open to France's financial offers had to be located, and then their safe passage to Paris under escort had to be assured, all without the knowledge of the Venetian Council of Ten. The efforts lasted many months and were fraught with obstacles.[4]

Bonzi first turned to a shrewd and discreet *mercante di marzaria*—a junk shop merchant—to gain entry into Murano. Three months later, the merchant announced that he had found some master workers tempted by the offer, over whom the Republic kept a watchful eye, and of whom it would be glad to rid itself. Colbert was informed in April of 1665, and the second phase of the operation began. In May a certain Jouan, who was given the sum of 2,000 pounds for his expenses and those of the Italians, was put in charge of ensuring the security of the convoy. At the beginning of the summer, three workers from Murano—La Motta, Pietro Rigo, and Zuane Dandolo, masters in crystal work—reached Paris safely and without incident. According to their conditions of employment, they began to build their ovens in a temporary space.

Their escape, however, did not go unnoticed back in Venice. The masters of the corporation of mirror makers alerted the authorities as soon as they themselves discovered the departure. A search was made of the home of the intermediary agent and their paperwork was found, but it was too late to arrest the renegade workers. Venice's ambassador to Paris was notified and was asked to find the workers upon their arrival and to persuade them to return to the fold, promising them safe transport and suspended sentences. But the investigation by Ambassador Sagredo did not achieve the expected results: the fugitives' trail had gone cold.

Encouraged by his initial success, Colbert made contact with Castellan, the master Italian glassworker in Nevers, and offered him 4,600 pounds for a recruitment expedition to Italy. Instead of going himself, Castellan sent his son-in-law, Marc Borniole, who arrived in Venice in the spring of 1665. Although they were conducted with the greatest discretion, the comings and goings of the French did not escape the notice of the Venetian police. One day, as he was crossing a canal in a gondola, one of Borniole's men overheard fragments of a conversation between two Venetians "who were saying just between themselves that a man of a certain hair color, wearing certain kind of clothing had arrived in Venice to hire away mirror workers," and that the authorities should be warned. Borniole, to whom the story was relayed, decided to expedite the group's departure and warned the head of the small cadre of emigrants, Antonio della Rivetta, to hasten the preparations. Luckily, in one of Murano's cabarets a brawl broke out that left several people injured, and the police were distracted by thier unsuccessful attempts to control the unruly mob. Despite this opportunity, Borniole's scheme still nearly failed due to a lack of money, for he had only 20 pistoles in his pocket. At last everything fell into place, and at four o'-clock in the morning, after bidding their families farewell, the men boarded a small boat. At daybreak, they reached Ferrare, where carriages were waiting to take them to Turin. From Turin they reached Lyon, but there encountered another setback: several workers were approached and were offered 2,000 pistoles to remain in that city. Confusion, hesitation, and heated discussion ensued. A few workers were tempted by the offer and a fistfight nearly erupted in the horse-drawn barge that was carrying the group to Nevers. Finally, four workers decided to return to Lyon, but there they were abruptly detained and questioned by men from the archbishop-governor for a few hours in the prison of Pierre-Suze. Once released, they returned to Venice.

The rest of the group arrived in Paris and were put to work immediately, boasting that they could execute panes of six or seven feet at once! A few weeks later more workers arrived from Venice through the aid of a new agent, Pierre Flament, who received a commission of 400 pounds. Thus, by the fall of 1665, Colbert felt confident enough to open the company in the hope that it would soon produce mirrors and glass, thanks to the twenty-man Venetian team hired to train and supervise the French workers. In fact, the first flawless mirror to come out of the company appeared on February 22, 1666, and Dunoyer sent it proudly to Colbert.

Difficulties of the Royal Company

Despite appearance of progress, however, little had really been made. Venice continued to discreetly pressure the émigrés with promises, threats, secret agents, fake letters—any ploy was considered fair game. For a whole year Colbert and the Venetian ambassador exchanged an escalating series of salvos and retorts, and Colbert was able to keep the Italians only by offering them substantial salaries. On October 21, 1665, an allowance of 1,200 pounds a year was accorded to the senior master, Antonio della Rivetta, and his three senior journeymen, Morasse, Barbini, and Crivano, were allocated 800 pounds per year. In addition, the factory received 3,000 pounds for workers' room and board. La Rivetta, on whose talent everything depended, earned 40 doubloons a month, in exchange for a pledge to serve the king of France for four years. But at the same time, Sagredo, the Venetian ambassador whom the Murano workers encountered upon their arrival in France, tried his own brand of intimidation, emphasizing the risks that the workers' flight would bring to their families and property back in Venice. The Murano workers were not overly impressed and remained more interested in the advantages of their immediate situation than in far-off threats. Sagredo was soon recalled to Venice and replaced by the ambassador Giustiniani.

Giustiniani received the same instructions as his predecessor: to obstruct by all possible means the progress of the French Royal Company, and to keep himself constantly informed of the situation through his secret agents. For his part, Colbert's mission was to make the establishment of the company irreversible. In order to raise the profile of the mirror enterprise, he organized a visit by the Royal Court to the faubourg Saint-Antoine and on April 29, 1666, the king, accompanied by Colbert and numerous members of the court, made a solemn call to the rue de Reuilly address to inspect the glassworks. The king strolled through its rooms, examined the tools, and asked numerous questions. A mirror was blown, polished, and silvered before the dignitaries' eyes. Satisfied with his visit, Louis XIV left a 150-doubloon *buona mancia*—a bonus—for his workers.

Giustiniani's pressures and repeated threats had some effect. Several workers, feeling troubled, suffered "breakdowns" and asked their ambassador for safe passage back to Venice. Fortunately for the company, they were underlings, but their desertion revealed that the team was still vulnerable. In order to keep them on French soil, Colbert had the idea of inviting all the wives still in Murano to come to Paris and reestablish their family life there. A nephew of Antonio della Rivetta, given the responsibility of acting as intermediary, procured letters from Antonio that were then passed on to his wife. But this traffic was intercepted by the Venetian police who, with couriers twice as fast as those on the French side, delivered false replies: no, the wives would not start out without an express order from their husbands, and their husbands would do better to come and fetch them themselves so that they might consult together on how best to proceed! Giustiniani had the fake letter delivered to the rue de Reuilly by his valet, in whose presence the letter was read; the valet then reported to his master the reactions he had observed. The workers were skeptical. The Murano men weren't fooled by the strategy, for they noticed that the letter had been written by "a person of superior knowledge and intelligence" and that "they shouldn't lend it any credence." Unfortunately, Venetian archives do not possess any letters written by Colbert to the Murano workers and their wives, although a collection of Colbert's correspondence supplies the other side of the exchange.

The story of fake letters doesn't end there. Life in the French capital, even without one's wife, was not without charm in the eyes of the Venetians. Pretty Parisian women whose curiosity brought them to the neighborhood offered them an *attrativa molto gagliarda* [a very delightful and lively sight]. Fed and generously paid, the workers had grown accustomed to receiving "sociable" women in their lodgings. It didn't escape their notice either that France believed their presence to be of considerable value. Royal favors gave rise to more and more demands and indulgences. The workers became difficult, impetuous, and hotheaded subjects, and yet there was no thought of doing without them—at least that was what was believed. In order to calm them down, Colbert decided, in the summer of 1666, to once again take up the matter of wives and to bring them to Paris whatever the cost. New secret emissaries left for Murano, but were intercepted by Giustiniani. The Venetian police received their descriptions and increased its surveillance efforts; the police even searched the wives' homes to verify that they had not fled. They were of course at home, resigned to patiently awaiting the return of their husbands. One of the women was resting in bed, in serious pain. Another begged the inspector to intervene so that her husband would return to the "nest." Everything seemed in order. But a few days later, when the inspectors returned to investigate anew, they were stupefied to find the nests completely empty. Their good health suddenly restored, the women had left with one of Colbert's emissaries and were too far gone to be captured!

The Venetian police had been tricked, and there can be no doubt that more radical measures against the *scelerati vetrieri* were soon considered. While waiting for a propitious moment,

Venetian officials started a rumor that the glasses coming out of the French workshop could not resist either cold or heat, and encouraged the Venetian workers to make exorbitant claims about the high quality of their own product.

Colbert, for his part, was only half satisfied. Dunoyer had just reported to him some somber news regarding the company: as of November 1666, it was a financial disaster. Certainly "the possibility of making glasses in France as beautiful as those in Venice was no longer called into question, as long as Venetian workers were willing to do the work." But these workers, always defiant and protective of their knowledge, refused to allow any French colleagues to work alongside them at the ovens—so much so that "all the expenses of this establishment, which have climbed to more than 180,000 pounds, and only about a third of which could be recovered if the enterprise should fail, depend on the whims of those gentlemen!"[5]

On the matter of whims, La Motta, one of the first foreigners to arrive, took offense at the success of Rivetta, who was particularly skilled at "pulling glass," and the restless immigrant community split into two camps. Naturally, Venetian emissaries threw oil on the fire. The rivalry turned to violence as both gangs armed themselves with matchlock guns. When gunfire broke out, La Motta was wounded in the shoulder, one of his companions in the hand. The royal guard had to intervene. In the end the workers received several days of imprisonment, and the company's production was halted. When it wasn't a scuffle, a work-related accident slowed glass and mirror production. In November, the worker who "stabilizes the mirrors on large pans" injured his leg, and no one had the expertise to replace him. Another worker was asked to attempt the job, but he refused, claiming that the task was so delicate that "it had to be learned from the age of twelve." The wasted days were expensive because the foundry continued to burn fuel; otherwise, "the hot ovens would be lost" and their contents worth nothing, "which would cause a loss of over

20,000 pounds." French emissaries attempted to hire another specialist from Murano, but without success: they were only able to bring back two polishers, since other workers they tried to lure abandoned them at the last minute.

In order to obtain better results, was it perhaps necessary to provide the Italian workers with greater financial enticements? Dunoyer gave this advice in a letter to Colbert: if the king, who had promised to take care of the workers, were to offer them a plot of land of their own, worth 20,000 ecus that would go to their widows and offspring when they died, if he could ensure a sort of retirement allocation for each worker's descendants, and if, for each French apprentice he trained, the Italian worker received a bonus of 2,000 ecus, the Venetian workers could master their ill will and lack of discipline.

That was where things stood at Christmas 1666. After eighteen months of expense and effort the company was running out of steam, but most thought time would vindicate it. In early January 1667, however, the first Murano worker, the one who made the preparation of molten glass possible, died. On January 25, a second worker, Domenico Morasse, also passed away. In Murano, investigators heightened their surveillance efforts: four glassworkers, suspected of wanting to emigrate, were imprisoned in Plombs.

In Paris, as well, the situation at the factory was tense. The Murano workers feared for their lives, and their generous benefits carried little weight in the face of such dangers. If even a few of them were to give in to the pressure, the entire community would follow. Giustiniani became more insistent: he milked the threat and promised amnesty to workers who returned home. La Rivetta, Barbini, and Crivano, worked to the bone, decided to abandon ship. In the early days of April 1667, they left France and reached Besançon where their ambassador made sure they were given safe conduct and a little money; their wives were to join them later. Venice, true to its promise, did not interfere when they went back to work, but their Murano colleagues made life so difficult for them that they eventually called upon the Council of Ten for support.

Was this a failure for the Royal Company? Only partly. The insubordination, financial demands, and refusal to cooperate on the part of the Italians eventually wore down many of their French counterparts, and Dunoyer let them go without much regret, as the factory began to look elsewhere for solutions. Then, in the spring of 1670, just three years after their return to their homeland, the same renegade Murano glassworkers, appalled by the terrible treatment they received at the hands of their compatriots, requested permission to return to work in Paris. When their request was mediated by the French ambassador, Saint-André, Colbert answered dryly: "They gave us so much trouble when they worked in the factory and were so full of ill-will that I don't believe it advantageous to call on them a second time."[6]

After such a troubled inception, how can we then assess the role Venetian workers had in the manufacture of mirrors in France? It was in 1670 that the French company recorded its first successes when, through a combination of experience and accident, many technical difficulties were resolved. Even before 1665, some isolated attempts at producing blown mirrors had succeeded in France, like Lucas de Néhou's glassworks in Tourlaville, Normandy, which were especially renowned. The Venetian contribution to French research was already in dispute, but this did not prevent the Italian ambassador from complaining to his government in 1680 over the progress he observed the French industry making thanks to Venetian help: "I repeat to your Excellencies that I have tears in my eyes when I see how these many factories, which by an admirable gift that Providence, nature and hard work had granted particularly to us, have been so easily transported and sustained by the unpunished spitefulness of a few of our fellow citizens."[7]

In fact, it would be processes entirely different from glassblowing that just a few years later would bring glory to French glassworks. "From 1666 on," Voltaire later wrote, "We began to make glass panels as beautiful as those of Venice, which had previously furnished them to all of Europe and soon we made some whose size and beauty were never imitated elsewhere."[8]

Toward Saint-Gobain

The Hall of Mirrors

When the Hall of Mirrors at Versailles, a joint project of architects Charles Le Brun and Jules Hardouin-Mansart, was presented to the public in 1682, it met with resounding admiration: "The most beautiful things are not always the easiest to portray—their glory and splendor are sometimes overwhelming," wrote the *Mercure Galant,* the weekly gazette founded by Jean Donneau de Visé, in December 1682. Everyone found something to praise. Official chroniclers and panegyrists could not say enough in honor of the "palace of joy" which enchanted "sight, hearing, taste and even smell" all at the same time. It was "a dazzling mass of riches and lights, duplicated a thousand times over in just as many mirrors, creating views more brilliant than fire and where a thousand things even more sparkling came into play. Add to that the splendor that the court's finery adds to this and the gleam of their precious jewelry . . . "

What more perfect symbol could be found for the dazzling reign of the Sun King than this prestigious hall, where court members dripping with jewelry could look at and admire themselves and one another from head to toe in all their splendor? In December 1682, the far end of the hall had not yet been unveiled, but the décor commissioned in 1678 for royal gatherings was in place. For those subjects who weren't fortunate enough to be invited to one of these brilliant displays of court pageantry, the *Mercure* served as a mirror detailing the ornament, finery, and beauty of the hall that those who didn't have access found difficult to imagine: "The mirrors are false windows facing the real ones and expand this hall a million times over so it seems almost infinite . . . " Chandeliers supported by silver posts alternated with casings of silver orange blossoms; all kinds of light fixtures—cressets, candelabras, and fountains resting on pedestals in front of the glass—sparkled with a thousand flames, and their reflections carried off repeatedly in all directions.[9] All that human art and ingenuity could bring to interior decoration—paintings, marbles, bronzes, carpets from Savona, white damask curtains, and mirrors—all were assembled in the service of royal glory.

The hall was completed in November 1684, and the last mirrors placed in artificial window casements the night before its inauguration. Discovering the series of corridors for herself in the spring of 1685, the marquise de Sévigné, famed for her letters portraying court life, was not sparing in her admiration: "This sort of royal beauty is unique in the world."[10] The bold design of the hall startled even those who had experienced similar glass paneled chambers. Each of its seventeen false window casements, opposite seventeen real windows, was covered with eighteen mirrors placed side by side, unframed, joined by finely carved gilded copper frames. There were 306 panes of glass in all, but they blended together, so that each gave the appearance of being a part of a much larger single pane. The structure of the hall itself vanishes in the radiance of such shimmering surfaces and bursts of light; visitors described it as an architecture of emptiness. Jean Baptiste de Monicart, while imprisoned in the Bastille in 1710, wrote a poem enumerating the beauties of Versailles in which the furniture and rooms speak for themselves. The hall itself remarks:

> My ceiling and its contour seem to have little holding them up for the high walls of mirrors and transparent panes appear as the

> only support for this large expanse and yet these sections are all the better for letting me see the scenery within my view.

Like most chroniclers, Monicart described the surprise provoked by the fracturing and duplication of objects in the hall's mirrors and noted visitors' "uncertain and awkward state."[11]

Colbert, a master of promotion, brilliantly manipulated the magnificent hall of Versailles to help launch the Royal Mirror Company. The hall gave considerable momentum to the young industry and increased public awareness of its successes. If neither the dimensions of the mirrors nor the Venetian glassblowing technique used to produce them was revolutionary, their cumulative effect in the hall was stupefying. The Royal Buildings Accounts for 1682 noted that Versailles had already devoured 38,000 pounds' worth of glass (mirrored and otherwise) and, in 1684, it was revealed that the great hall alone had cost 654,000 pounds, although it is not known how much of this total sum was spent on glass.[12] Year after year, beginning in 1666, orders for mirrors are listed in the royal accounts in increasing quantities. Such demand was an indispensable godsend for Dunoyer's company, whose best customer was the king.

Competition and Contraband

In 1685, however, despite royal patronage and the protection of Colbert, and the careful attention paid by the five chief associates, the fate of the company was still far from certain. The difficulties that threatened its future were many: first, a lack of capital, especially crucial since the company needed to grant large lines of credit to its customers; second, the need for a stock of mirrors of all qualities and formats adapted to diverse tastes and incomes (reserve stocks often represented two or three years of sales); and finally, the competition from numerous black-market mirror makers.

Without a doubt the advantages granted to the company in 1665 were immense: in addition to its twenty-year monopoly, the glassworks had also obtained the right to expropriate any necessary raw materials (soda and natron [sodium carbonate], for example), and to transport these materials with a complete exemption from customs laws and tolls within the kingdom. Moreover, the king had exempted the chief associates and their workers from the ordinary duties of his subjects: milking cows, *corveé* (menial, uncompensated labor for the state), and guard duty, and he authorized them, in the event of a trial, to have their cases sent before the king's counselors rather than to submit themselves to ordinary justice.[13]

But the Venetian episode had cost the company a great deal. By November 1666, it had already spent 180,000 pounds to achieve only mixed results. Dunoyer complained in a letter to Colbert that his personal fortune wouldn't cover expenses and requested new subsidies, which were eventually granted. Discussions sometimes became so bitter among the associates that a reorganization of the company's structure became necessary. Two newcomers joined the initial group of partners in return for financial investments roughly equal to half the company's capital. The new partners, P. Pocquelin and P. Jousset, both bourgeois from Paris, were the biggest mirror merchants in the kingdom, and practically all trade with Venice was conducted through their firms. In addition to their financial resources, they brought useful competencies to the company and on occasion served as negotiators with the mirror makers of Paris. Despite the reorganization in 1667, the king still had to allow forty cases of Venetian glass to be imported that year while he waited for the company's supply to meet French demand.

Despite the monopoly granted to the company by royal decree, illicit competitors often succeeded in avoiding sanctions. The first official takeover to eliminate the threat posed by a rival glassworks took place in 1670. In Tourlaville, near Cherbourg, one Lucas de Néhou, the very skilled artisan under the protection of the Marquis de Seignelay, had obtained excellent results sometime before 1667, successfully blowing a twelve-inch-square pane of glass. Situated near the coast, close to land rich in raw materials and wood, Tourlaville was in a good position to export its products either by sea or via the Seine. De Néhou's glassworks were particularly damaged by the decree protecting the Royal Company. In order to avoid useless conflict, Dunoyer and Néhou agreed to unite their efforts, and pressure from Colbert helped close the deal. Letters of patent from Louis XIV confirm the establishment in December 1670 of the glassworks at Tourlaville as a subsidiary of rue de Reuilly, which took over the ownership of the site's twelve acres of land. Néhou joined the company on the same terms as Pocquelin and Jousset, and Colbert granted the enterprise a subsidy of 15,000 pounds from the state treasury to proceed with new innovations, in Paris as well as Normandy.[14] Under the new arrangement, the glass was blown at Tourlaville, and abraded and polished at rue de Reuilly in Paris.

Other conflicts were less easily resolved. In the provinces, lesser glass factories continued to produce small-scale glass for eyeglasses, window panes, and little mirrors in order to avoid financial ruin. These factories were fairly numerous in western France, in the forest of Lyon, and they also supplied the vendors of Rouen. At first, the company tolerated this competition without concern, at least as long as the mirrors that were produced did not surpass eight inches in size. But evasion soon became rampant, and the courts stepped in. Offenders were forced to destroy their ovens and to submit their tools and their glass products to the authorities. Some of them were repeat offenders: records of the last twenty years of the seventeenth century are full of these largely ineffectual punishments.

The case of Bernard Perrot was rather different. As the nephew of Castellan, the glassmaker who had helped Colbert recruit the Murano workers, he had received aid to revive his factory on several occasions. In 1661, 1668, 1671, and 1672, letters of patent authorized him to operate his glass factory in Orléans. A remarkable artisan, he carried out all kinds of research and in 1680 had the idea of "casting" glass on a flat table, as was done with metals, a technique that would allow him to produce much larger pieces than was possible with blown glass. In 1687, Perrot gave a much commented-on presentation before the French Academy of Sciences on the subject of casting. His presentation was perhaps too noteworthy because, when he requested a royal privilege for patenting his discovery, other artisans got wind of his experiments and tried to imitate them. Louis Lucas de Néhou, in particular, succeeded in perfecting the new technique. Perrot did obtain his royal privilege, but four years later, when the Royal Company was facing tremendous difficulties, all promises were forgotten. The operation of Perrot's glassworks was forbidden, and he himself was threatened with a 3,000-pound fine for each declared infraction. In the end, he was granted an annual pension of 500 pounds as compensation, a purely moral and symbolic gesture.

Nonetheless, Colbert and his successors found that protective measures and increased penalties did not always produce the desired effect. Glassworks sprung up all around the perimeters of the kingdom and recruited renegade workers. In 1700, a decree was necessary to prohibit the export to the frontiers of raw materials needed for glassmaking. In the principality of Dombes, at Beauregard, the duke of Maine, the legitimized bastard son of Louis XIV, founded a glassworks in 1700. In Savoy, Genevans and Italians joined to set up their own glass factory, and despite strict controls on transport, their products managed to seep into the French market.[15]

Even so, the most serious competition still came from Venice. Beginning in 1672, the king forbade all imports of Italian glass in the hopes that the Royal Company could meet French demand. But in fact, numerous merchants from Paris and the provinces continued to buy their supplies from the sources to which they were accustomed, particularly in Marseille, the port of transit for Venetian mirrors destined for Spain. Marseille, a free port open to the entire Mediterranean, became a hub of mirror traffic as merchandise could be stored without suspicion while it awaited shipment. French authorities tried to infiltrate these networks and asked their ambassadors to Venice, first Saint-André and then d'Avaux, to closely monitor correspondence exchanged between the Murano glassmakers and French merchants. From 1669 through 1671, Colbert wrote several insistent letters to Saint-André: "I beseech you to get to the bottom of all that is going on in this matter" and "I beg you to keep an open eye on all that happens in this regard." The ambassador was able to put together a fairly large dossier and provide a list of all suspect merchants, but he begged Colbert not to reveal his sources for fear of reprisals: "The men of this Republic will view me much less agreeably."[16]

Meanwhile, the Royal Company and the mirror makers of Paris managed to persuade the king's police lieutenant, Gabriel Nicolas de La Reynie, to name two commissioners at Châtelet, responsible for searching the shops of haberdashers and used clothing merchants suspected of housing smuggled glass. The archives are full of references to this type of confiscation including the following case in July 1965: "Having encountered a thief in possession of four pieces of glass belonging to the king and that had been sent under escort to a worker to be silvered, . . . the pieces were seized and removed to their nearest office."[17] Then the company assigned its own employees to the task, aided by a bailiff and another judicial officer. In the free ports, and at Marseille in particular, new rules were decreed by edict in 1703, to be enforced by an officer of the Admiralty: if a boat carrying foreign glass was detained for reasons of war or inclement weather, and had to drop anchor in one of these ports, the captain was required to declare his cargo immediately and to leave it in a designated area until his departure. An officer of the Admiralty would enforce the rule. In 1701, 588 pieces of glass were seized at the port of Saint-Malo.

Still, smugglers nearly always managed to slip through the net, and there is no way that the extent of their activities can be ascertained. In 1674, for example, a merchant from Lyon bought forty-eight cases of glass imported through Marseille, where they were confiscated. Because the merchant was unaware of the ban, or so it seemed, the French company made a one-time exception and allowed him to resell his merchandise in Languedoc and in Provence. Eventually such leniency disappeared, and the penalties became more severe. The banker Pierre Formont, in exchange for drafts on a foreign account, had ordered two cases of glass from a merchant in Genoa, pleading for exceptional authorization because of his debts. He was suspected of being an intermediary for two wily merchants from Marseille who were hoping to get around the ban, and the cases were confiscated from a Genoan galley and returned to an agent from the Royal Company. Most often the lawbreakers were wholesale traders who were well placed to take advantage of their business abroad and to obtain supplies of merchandise; in fact, some were too well connected to worry about the consequences. Others attempted all sorts of ploys. On one occasion a carton of mirrors was discovered in a well-wrapped package labeled "paintings." In 1685, the company organized the inspection of a dozen Parisian mirror dealers' inventories and confiscated numerous Venetian glass panes. There was even fraud within the French company itself. At certain property seizures, informers, representatives of the offices of the *Cinq Grosses Fermes* ["The Five Great Farms": the tax agency that had jurisdiction over central France] and agents from the French company set aside a portion of the goods for themselves: thus an employee would confiscate glass in order to resell it for his own profit![18]

In 1680 Colbert estimated the losses to Venetian trade at 1 million pounds. For the next ten years, Venice made glass half as expensive as French glass and profits to retailers, despite the transportation costs and risks, were substantial. Around 1700, the south of France was inundated with Venetian glass and the French company sold almost nothing there. It wasn't until the following decade—with the invention of casting and the production of large mirrors—that the situation was reversed.

The Birth of Saint-Gobain

Contraband was not the only explanation for the extreme financial difficulties confronting the French glassmaking enterprise. When Dunoyer died in 1679, the company was 50,000 pounds in debt—hardly a brilliant record considering all the efforts made on its behalf. Thus, when the company's royal privilege came up for renewal in 1685, the partners were hesitant. Colbert had died in 1683, depriving them of a powerful protector. Nonetheless, new support materialized, and the company managed to obtain the essential letters of patent that renewed its 1665 privileges, this time with the aid of a figurehead, Pierre de Bagneux. But other troubles arose from an unexpected source, Louis XIV's minister, the marquis de Louvois, who agreed to sponsor a young competing glassworks in the faubourg Saint-Germain. Located in a place called the "Grenouillère" on the banks of the Seine between the rue du Bac and the rue de Bellechasse, the site was highly convenient for the loading and transport of goods by boat.

The director of the Saint-Germain glassworks, a certain Thévart, became especially adept at making glasses of exceptional size—reaching nearly five feet high—a size heard of previously only in fairy tales.[19] This same Thévart had earlier hired away an expert from the Tourlaville glassworks, the nephew of Lucas de Néhou, who had learned to work molten glass by employing the method used by Bernard Perrot in Orléans, with encouraging results. Thévart's self-assurance and confidence in the new process earned him the support of Louvois, who sent him letters of patent in December 1688 and granted him a privilege of thirty years.

Nevertheless, in order to avoid harming a Royal Company already in a sorry state, an unusual condition was added that stipulated that Thévart agree to produce only glasses larger than those of M. de Bagneux, Dunoyer's successor, namely ones larger than sixty by forty inches. Thévart was prohibited from selling smaller sizes and "if the large glasses broke, he was not allowed to use the pieces." Upholding this condition, although laudable, proved impossible: breakage was such that Thévart's company was driven to the brink of bankruptcy, and in 1691, fearing total collapse, the company managed to acquire authorization to sell its small, broken glasses outside of France and to have the size threshold for its products lowered to fifty-four inches in height.[20]

Thévart rather quickly succeeded in presenting the king with the first cast glass, although it was hardly impressive in size. A report from the architect Mansart made an alarming assessment of ten years of production: "Since 1688 when large glasses were invented, we have only managed to make three from 80 to 84 inches high and 40 to 47 inches wide that are still in one piece. Although a total of more than four hundred were produced, most of them were thrown back to be melted down and the rest were salvaged for pieces between 40 and 60 inches in height."[21]

Intoxicated by his initial successes, Thévart did not sufficiently take into account the technical challenges he faced, and was also unprepared for the economic decline triggered by wars and other crises. He eventually would pay for his management errors. Heavily in debt, he decided to leave Paris in 1693 and start over in a more spacious and favorable location. He chose the ruins of a château in Picardie. Called Saint-Gobain, the château was located near the Oise River, in the middle of a forest, where a small glassworks had existed two centuries earlier. Aside from convenient boat transportation, the close proximity of fuel (wood from the forest) constituted a precious asset.

The Royal Company of faubourg Saint-Antoine derived no advantages from these ill-fated episodes in Thévart's career. The company also suffered during the times of crisis, and its excessive expenses, poor judgment in selecting administrators, and faulty assessment of demand all weighed heavily on its management. The treasury now had two subsidized companies on its hands! In order to end this rivalry, Louis XIV requested a general report from his financial controller, Phelypeaux de Pontchartrain.[22] When the study was finished in the spring of 1695, the king decided to put the anarchical situation in order. He canceled all the privileges hitherto accorded to both Bagneux and Thévart, and the two companies were dissolved and their debts liquidated. Once all was free and clear, he created a new company, the Manufacture Royale des glaces de France [Royal Glass Company of France], which received a privilege of thirty years awarded to another figurehead, François Plastrier, behind whom several competent associates worked. A monopoly was reestablished with an aim toward producing "glass for mirrors of all heights, lengths and widths, transparent panes for windows or doors, lights and vases of all sorts, cornices, strips and mouldings, glass jewelry for the Indies, enamels, mantelpieces, white glass and glass for spectacles, crystal glasses, entire table settings," and so on. All outside glassmakers were prohibited from making any of these objects under penalty of fines, confiscation of tools, and demolition of ovens.

The decree annoyed mirror- and glassmakers who felt that the past performance of the two companies did not make them deserving of such special treatment. There was so much recrimination that the king made a concession: master mirror makers and eyeglass makers would be authorized to silver mirrors destined for sale to individuals in Paris and to create ornamental motifs for building projects. Bernard Perrot, despite the success of his presentation before the French Academy of Sciences, was the first to suffer from the royal decision: all of his tools were confiscated in March 1696, to the benefit of the new company.

In 1700, the goal was in sight. The new Saint-Gobain factory produced a cast pane of glass that was a remarkable feat: it measured almost nine feet tall and more than three feet across. An English traveler to Paris, Martin Lister, visited the faubourg Saint-Antoine glassworks in 1699 and noted with admiration: "There I saw, fully complete and silvered, a mirror measuring 88 by 48 inches, and only 1/4 inch thick. I don't think anyone could obtain such dimensions by blowing."[23]

A Great Enterprise of the Ancien Régime

A State-of-the-Art Enterprise

One anecdote perhaps best illustrates the vulnerable, insecure state of the young company. On the morning of July 12, 1700, a master *tiseur* (a worker responsible for building and controlling the fires in the glassworks' ovens) named Bellemanière could not be found. He had left Saint-Gobain the previous night and had crossed the border to get to the Dombes in Burgundy where the director of a competing glassworks had offered him a very large salary. As the leader of a team of eight assistant *tiseur*s, Bellemanière had mastered the technique of casting, and his flight from Saint-Gobain would seriously compromise deliveries, force one of the ovens to shut down, and cost the company dearly. The civil and criminal lieutenant of the bailiwick territory of La Fère was immediately alerted and duly began his investigation, but the fugitive was never caught.[24] This defection, such a setback to Saint-Gobain, was not the only one; now many foreigners sought to hire away French workers, just as the French had done with the workers from Murano. "Nothing one could have done to keep the beautiful and ingenious secret of casting glass in

France," wrote Germain Brice in the middle of the eighteenth century, "could have prevented it from being exported to foreign countries such as England, Brandenburg and Saxony."[25]

For a long time the French jealously guarded the revolutionary process of casting glass as the Venetians had done with their glassblowing technique. No theoretical works on the subject existed and the various treatises on optics or manuals on the art of glassmaking did not address its practical aspects. In 1746, when Abbé Pluche published his massive *Spectacle of Nature*, in the seventh volume devoted to "arts that educate man," he praised the caution of the directors of the French company, who, he said, reserved "for our nation and for themselves the knowledge of certain preparations," but even while educating his readers with the help of plates and engravings, he omitted some essential details, such as the construction of the ovens. "I even left out what I was able to learn about the nature of the stones that form the base of the oven," he said. He also omitted "the mixing and preparation of materials and the exact measurements of the instruments."[26]

The manufacture of large cast mirrors required five particularly delicate stages: the building of the ovens and crucibles, the pouring, the flattening, the refiring, and finally the silvering. The composition of the glass itself changed little over the centuries, even if the precise role of each element in the formula—silica, sodium oxide, and lime—was not entirely understood (lime's action on the process was not fully identified until the middle of the eighteenth century). The quality of the glass was improved gradually through trial and error by varying the proportions of the ingredients.

Abbé Pluche describes in detail the different steps in the manufacturing process. After extraction, two hundred workers cleaned the white sand and soda, sifting the material to remove waste and foreign bodies. What remained was then washed, dried, and pulverized in a gristmill drawn by horses. Next the sand was filtered with water through a sieve of silk and then dried. Glass was produced by combining the various elements through melting, which at the temperature of 1,500 degrees Celsius created a viscous, half-liquid, half-solid mixture. Melting took place in heat-resistant crucibles called *pots* that held up to 300 kilograms of glass each. Because the raw materials took up twice the volume of molten glass, large quantities could not be placed in the oven at once. Two men in protective clothing, who worked in six-hour relay shifts, kept the oven lit. The oven itself had a life of only seven to eight months, after which time it was refitted completely, which took another six months.

The oven contained several crucible-shaped *pots*, and the *pots'* resistance to heat was one of the keys to the success or failure of the glassmaking process. They were made from a special white clay that could withstand direct firing up to a temperature of 1,800 degrees Celsius without softening. (Abbé Pluche revealed nothing about their manufacture.) When first fired, this clay produced small grains called *chamotte*, which were then mixed in with fresh clay, the proportions being kept secret. When the *pot* was placed in the oven, the fresh clay expanded, whereas the *chamotte*, which had already been baked, did not, thus preventing any cracks. The vessel was placed in a mold, dried over a period of several months and baked at a low temperature before being used for the fusion of glass. Generally vessels were made as needed and could be used only for a few weeks to three months maximum. Sometimes the vessel would shatter while full of molten glass, an absolute loss for the company. In 1705, Saint-Gobain had only ninety-five vessels in stock for its two working ovens.[27] For its part, during the last decades of the seventeenth century, Tourlaville worked with one oven and four vessels at a time, the operation of the oven requiring three master *tiseurs* and ten master blowers.

A good part of success in glassmaking depended on the skill of the master *tiseur*, who kept the ovens fired and at a constant temperature that maintained the regularity of combustion. With a shovel resembling the scoop for bailing water out of a boat, the *tiseur* placed a certain quantity of material in the vessels, in proportions known to him alone. The sand and soda remained there for thirty-six hours; the melting point temperature was strictly controlled. Then the mixture had to be refined and transferred into new crucibles made of the same substance as the first *pots*, where it was steeped in order to eliminate volatile elements—a process called sintering (or *frittage*). The molten glass was then ready to be poured.

The temperature of the oven was lowered, which brought the glass to the appropriate viscosity. A cart equipped with a forked holder was used to carry the vessel from the oven to a metal table on which the workers, at the signal of a whistle, poured out the viscous substance. The glass spread across the table, which was equipped with iron rods of a specific diameter around its edges. The workers balanced a cast iron roller on the rods to even the thickness of the sheet of glass. Those who operated the roller were protected from the heat by thick fabric covering their faces and chests. The use of the laminating roller appears to have been one of Néhou's inventions, and we know that the first casting table at Saint-Gobain was about ten feet long. Finally, the poured glass had to be refired or it would shatter with use. It was reintroduced into a large oven called a *carcaise*, where it remained for three days, cooling in gradual stages.

These delicate manipulations were far from successful every time, and in the early days of production at Saint-Gobain, few glasses successfully withstood the test of refiring; broken shards were converted into smaller-sized pieces. Moreover, it was fairly rare to obtain flawless glass: marbling, clouds, grease, rust, rusty or lead-darkened fibers, veins, "teardrops," and muck often compromised the clarity of the glass. In 1699, a flawed firing table caused months of production to be lost. Quantity and quality never went hand in hand, and merchants regularly complained about the poor grade of the glass destined for their private clientele. In 1752, one of the company's directors tried to make more profitable use of his equipment by setting four sheets of cast glass instead of three in an attempt to get twenty-four more sheets a week. The casting and the refinement of the first firing took twice as long as usual and, when the finished glass sheets were removed from the ovens, they were a dirty green, coarse and pocked with small stones and grains of sand. When they arrived in Paris to be polished and buffed, nearly every one broke. In fact, the oven and the degree of heat were meant for forty-eight hundred pounds of glass, not for sixty-four hundred.[28]

To be transformed into a mirror, cooled glass had to undergo a mechanical process in two stages: polishing and buffing. These two operations were carried out not at Saint-Gobain, but in Paris, at the rue de Reuilly. Glass arrived unfinished at the port Nicolas du Louvre and from there was sent along in carriages to the faubourg Saint-Antoine works. The transportation incurred great risk, and breakage was common. Once, out of a load of seventy-two sheets of glass, only twelve arrived intact! It is not hard to fathom why the directors preferred sending only the rough, unpolished glass into the capital.[29]

For the polishing process, a sheet of glass was attached to a stone table, then a second sheet was set on top of it with wet sand spread in the gap between them. For several days, men rubbed the two pieces of glass back and forth on top of each other. The process was finished by using emery paper. Buffing gave the glass its transparency and was done by hand. The glass was rubbed with an abrasive agent called *potée*, made of a very fine iron oxide powder. "Six hundred men work at it daily," wrote one visitor to the factory in 1698, "and it is hoped that we will soon have enough work for a thousand. On the floor below, they put rough glass in with pulverized sandstone. On the upper floors, where the glass was buffed, the workers stood in three rows, two men for each piece of glass that they wiped with brushes. The noise is most unbearable."[30]

The last stage was the silvering. "This wonder that has tormented more than one philosopher," wrote Pluche, "is nothing but a bit of tin and quicksilver cleanly applied to one of the two sides of the glass." The sheet of tin, about the thickness of a thumb, was pounded with a roller and stretched out in all directions. When it was even less than a tenth of an inch thick, it was spread out flat on hard limestone with a ruler and was rubbed with a chamois cloth soaked in quicksilver. The entirety was then submerged in quicksilver during which the glass was placed on top with tremendous pressure so as to expel any air bubbles. After resting under weights for twenty-four hours, the assembly was then gradually elevated at one end over a period of several days until it was vertical, thus draining off the mercury. The mirror could not be moved for another fifteen to twenty days so that the amalgam could stabilize. Then it was ready for sale. Aside from the toxic fumes it produced, this silvering process allowed for only a very fragile layer of silver, susceptible to humidity and hardly durable. Moreover, a darkness lingered in the tain (silver layer) and did not offer the clarity that we take for granted with mirrors today.

Modernizing the Process

During this period, no revolutionary strides in the manufacture of glass occurred until 1830, but there were a number of small improvements in quality and working conditions. Bosc d'Antic, one of the directors of the French company, perfected the large tables of allied copper. The use of sodium carbonate, from 1752 on, and that of coal instead of wood to fuel the ovens, brought about some progress. In 1763, the Saint-Gobain glassworks gave up glassblowing to concentrate solely on casting mirrors and built new halls with wide corridors to accommodate this process.

Popular interest in the glassmaking enterprise can be measured by the great number and variety of experiments undertaken in its name by serious scholars and amateurs alike.

Deslandes, an erudite director of the company in 1758, dedicated all of his learning and efforts to the industry, but there were also scholars, alchemists, and handy do-it-yourselfers who set up, as was the fashion, their own little laboratories. The *Almanach sous verre*, a periodical that collected information on "recent discoveries, inventions or experiments in the sciences, arts, trades and industry," regularly published the most recent industry news and provided encouragement.[31] In 1781, a Bourbon gentleman believed he had discovered "a glaze that protects mirrors from all humidity and makes it easier to put them in entry halls," (from which they were usually excluded because of their fragility), and "even to transport them by sea, without causing the tain to deteriorate." Another researcher invented a type of varnish intended to attach the tain to the glass. In 1785, Pilastre des Roziers, an amateur chemist famous for his flight in a hot-air balloon, claimed that he had found an infallible process for detecting hidden imperfections in glass. Such fanciful claims circulated freely, but the magical discovery sought by all, and in whose quest all inventors (serious or not) worked themselves to exhaustion, was a means of repairing broken glass and making it whole and clear again. What an elusive dream! A Parisian mirror maker staked his fortune on such a claim in 1692, advertising that "For private citizens, he can repair looking glasses that have been ruined."[32] A century later, in 1786, rumor had it that the secret of "making glass from broken pieces of glass that have the same appearance and polish as those that are whole" had been discovered.[33] The same hope was expressed by the citizen Pajot-Descharmes around 1800: "We finally have mastered welding broken glass together in such a way that breakage lines completely disappear; we can fuse the large pieces to make a single pane; we are able to make the air bubbles disappear and lighten the tain of a mirror that is a bit too green."

The problem of the tain was the prime objective of all research. Aside from its fragility, the mercury silvering also emitted dangerous vapors that made workers sick. The *Bulletin d'encouragement pour l'industrie nationale* reported efforts made to remedy these problems throughout the nineteenth century.[34] In 1812, a sum of 150 francs was granted to a certain M. Véréa, who declared that he was able to "give glass a new tain which does not adhere like ordinary silvering: it is a sheet of tin alloyed with other metallic substances; it can be placed behind the glass and removed at will." Ravrio, the bronzeworker Honoré de Balzac mentions in his short story "Domestic Peace," offered a prize in 1814 to whomever could remedy this "criminal poisoning" by mercury fumes. Again in 1842, a mirror maker from the Boulevard du Temple in Paris received a patent for his method of conserving a mirror's tain: "Mirrored glass can finally be kept in humid places," he announced in his advertisements, a now familiar boast that served as proof that progress was not being made quickly.[35]

Only in 1850 did problems with the silvering process begin to be resolved. In England, a researcher named Drayton perfected a method of silvering without mercury. He exported his patent to France, but in 1858 the *Dictionnaire abrégé des sciences, lettres et arts* made no mention of any silvering method other than with mercury. Twenty years after that, the *Dictionnaire des arts et manufactures* offered a detailed description of the English silvering process. At last, the mirror lost the grayish tint so detrimental to the clarity of its reflection.

The principal changes that modernized the mirror and glass industry in the nineteenth century came about in the realms of polishing and buffing, when the paddle wheel allowed for the mechanization of some forms of manual labor. The workshops of the faubourg Saint-Antoine proved neither sufficient nor convenient for the installation of this new technology, so the company bought the Chauny windmills and had the works installed there, where machines were powered by seven water wheels on the Aisne river. So as not to increase the geographic distribution of labor, most of the essential polishing was done at Chauny, and the role of Reuilly, where the workforce never surpassed four hundred people, was reduced.

Another innovation was that of artificial soda, invented during the Napoleonic era. Toward 1860 an equally important advance was made: the use of Siemens ovens made it possible to obtain much higher and more evenly distributed temperatures, thus reducing flaws in the molten glass. Gradually certain manual tasks disappeared. Mechanical cranes replaced men for transferring the vessels to the ovens, pouring out their contents onto the tables, and for rolling and laminating. Savings were made in time and in quality. Saint-Gobain was entering the modern age.

The Social Aspects of Saint-Gobain

In comparison to other industries of the ancien régime, Saint-Gobain was a gigantic enterprise. Yet it had to overcome many obstacles before realizing its astounding successes. At the beginning of the eighteenth century, it nearly perished from management errors when no one knew enough to evaluate orders and schedule them over time. Vigorous royal intervention was necessary to save the company, including Plastrier's dismissal from his post and the suspension of his partnership. A group of Protestant financiers supported by Minister Chamillart, including some from Geneva, then took a gamble on the future and began reimbursing the company's creditors. Under the name of a nominal partner, Antoine Dagincourt, a bourgeois Parisian, they shored up the company's finances and began anew with a more solid foundation.[36]

The company also needed to be protected from increased competition across the border, such as the glassworks in Saint-Quirin in Lorraine and Rouelles in Burgundy, for example—Saint-Quirin made cast glass in the early years of the nineteenth century by hiring away a foreman from Saint-Gobain—and to withstand the anger of mirror makers penalized by Saint-Gobain's monopoly. The English, for their part, developed their industry throughout the eighteenth century. After the success of the Vauxhall factory near London, created in 1701, the Ravenhead works opened in Lancashire in 1773 where two defectors from Saint-Gobain were employed. But British mirrors remained more expensive than French ones for quite some time. Until 1830, when Saint-Gobain was returned to the private sector and its privileges ended—the revolutionary years aside—the French industry improved its output and stayed competitive.

When Louis-Sébastien Mercier, the writer famed for his science-fiction novel *Memoir of the Year 2500*, visited the studios at Saint-Antoine shortly before the Revolution, he was at once indignant and filled with wonder. He was indignant because, he said, he saw the employees "subjected to work to which a tyrant wouldn't have dared condemn [them]." This spectacle inspired a harsh couplet regarding the whims of the idle youths at the end of the century who could not forgo looking at themselves "in four mirrors at once to see if their breeches are tight against their skin" and who were unaware of the cost in blood, sweat, and tears of the pleasure of admiring oneself in a looking glass.[37] But the efficiency of the work and the size of the factory also drew a cry of respectful admiration from Mercier: "The workshop will surprise you by its size, by the multiplicity of wheels and stones that more than four hundred workers standing in parallel lines slide and twirl across the glasses in order to polish them." What might he have said if he had visited the Saint-Gobain workshops later in the nineteenth century when more than eight hundred people rushed about night and day in royal garb of long white linen shirts and blue linen breeches, white gaiters and a large, turned back felt hat, their faces protected by an armor of light cloth![38]

The Saint-Gobain hiring contract imposed draconian rules on the apprentice worker. Hired for a one-week trial period at the meager salary of 10 sous per day, he was expected to work from five o'clock in the morning until seven o'clock at night, summer and winter, with three breaks during the day, a half-hour in the morning, an hour at lunch, and a half-hour at four in the afternoon. His salary rose to 15 and then 20 sous in the month after his hiring, with the cost of mirrors he broke either through his lack of experience or by accident deducted from his pay.[39] If the apprentice survived the one-month test, he was hired for a year, with the possibility of a two-year renewal. A good worker often remained in the same position for thirty years but had no right to be absent during this time without permission, nor to travel more than a league from Saint-Gobain, measures designed to keep him away from any possible job offers with rival glassworks. To leave the company, permission had to be requested in writing two years before the date of departure.

The company invested a great deal in the long and expensive training of its employees (at least 1,000 pounds each), and desertion met with severe penalties, fines, or corporal punishment. In 1693, three *tiseurs* abandoned their ovens and ran off one night. Right away the town's cavalry set off in pursuit, captured the men, and led them off to prison. In the beginning, the company was merciless. Le Pommeraye, a former director of Saint-Gobain and protégé of Louvois, but who had had a falling-out with his old friends from the company, was sentenced to pay large sums of compensation in 1714 for having started a rival company in Dombes and then in Spain. He was eventually imprisoned.

Salaries varied according to the qualifications, seniority, and skill of the worker, and they were generally slightly higher than in other professions. Personnel were ranked according to a strict hierarchy: directors earned 2,400 pounds per year plus benefits. Next came the managing officers at 1,200 pounds, the clerks at 600 pounds, and the warehouse guards at 400 pounds.

Among the workers, who were paid weekly, a distinction was made between the interior hall workers and exterior courtyard workers. The former, highly qualified, prepared the molten glass; the latter oversaw the care of materials. A master *tiseur* could earn as much as 600 pounds; those who poured the glass earned a bit less. Then came the fire stokers, the men in charge of the embers, the square cutters, the polishers, and the buffers. Each affixed his symbol on each piece of glass that passed through his hands, hoping to earn the bonus offered for the highest-quality product among them. A night team that changed shifts every week slept on straw mattresses in the large rooms near the ovens and monitored security. Women and children also worked as day laborers at small jobs and earned a few sous per day.

Workers lived cloistered within the walls of Saint-Gobain, and many of them complained about it. In order to avoid conflicts, the company had banned the sale of alcoholic beverages and reduced workers' idle time, removing all opportunity for distraction. The doors of the establishment were locked at eight o'clock in the evening in winter and at ten in the summer. After closing, the doorman was required to lock the door and give the key to the director. Workers had to return at least fifteen minutes before closing time, and any infractions—drunkenness, tardiness, or truancy—were punished by a reduction in wages proportional to the seriousness of the offense.

The organization of labor at Saint-Gobain was rigorous because of the indispensable protections inherent in a state-of-the-art industry. Workers enjoyed both advantages and restrictions greater than workers in other industries. But all in all the situation for Saint-Gobain personnel must have been fairly enviable for the time, for job applications never ceased to pour in, and this severe regime did have its advantages, not the least of which was job security. Even in periods of stagnant sales and during times of political upheaval, the company refused to lay off workers. During the Revolution, when Saint-Gobain was forced to shut down its kilns for lack of orders, workers were kept on and assigned to other tasks without a reduction in salary. The reason for this was that management, while waiting for better days, feared that its workers would otherwise be hired away by foreign competition. During shortages, provisions were distributed, and smocks, mittens, and clogs were furnished free of charge. Workers also benefited from lodging, heat, and medical assistance; their total care was assured. Architects had even dreamed of building an extremely functional and modern "apartment building" in Bel Air, at Saint-Gobain, to bring workers together under one roof, but the project met with violent opposition because such close quarters ran the risk of aggravating tensions inherent in the already concentration camp–like conditions, and had to be abandoned.

Saint-Gobain was ahead of its time regarding social legislation for workers, perfecting a system of insurance against the risks of accidents, illness, and old age. In case of illness, workers received half their salaries, and if they were injured in the course of their work, they received compensation proportional to the length of their disablement. In 1760, management decided to grant retirement benefits to workers with twenty-five years of service and to those disabled through occupational injury, as long as they were "industrious, sensible, and orderly." Retired workers retained possession of their lodgings and received a lifetime annuity. The worker could also increase his salary by producing, on certain authorized days, small works of glassmaking on his own. Finally, he could receive special compensation for the most backbreaking tasks, such as cleaning out the ovens. Despite the difficult living conditions and the strict supervision, Saint-Gobain was considered a pioneer in matters of social protection.

3

From Luxury to Necessity

An Expanding Trade

Decorating in the Century of Louis XIV

In 1685, while Madame de Grignan was furnishing her new residence, her mother, Madame de Sévigné, who followed the work closely, gave her some advice as the bills piled up: "I know the pleasure of decorating a room," she conceded. "I would have given in to it as well, but I have always experienced misgivings about having things that aren't necessary when one doesn't have those things that are! Thus, both maternally and as a good friend," she added firmly, "I reprimand Monsieur de Grignan for his desire to give you another mirror. Be satisfied, my dear, with the one you have. It belongs in your bedroom, which still needs improvements."[1] One mirror and not two: her words convey the rarity and price of the object.

Her maternal advice is all the more commendable given that the marquise could see for herself the marvelous decorative effect of glass-covered walls in the most beautiful Parisian houses of her time. The chamber in which "the new Madame de Lafayette" received visitors was full "of mirrors, chandeliers, panes of reflective glass and crystal after the current fashion." In

1689, Louis XIV ordered that silver be melted down for coins to help pay for his military campaigns. As for the duchess of Lude, she obeyed Louis XIV's decree by reducing "all of her beautiful silver furniture to bits and pieces. . . . But since the silver was of such a fine quality, she received 27, 000 ecus and refurnished her home with all sorts of wooden and glass or mirrored furniture."[2] One can only imagine what the psychology was like in an era in which people had to surrender their wealth to support royal ambitions and to console themselves with the illusion of infinitely multiplied reflections.

The aristocratic society of Louis XIV had a passion for mirrors. Associated with light—the seventeenth century emphasized the optical and visual—mirrors lit up dark rooms, lightened thick walls, simulated window frames, and resembled precious jewelry in their elegant gem-encrusted box frames. When placed opposite windows, they reflected the scenery of the countryside and served as paintings, perfectly adapted to the subtle alliance of art and nature called for by the social proprieties of the time. Renovations on the le Pelletier de Saint-Fargeau residence in Paris in 1989 uncovered, beneath mirrors mounted on the walls, painted scenes of the countryside and of the townhouse across the way. The drawings are exact reproductions of the mirror's image of the scene and demonstrate the meticulousness of the interior decorators when choosing the best location for the glass.

Nature itself was fashioned as an element of interior decoration. Thus Mademoiselle de Scudéry modeled her ideal country house after the model of the palace in Francesco Colonna's pastoral fantasy, *Hypnerotomachia Poliphili*, endowed with numerous mirrors placed opposite the windows "that duplicate the view of the countryside and make this admirable salon appear entirely open on three sides."[3] Between the sculpted wood paneling and the marble pilasters, the court was able to view the brilliant reflection of the countryside, whose varied effects contributed to the stimulation of the eyes and of the intellect. Mirrored glass was found everywhere, in châteaux and even in parks. According to one observer, the grotto in the park of Saint-Germain had walls covered in glass: "When water is poured in, a hundred waterfalls suddenly appear where there is really only one and infinite jets of water appear on all sides. Each mirror returns to the others the image it receives, and what it cannot have directly, it takes from one of its neighbors." The simplicity of the real vanished before the multiplicity of the artificial. The empire of the sign, where opulence spread and multiplied, had begun: "Thus nothing is lost in these mirrors."[4]

The Price of the Reflection

By purveying these dreams, the Saint-Gobain company also made its own fortune. Orders poured in: half of the homes in Paris acquired a mirror in the last two decades of the seventeenth century. When the company first got off the ground, the directors had expected to produce between eight hundred and nine hundred sheets of glass a year, a forecast that fell well short of actual demand. They were soon disillusioned, however: the transport from Saint-Gobain to Paris caused significant breakage, and the mirrors were often so defective that clients refused to accept them! The company came close to bankruptcy in 1699, when princely mansions refused their poorly silvered mirrors of an ugly yellow color, and the company's dealers had to act quickly to grab up the stock of good glass from the small merchant–mirror makers of Paris in order to honor royal commissions. In addition, despite regulations forbidding importation, Louis XIV himself often turned to the Murano production. In 1686, the Venetian merchant J. B. Patriarche gave him glass worth 3,478 pounds and another 4,800 pounds the following year.[5] Once again, in 1714, shops that were out of stock turned to the Italians.

The uncertainties of production heavily influenced prices. A pane of glass was assessed according to its size and purity, and official tariffs were calculated on the basis of absolute perfection, a standard that was in fact never achieved before certain advancements in the field of chemistry around 1830. Every Friday, the glass produced that week left the polishing workshop at the rue de Reuilly and was presented to the assessors, who, in the presence of the directors, decided which price reductions should be made due to flaws.[6] Even at reduced prices the French mirrors were more expensive and less beautiful than those from Venice for quite some time, and it wasn't until the end of the century that the price of French glass was truly competitive.

From about 1700, the technical advances at Saint-Gobain gave French glass the upper hand, by allowing for panes greater than seventy inches tall, the maximum size attainable by glassblowing. Prices dropped: the same five-by-three-foot looking glasses worth up to 2,000 pounds in Venice sold for a quarter of that price in Paris, although the clarity of the Italian product remained superior. Delahaye, the French ambassador to the Venetian Republic, noted in 1697 that the Murano glassworkers had given up trying to make large looking glasses due to a scarcity of workers capable of blowing them.

In 1682, the Royal Company introduced two rates: the first aimed at royal houses (its best clients), and the second at private demand. Based on volume orders, these rates were adjusted according to different authorized rebates. The glasses were classified into three categories, and their worth increased in proportion to their size. Anything smaller than forty inches high was either blown glass fabricated at Tourlaville, or "scraps" from larger broken glasses. Panes larger than eighty inches were always cast. At the bottom of the scale, grooming mirrors and pocket mirrors were usually designated by numbers that went from one to fifty.

Advances in glassmaking can be measured by comparing rates: In 1682, the largest pane was forty inches tall and cost approximately 140 pounds, a price that remained unchanged for some time. At the beginning of the eighteenth century, sizes as large as seventy by forty-five inches and ninety by fifty-five inches were obtained and priced at 750 and 3,000 pounds, respectively, when sold to a private buyer. Not until thirty years later did prices drop significantly; in 1734 a seventy-by-forty-five-inch looking glass was worth no more than 425 pounds—a price that corresponded to the annual salary of one qualified Saint-Gobain worker. A century later, the mirror was still a luxury product that sold for 90 francs per square meter, not including framing costs or retail markup—and a worker's average salary was 45 francs per month.[7]

Louis XIV, the company's principal client, benefited from preferential rates that were approximately half those for private customers. Looking glasses that were forty by thirty inches cost him 126 pounds, those seventy by forty-four cost 381 pounds, and those eighty by forty-five, a little less than 500 pounds. The annual commission for decorating Versailles, inventoried in the *Comptes des batiments royaux*, reached 40,000 or 45,000 pounds in its peak years! The king had the apartments of his favorite mistresses, Madame de Montespan and Madame de Maintenon, decorated according to the mirror-obsessed fashion of the day. For his various secondary residences—Versailles, Trianon, Saint-Germain, Glagny, and Meudon—he bought some 375,000 pounds' worth of glass between 1667 and 1695. Mirrors also figure among the gifts he offered to foreign dignitaries, including the ambassador from Siam and the sultan of Turkey: in effect they served as promotional gifts as the Siamese government bought four hundred mirrors from Saint-Gobain in return.

The royal family and the court imitated their monarch by taking advantage of the slightest discounts. In 1717 the duke d'Antin and the marquis de Lassé demanded the same rates as his majesty, but their request was denied. The duke of Orléans bought some 30,000 pounds' worth of glass between 1696 and 1700, and the duke of Anjou had 109 mirrors worth some 26,000 pounds sent to Spain in 1713. The company might well have feared that once royal residences were furnished, the number of orders would plummet, but such was not the case: nearly 300,000 pounds were billed to the treasury in the period between 1747 and 1764, and nearly 500,000 pounds in the twenty years that followed.[8]

The company's private clientèle, an increasingly diversified group, was poised to continue the buying trend. At the end of the century nearly all of the bourgeois in Paris were procuring decorative glass, this indispensable element of décor, a testament to their elevated standard of living. Those of lesser occupations soon followed suit. In 1684, when the company's privilege was renewed, Louvois required the directors to drop prices of small looking glasses by 25 percent, and from this point on, the market expanded. British naturalist Martin Lister, during his stay in Paris, was astonished at the low price of glass: "They have succeeded to such an extent that they are able to sell it at such a low price that nearly all delivery carriages and most horse-drawn cabs are enclosed in the front by a large pane of glass."[9] From 1698 to 1700, sales quadrupled, reaching 750,000 pounds on average per year; if there were a few periods of stagnation caused by war or crisis, there were also times of incredible prosperity in 1700 (954,00 pounds), 1713, and 1714. In 1722, the rates were printed. Even during times of crisis, certain speculators chose glass as a safe investment.

In the middle of the eighteenth century, Saint-Gobain reached new heights: sales doubled between 1745 and 1755, with record sales of 1.182 million pounds in 1750.[10] During the same decade, the glassworks of Murano were barely surviving, despite orders from England.[11] Italy's production, valued at 584,000 ducats in 1743, fell to 314,000 in 1761, an average loss of 50 percent in less than twenty years, and their glasses were less and less esteemed. According to the French naturalist Louis-Augustin-Guillame Bosc d'Antic, by 1780 there was only a single artisan making crystal in Venice, "and he sells it at excessive prices!" Once again in 1770, a good year, Saint-Gobain couldn't fill all its orders and reluctantly had to reduce exports abroad. Sales surged under the Restoration in 1820 and in 1825.

The Organization of Sales

How were such vast quantities of glass sold? The company may well have wanted to reserve all distribution channels for itself, but was forced to yield to strong opposition from merchant–mirror makers, who had already been financially ruined by Saint-Gobain's monopoly. Ultimately the two sides arrived at a compromise: Parisian mirror makers obtained the right to do the silvering themselves and to sell mirrors destined for individual customers, whereas the company kept all of the public trade plus foreign exports. Mirror makers from the provinces, less numerous and less united, did not benefit from this arrangement.

The fairly complex system of sales changed on several occasions.[12] At first, the company assigned several agents to ply the commercial trade. These "representatives" would take all the glass the company made, even that which was destined for royal houses, and arranged for storage with the merchants. Their profits came from a commission made on each sale, a commission that increased progressively if the total sales surpassed 600,000 pounds. However, the value of all unsold glass was withheld against profits. This system was dissolved in 1701, and the following year, the company created a central sales service in the rue de Reuilly consisting of two offices under the management of a general cashier: one for sales in Paris, and one for royal sales and those in the provinces and abroad.

Responsibility for the purchase of the king's looking glasses fell to the royal mirror maker, who called at Reuilly. He made his choice after the polishing stage, then his selections were taken to be silvered. For the Parisian merchants, sales took place on Fridays, after the assessment. Mirror makers examined the glass available in the different exhibition halls at Reuilly and indicated those that they wanted. When the company did not have the requested sizes in stock, it was obligated to cut a larger one down to size, as long as the reduction did not surpass four inches. A porter would deliver the order to the mirror maker's shop, where the silvering took place. The shipping of mirrors from the factory was strictly monitored by a general inspector. Every year a detailed inventory was drawn up, listing everything in the warehouse and in the workshops.

Parisian Style

The Empire of the Merchant–Mirror Makers

Mirror makers, who were represented in trade guilds beginning in 1581, formed an important class of haberdasher-merchant in Paris, comprising an active, informed body of some three thousand members in two thousand shops.[13] "Merchants of everything, makers of nothing," was how Diderot's *Encyclopédie* defined the haberdashers, because they gladly modified their wares to conform to the tastes of the day and could charge tenfold the value of the raw product on account of this. Always on the lookout for novelties, haberdashers dictated fashions, and the most skillful among them scoured for wares abroad. Upscale haberdasher–mirror makers or jewelers imported mirrors for years, doing their part to help Paris earn its reputation as the capital of luxury. A trend often faded within twenty or twenty-five years (faster still in the eighteenth century), so haberdashers worked incessantly, proposing new and original fashions, creating new demands. A Sicilian strolling in Paris in 1714 was astounded: "There shines here an infinity of shops where only those things that are not needed are sold!"[14] While an article of clothing became outdated faster than a flower could wilt, buying trendy luxury goods was the favorite pastime of "people of quality."

The best shops were those of the Palais-Royal, the Pont-Neuf, the pont Notre-Dame, and the rue Saint-Honoré, where Lazare Duvaux, purveyor of furniture and gold for the king and Madame de Pompadour, and the jewelers Ericourt et Desguerres were located. The *Livre commode des adresses de Paris* by Abraham du Pradel (1692), a veritable Who's Who of the most stylish addresses, mentions several haberdasher–mirror makers who sold panes of glass from the Royal Company, Venetian-style glasses, and secondhand mirrors at prices to match all incomes. The Sun and The Crown of Gold on the quai de l'Horloge sold mirrors, telescopes, and microscopes. In the rue Saint-Denis, Madame Delaroue sold lights and crystal candelabras and also rented chandeliers for parties.

The boutiques of the pont Notre-Dame, according to the *Livre commode*, were the best stocked and the most renowned. In 1682, for the sumptuous parties that accompanied the dauphine's labor and the birth of her child, the haberdashers of the pont Notre-Dame swathed their shops in bunting and turned them into veritable palaces by lighting their windows with "a nearly infinite number of lights: mirrors of all sorts, in crystal or gilded frames that reached to the ceiling."[15] One of these shops, hung with tapestries and ornate with mirrors, was so well decorated that it was chosen as a ballroom. The same spectacle occurred in 1686, when the king came to Paris after his great illness. The mirror makers on the pont Notre-Dame, which Louis XIV needed to cross in order to get from the Palais to the Hôtel de Ville, set up a hedge of mirrors in his honor "in order to multiply his image."

Some rich merchants, like the Darnaults at rue du Roule, or the Delaroues, established veritable business dynasties, passing their enterprises from father to son. Sensing the tastes of the moment, they made a specialty out of discovering and dictating the "must have" fashions of the time. Through the famous painting by Jeanne Antoine Watteau, we are familiar with the interior of Gersaint's shop on the pont Notre-Dame: this jeweler-merchant sold "all sorts of new and tasteful metal jewelry, mirrors, paintings, pagodas, laquered items and porcelaine from Japan." From the top of an invoice from the Darnaults, in the rue de la Monnaye, we read: "Darnault father and son, ordinary merchants and mirrormakers of the King keep a shop of looking glasses, stoves, handles, cabinet works, china and clocks."[16]

In the richness and beauty of the mirror's frame, too, one sees the stamp of the leaders in the mirror trade. After buying silvered glass from the mirror makers, merchants would set it in a frame and decorate it. Frames were made of ebony, cedar, and violet wood, and adorned with brass plates and bronze hinges. Decrees that prohibited the use of precious metals forced mirror makers to be twice as imaginative with regard to materials and shapes: leather, tortoiseshell, and sculpted wood were used, and in 1770, round or oval shapes were invented—also rectangular ones with cornices said to be *à la Dauphine*. The mirrors were protected by small curtains of silk or taffeta with ribbons or cords; their wooden pediments were decorated, in the eighteenth century, with fantastic animals and figurines; the frames copied Chinese motifs, the rococo style with intertwined branches, foliage, and garlands of flowers.[17] The scalloped capitals emulated the sober moldings of the classical era. Their size varied—the most ordinary models measured roughly one foot high and were made of a single pane of glass, but there were also some made with several juxtaposed panes.

The Mirror and Furnishing in the Eighteenth Century

The mirror was often embedded in furniture, decorating writing cases or desks, the compartments of wardrobes, centerpieces, corner cupboards, and candelabra holders, and it was an obviously indispensable complement to grooming and shaving.

Lazare Duvaux specialized in delivering expensive dressing tables with mirrors to his aristocratic clientèle, and those of Madame de Pompadour were particularly sumptuous, with their ensemble of brushes, perfume flasks, and carved mirrors and cases. For a long time, "la toilette," or dressing table, was nothing more than a piece of cloth—made of canvas, serge, wool, satin, muslin, or lace—that covered a chest upon which the necessary accessories for the care of the face and hair were placed. It was set up in a small closet or room, a wardrobe, where a servant might sleep or where the household linens might be stored. Such chests, still rare in the seventeenth century, became more commonplace in the eighteenth. The use of small, portable stands composed of a frame and a tabletop also spread toward the middle of the century.[18] They progressively became true furniture with drawers and inclining mirrors, called *coiffeuses* (dressing tables) or *poudreuses* (powder tables) and beautifully decorated with marquetry.

These pieces of furniture that assisted grooming were found in corners reserved for personal care and dressing. Architects recommended putting vanities in large rooms (roughly sixteen by thirteen feet) that faced north and tiling the floor of the room with hard limestone. The room had to be equipped with at least three mirrors, mounted as low as possible so that people could see themselves from head to toe. Thus the "cabinet de toilette" (or what today might be called the bathroom) was born. This eighteenth-century innovation spread slowly: it was found in only 6.5 percent of Parisian households inventoried following 1750 (among a total of eight hundred surveyed).[19] Visitors, be they gentlemen or women friends, were admitted into this sanctum, the mirror serving another purpose while grooming, for "it is of some importance to watch the arrival of those who come to pay homage to you." The bathroom proper was a nineteenth-century development, although certain architectural treatises trace its roots to the end of the eighteenth century. The architect and writer Nicolas Le Camus de Mézières advised fashioning the room out of marble, calling it "the bedroom of the baths" for its mirrors "imitate a beautiful room of water whose tranquillity seems to summon sleepiness and make it stay."[20]

Mirrors thus invaded household decor and transformed furniture throughout the eighteenth century. A certain amount of time was needed to acclimate to them, however, for their visual effects turned the relationship between empty and full surfaces on its head and defied equilibrium. But soon people could not do without the light brought by looking glasses; they gave life to surfaces, replacing paintings and tapestries to the point of alarming one contemporary art critic, La Font de Saint-Yenne, who regretted what he called the "disastrous blow" that mirrors delivered to historical painting. But he did admit that

> the advantages of these mirrors, which are something of a miracle, were in many ways deserving of the favor that fashion granted them: piercing walls to enlarge rooms and to join them with new ones; returning with high rates of interest the rays of light they receive, whether those of daylight or of candelabras. How could man, from birth an enemy of darkness and of all that can bring about sadness, have refrained from loving an embellishment that cheers him while lighting his way, and that, in deceiving his eyes, never deceives him in the real pleasure he gets from it?[21]

Such were the profound reasons for the success of the looking glass.

The Triumph of Overmantel Mirrors

In the late eighteenth century, the invention of overmantel mirrors, generally attributed to Robert de Cotte (1656–1753) launched a major trend in the decoration of private Parisian mansions. The architect J. F. Blondel expressed the anxiety incited at the start of the overmantel mirror trend: "Many people protested, as is the custom, the use of mirrors between window openings, claiming that since the mirrors represented emptiness, it was hardly natural to express something as though it were an opening when it should have been filled."[22] Mantelpieces were lowered and mirrors, sometimes framed by painted scenes, were mounted above them. Inventories of Parisian houses begin to list such mirrors beginning at the end of the seventeenth century, but they became especially widespread under the Regency and multiplied in bourgeois homes after 1750.

Overmantel mirrors (*trumeaux de glace*) could also mean mirrors placed between two windows, up to six and a half feet in width, sometimes composed of two or three small mirrors fit together, and sometimes of a single large pane, encased in a frame of painted wood, and sometimes decorated with pilasters or other motifs. The widow of an officer of the *Chancellerie du Palais*, Lady Terneau of the rue de la Harpe, hung two mirrors over her mantel in 1695, one made of three fourteen-by-ten-inch pieces of glass, the other of "three mirrors of five 10 by 6 inch panes," as well as a large sixteen-paned mirror framed by gilded wood. Another decorated the main room of his house with "two over mantel mirrors, each one foot, eight inches wide by one foot, four inches high," with two arms of copper candlesticks.[23] Sometimes up to eight mirrors were placed one above the other. Candelabras and wall lamps, often mounted on mirrored plates that refracted and multiplied light, framed mirrors and mantelpieces.

Germain Brice's *Description de Paris*, published in twelve editions between 1684 and 1752, a veritable guide to taste and luxury and an inventory of the beautiful townhouses of Paris, enumerates the most delicate inventions, the most beautiful decorative effects of contemporary architecture and all "that the caprice of time has changed." Mirrors top the list. Brice's book notes that in 1698 two prominent gentlemen had their residences redecorated at the end of the seventeenth century with all the "singular and beautiful things one could imagine, especially mirrors of an extraordinary height," framed in tortoiseshell. The townhouse of J.-B. Terrat, the chancellor to the duke of Orléans, included "a room with mirrors everywhere." In Pierre de Quency's mansion, at the place Louis-le-Grand, "everything shines with gold and large-sized mirrors." In the new hall of the Richelieu townhouse, also called the Cardinal Palace, the mirrors above the fireplace reached to the cornice. Placed advantageously, they reflected "all the beauties of this place and a part of the salon that serves as an entryway." At the home of the duchess of Bouillon, mirrors framed in small Corinthian columns of jasper rose above the fireplace. The same effects could be found in the small Bourbon townhouse of Princess Anne of the Bavarian Palatinate, where "extraordinary embellishments" were made in 1710: "the fireplaces were trimmed with select marble and mirrors."[24]

In truth, there was no longer much in common between Madame de Grignan's rare and precious mirror valued for its sculpted frame, not for its size (just that of a dinner plate), and the panels of glass encased in gray or green floorboards that later decorated the homes of the modestly well-to-do. The mirror craze showed no sign of faltering; instead it grew as the century advanced. A notice in the periodical *Annonces, Affiches et Avis divers* in 1754 noted, as if it were of exceptional interest to Parisians, a mirror sale of guaranteed quality to take place at the château de Bagnolet over several days: "There are more than two hundred pieces that the now deceased Duke of Orléans, regent of the kingdom, had had installed by contractors from the Company."[25]

A celebrated architectural treatise written by Nicolas Le Camus de Mézières devotes more than ten pages to the indispensable rules governing the installation of mirrors: their color, purity, and regularity must be checked while they are being assembled, for "it would be ridiculous if a nymph who wanted to consult the charms of her beauty should meet, instead of a regular figure, a face that is squashed and crooked."[26] Such infatuation with mirrors incited this amused commentary from Louis-Sebastian

Mercier, subtly mocking the bourgeois pretensions of the fin de siècle: "When a house is built, nothing is yet done, not a quarter of what is necessary has been spent. The carpenter, the tapestry maker, the painter, the gilder, the sculptor and the cabinetmaker must do their part. Mirrors are needed next, and doorbells put everywhere."[27]

In this passage, mirrors double the owner's proprietary pleasure while the bells indicate the attentive presence of numerous valets. A house could not be pleasing unless it was endowed with mirrors. Issues of *Annonces, Affiches et Avis divers* always mention, as an added attraction, those houses for rent that had mirrors. The provinces were not yet familiar with the refinement of luxury that was the delight of Paris at the beginning of the eighteenth century, so advertisements were especially insistent. One advertisement notes a beautiful house in Orléans, with its outbuildings "built in a modern style. The lodgings are beautiful and practical, they are full of woodwork and decorated with mirrors." A house in Nantes is described in 1758, its principal room "with parquet floors and plastered ceilings . . . embellished with mirrors." Or yet again, near Lyon, a country residence, furnished in silks, has "mirrors and overmantel mirrors in its rooms." It is no surprise that in the nineteenth century, in Paris, rental signs still advertised apartments "lined with mirrors."

Mirochons et Mirelaids

The Trivialization of Mirrors in Paris

"Soon the boudoir of any cloth merchant will be covered with mirrors. . . . Where would one not put them?" To a historian of sensibility, this quip from Louis-Sebastien Mercier is worth numerous surveys and statistics. An expensive and rare object reserved for a small elite under the reign of Louis XIV, the mirror could be found in more than 70 percent of Parisian homes one hundred years later, as well as in a substantial number of homes in the provinces. The public imagination was not short on decorating ideas. Women covered their salons, sleeping alcoves, offices, ceilings, stairwells, wardrobes, and other furniture with them.

At the end of the eighteenth century, the *psyché*, or free-standing mirror, had a place of honor in many sitting rooms and became the symbol of an era. Similar in design to the *miroir de toilette*, or grooming mirror, the *psyché* was an enlarged version, and first called a "glass screen" for its resemblance to the screens mounted on stands and covered with upholstery and placed in front of fireplaces. A visitor to France in 1787 was surprised by this "pleasing invention" consisting of "mirrors in front of fireplaces instead of the various folding screens in use in England."[28] The *psyché*, a sort of two-meter high dressing mirror without a table or a drawer, flanked by two sconces for lighting, enjoyed all sorts of improvements over the years, such as side mirrors and small panels. Around 1810, the *psyché* came to be known as a piece in which the central pane of mirror could pivot around a horizontal axis to modify the angle of vision. It soon became an indispensable beauty aid during the Empire and the Restoration.[29]

The status of this full-length mirror changed as it became accessible to the population at large. A more commonplace item, the mirror blended into a home's interior decor and its frame became more subdued. J. Callot, a student of past mores, correctly observed in 1827 this metamorphosis at the end of the century:

> Mirrors played a great role in the new mode of decorating, not mirrors surrounded by large carved and gilded frames in the style of immense historical paintings, hunting scenes and still lifes, but mirrors secured by and enclosed in strips of wood, whose light gilding no longer attracted one's gaze at the mirrors' expense. In between windows and above fireplaces, almost

wherever they turned, ladies could look at themselves from head to toe at leisure.[30]

At the end of the eighteenth century, mirrors brought an element of a fairy-tale dream to life as they invaded all spaces of social interaction, where they replaced tapestries. They decorated stylish new cafés, soda shop counters, and covered the walls of lovers' discreet meeting places.[31] As the costly craze traveled across Europe, governments began to take notice. The Republic of Geneva went as far as enacting a law that prohibited its citizens, under penalty of a fine, "from having more than one mirror in each room and from having any in excess of thirty-two inches in height." The law even forbade nobles from having more than two large mirrors and the bourgeoisie from having one more than twenty-four inches in height.[32] The legislation combined fiscal concern with the maintenance of propriety.

Nonetheless, the art of "the good life" spread through bourgeois circles, and then to the masses. From 1730 onward, the class of domestic servants imitated their masters' consumer spending, and artisans followed in turn. The estate inventories of small wage earners, those at the bottom of the social ladder, begin to include small mirrors. The famed libertine novelist Restif de la Bretonne, describing the room of an eating house that rented for 4 pounds a month, listed the simplest of furnishings—a bed, a table, two chairs, a pitcher and washbowl, as well as a small mirror.[33] Overmantel mirrors, however, were still unusual, and often carried certain associations: a young girl in Restif de la Bretonne's *Les Contemporaines [Contemporary Women]* who had turned to prostitution, saw herself made up for the first time in her madame's overmantel mirror without recognizing herself.

A third of Parisian lodgings in 1750 were made up of a single room and accommodated a family with several children.[34] Statistics compiled by surveying more than five hundred households have established that between 1695 and 1715, approximately half of all salaried workers and domestic servants possessed a mirror smaller than twenty inches in height, but that only 10 percent of them owned a larger one. In about 1750, two-thirds of the Parisian populace had a mirror, a quarter of those possessing one larger than twenty inches in height.[35] By the end of the eighteenth century, a significant proportion of Parisian homes contained several mirrors, though these mirrors were for the most part modest in size. The dramatist and writer Pierre Carlet de Chamblain de Marivaux has the heroine of his novel *La Vie de Marianne* complain that, in the house of her landlady (a linen seller), for trying on the lovely outfit given to her by her patron, she can only find "one ugly little mirror that showed me only half of my face."[36] Large mirrors remained scarce in the eighteenth century except in the grand townhouses of the aristocracy, like those described by Germain Brice. In 1759, at the estate sale of a Madame Hérault, a single-paned mirror sixty-five inches high by fifty inches wide, was exhibited as a veritable curiosity. Eight years later, at M. Delisle's home, rue Bourdonnais, a mirror seventy-eight inches high and forty-seven inches wide could be seen.[37]

Novelist Louis-Sebastien Mercier noted drolly that on the feast day of Saint-Louis, when the château at Versailles was open to the public, a mass of poorly dressed people rushed into the royal apartments and opened their eyes wide with stupefaction: "The Swiss laugh to see the flabbergasted artisan strain his neck to look at the ceilings and to see himself in the mirrors."[38] Clearly the large mirrors in which one could see oneself from head to toe were not yet widespread, even in Paris. They were associated with a certain idea of life, a taste for splendor and performance that only certain classes and professions could enjoy. They were a hallmark of social standing, and all beautiful houses had to have them. During the Restoration, Octave de Malivert, the hero of Stendhal's novel *Armance*, having admired the Hôtel de Bonnivet, dreams of decorating his own home with large mirrors: "I will have a magnificent drawing room. I shall have three mirrors in it, each seven feet high. I have always liked that kind of somber, magnificent decoration. I wonder what the measurements are of the largest mirror they make at Saint-Gobain?"[39]

A Slow Spread to the Provinces

Within a few decades, the provinces followed Paris's lead. The aristocrat who frequently visited Versailles had undoubtedly brought similar refinements into his own surroundings. Ceremonial halls and bedrooms were almost always decorated with mirrors above the fireplace and between the windows. But the provincial bourgeoisie, with its frugal and austere ways, was suspicious of the mirror's offering of prestige without substance. A fragile object that one clumsy slip could reduce to splinters, its triviality, the way it made thick protective walls appear empty, robbing the home of its secret and intimate feeling: these qualities rarely moved the noteworthy burgher to open his wallet. It was less a question of standard of living than of mentality.

Household inventories from the first third of the eighteenth century often mention simple *miroirs de toilette*, or grooming mirrors. One bourgeois woman from Saint-Malo, the widow of a rich shipowner, possessed only one small glass square valued at 10 pounds in 1729. Another woman from Brittany had "two small *miroirs de toilette* in addition to a larger mirror in her bedroom." In 1767, a merchant of fine china from Limoges, whose shop housed ten thousand items from Nevers, Rouen, and Holland, had only one mirror in his room, fixed with two small clamps, and a small *miroir de toilette*.[40] The pursuit of material comforts remained tentative, although evidence of a certain level of affluence can be detected in the accessories that promoted social interaction—cushions, armchairs, lighting, and china.

In Lyon, mirrors were hung on walls in the homes of certain silk workers whose standard of living approached that of the bourgeois classes. A master bread baker, whose annual income reached as much as 10,000 pounds, owned one tapestry, two clocks, and a framed mirror. At Ville-Dieu in 1744, a bistro owner and bailiff decorated his entry chamber with "a small mirror." At Chartres, sometime between 1780 and 1790, historian Robert Muchembled noticed, master craftsmen on average had two mirrors per household, but they were found in only half of the inventories of salaried workers.[41]

The insufficient or poor organization of commercial distribution bore part of the responsibility. Before 1695, when markets were limited, mirror dealers would buy their goods in Paris where heavy transport tolls forced prices up. After that date, the Royal Company ensured itself a monopoly on sales in the provinces by creating royal shops controlled by the general inspector in the principal cities of the country: Lyon, Lille, Nantes, Marseille, Montpellier, La Rochelle, Brest, and Rouen. These warehouses supplied nearly all the large regions. Polished and unsilvered glass arrived from Paris every three months in quantities that varied from city to city and were decided upon by the local officials. In the same year, Lyon bought 4,000 pounds worth of mirrors, while the Nantes shop ordered for itself only 1,500 pounds worth. The dealer received a commission once he exceeded a certain number of sales and he alone took responsibility for the silvering. In the first half of the eighteenth century, Lyon and Marseille had the most active warehouses; others foundered, while those in Bordeaux, Roanne, Saint-Malo, Dijon, and Clermont barely took hold.[42]

Even in the best of cases, retail sales in the provinces couldn't compare to those in Paris. At Clermont, it took three or four years for a dealer to sell some twenty mirrors, so in 1742 he began to reduce his inventory. As a result, clients often could not obtain the type of mirror they needed, and thus came to prefer dealing directly with a Parisian agent, bypassing the supposed monopoly of the Royal Company. Sometimes a single order of large glass completely depleted a dealer's stock. Delivery delays (often several weeks) and increasing competition from peripheral mirror-making factories—Rouelles in Burgundy and Saint-Quirin in Lorraine, for example—made the risk of bankruptcy quite high for provincial dealers. A final difficulty was that the main office in Paris all too often used deliveries to the provinces to rid itself of its most mediocre merchandise—defective and yellowed glass—and that engendered mistrust and a decline in sales. The disparity between Paris and the provinces is well illustrated by a couplet written by a Parisian mirror maker at the end of the eighteenth century: "Why are people more *poli* (polished/polite) in Paris than in the provinces? Because mirrors are less common there than in Paris . . . "[43]

Reticence in the Countryside

Did those living in the countryside even consider looking at themselves in a mirror? In rural society, the mirror was suspect, unsettling, and almost an enchanted object: "When a mirror is broken in a home, misfortune will follow," was a popular saying. The man who confronted nature on a daily basis was not interested in intangible reflections, or in encountering his wrinkled face, tanned and worn by his work. The peddler, winding his way through the countryside, sold him small mirrors—mostly of metal, but sometimes of glass—that he hung in the common room of his home, near the window. Mirrors were also used for women's grooming—proverbs associated them with coquetry, arousing the same suspicions as affected dress or overly contrived beauty. A mirror was, however, also the gift that parents gave to their soon-to-be-married daughter so that her gracious face might keep her husband at home. In rich families, the dowry mirror was engraved with the bride's maiden name and the date of her marriage.

Estate inventories list very few mirrors in rural areas. The famous 1792 fable of Jean Pierre Claris de Florian, *L'Enfant et le Miroir*, testifies to their rarity: "A child reared in a poor village returned to his parents' home and was surprised to find a mirror there."[44] In paintings, the mirror was hardly ever depicted on the walls of farmhouse interiors; instead, religious paintings are often seen. The countryside just outside Paris obviously differed from the distant provinces in this regard, as did the situation of the industrial laborer from the small peasant. The historian Albert Babeau, in his 1894 study of rural life during the ancien régime, found only three mirrors in the inventories he studied. The people whose belongings were inventoried, a miller, a gardener, and a laborer, all lived not far from the capital. In each case, their inventory listed a "small mirror," with the most modest of frames, in black wood. A weaver from Beauce who died around 1750 left a mirror to his widow, and in the household inventory of a manual laborer from Sancerre, whose total goods were estimated as worth 100 pounds, a mirror was also listed.[45] But these are exceptions. Until the 1730s, the mirror was more or less non-existent in rural life despite a rise in peasants' standard of living. In thirty-five household inventories compiled between 1695 and 1710, and thirty-five between 1710 and 1755 near the Meaux region, scholar Micheline Baulant found no glass mirrors.[46] It is possible that there could have been small pieces of broken glass or polished steel.

In the Haut-Maine region of the Loire valley, one hundred inventories drawn up in La Fontaine-en-Cérans between 1735 and 1755 revealed seven or eight mirrors with modest wood frames among the households in the most modest category (having less than 600 pounds of annual income, including profits from livestock)[47]—those of day laborers, sergers, weavers, and petty artisans. The mirror was sometimes a gift offered to girls. In the homes of more affluent laborers and merchants, with annual incomes greater than 2,000 pounds, mirrors were much more common, and more luxurious, too—with walnut or even tortoiseshell borders. Along with pewter dishes, a clock, or curtains, they indicated a concern for decoration and comfort and a way of life that was already bourgeois, centered on the charms of social relationships.

In a series of estate inventories of peasants in Normandy dating from 1700 to 1735, not a single mirror is mentioned.[48] It was not until the second half of the eighteenth century that they began to appear a little more frequently—barely ten between 1745 and 1783—of glass or metal, always small (less than ten inches in height), with frames of wood veneer. In Lower Normandy at the end of the eighteenth century, a few affluent farmers decorated the interiors of their homes with small wall mirrors, adorned with branches of laurel. Women used *mirettes*, or small, inexpensive hand mirrors, generally made of defective glass that provided a distorted reflection, to adjust their hair. Such mirrors were commonly found among traveling market vendors. Even haberdashers in this region who furnished ribbons, combs, lace, knives, gloves, and candles failed to stock mirrors.

In rural society people rarely looked at themselves, and the mirror, by whatever name or style (*miroué, mirail, miraou, mirei, mirette, mirelaid,* or *mirochon*) possessed a poor reputation among them. The body was a tool for work that needed care and managing, yet excess adornment elicited disapproval, except on a patron saint's day, when women dressed in special garments that had been stored carefully and handed down from generation to generation. Once a week on average, men showed up at the local barber's, who himself usually did not have a mirror at his disposal. This is why the young Corentin, a peasant from Brittany brought to life in Oliver Perrin's 1835 novel, *Galerie bretonne,* took special care to monitor the growth of his beard, which served as a passport to the world of adults. He borrowed a mirror from his girlfriend, the domestic servant Soizic, that was a small fragment that she herself used on Sundays, and that was undoubtedly given to her by her mistress, the lady of the château.[49]

Fifty years later, a poignant reminder of the rarity of mirrors in the countryside surfaces in a story by Guy de Maupassant. Rose, the heroine of *L'Histoire d'une fille de ferme* [*The Story of a Farmgirl*] becomes pregnant by Jacques, a valet who abandons her: "Thus began for her a life of continuous torture—if only they knew! She got up every morning well before the others and with relentless persistence tried to look at her waist in a little piece of broken mirror that she used when she did her hair, always anxious to know whether today would be the day people would notice."[50] This broken, mediocre mirror is so feverishly consulted! "The wild man who has only seen his face in the water of his fountains, concluded Perrin, would give all the wealth of Potosì for a mirror worth a few sous!" In *The Turn of the Screw,* Henry James makes a similar observation about rural England: a young schoolteacher who has always lived in the country arrives to serve as governess in a manor house and is stunned by the discovery of her own head-to-toe reflection in a mirrored armoire.[51]

Life in the countryside evolved at an exceedingly slow pace. Furniture stayed the same over a hundred- or two hundred-year span; when damaged by age, a piece was replaced by a new one, made according to the same techniques and decorated with the same motifs. It was not until the beginning of the twentieth century that the repercussions of industrial production became evident, introducing altogether new forms and materials. A historian of rural furniture, Suzanne Tardieu-Dumont, notes in her study of the Mâcon region that mirrors were almost completely absent from all rural interiors until the end of the nineteenth century, except in the homes of a few rich laborers, coopers, and wine merchants.[52] In the period from 1890 to 1950, however, she mentions 110 mirrored armoires, noting a substantial change in furniture purchases just after World War I. Several factors played a part in this acceptance of a more urban lifestyle: the reduction in prices due to mass production; a taste for exotic woods less expensive than mahogany, bamboo, rosewood, bubinga, and pine; and the distribution of catalogs and magazines aimed at women in the provinces—these included beauty tips, recipes, household advice, and furnishing ideas.

The Advent of the Mirrored Armoire

The birth of the great department stores in Paris—Le Petit Saint-Thomas in the rue du Bac, La Ménagère in the boulevard Bonne-Nouvelle, Le Louvre, and Le Bon Marché—had an enormous role in these changes. They introduced the concept of *chambres à coucher*, or bedrooms, offering sets of furniture at a wide range of prices to accommodate even modest incomes. The modern bedroom ensemble included a double bed, a night table, and the indispensable armoire, which replaced the linen chest. Soon, thanks to better prices at Saint-Gobain (throughout the Second Empire, the price of mirrors fell 30 percent each decade), every armoire was outfitted with two mirrors, one on each door.

At Le Bon Marché, a special furniture sale took place each September. Its printed catalogs spread new fashions to notable residents of city and village alike and offered dozens of models of dressing tables, *poudreuses*, mirrored armoires with pediments and one or two sculpted, arched doors. An aisle devoted especially to mirrors offered very modest German mirrors framed in fir wood, *demi-fortes* or *fortes* (magnifying) mirrors for slightly more money, and three-way mirrors in different sizes. From 1870 onward, the store operated a mail-order service, distributing a million and a half catalogs in 1894. Four thousand orders were received each day, and a million fulfilled orders were delivered to the hinterlands. The volume of mail-order sales grew sixfold between 1872 and 1902, when fifty million packages were shipped out to the provinces.[53] In 1840 Saint-Gobain's clientele was still two-thirds Parisian, but by 1860, Parisian clients made up only one-third of all customers.

The bourgeoisie set the rules of social etiquette, demonstrating to all how those who have succeeded should live and furnish their homes. The mirrored armoire, an emblem of affluence and prosperity, reigned supreme! Its solid mass spread light throughout a room, doubling bourgeois opulence. Beginning in the middle of the nineteenth century, it competed with the *psyché* and first was looked on as a *parvenu.* The *psyché,* a precious ornament that woodworkers decorated with art, aided the coquette in her grooming and lorded over the sitting room of the rich, leisurely, and sophisticated woman. The mirrored armoire, by contrast, held piles of sheets and household linens and attempted to conceal its tidiness and bourgeois coziness under a brilliant screen that reproduced the eighteenth century's games of light. In his *Education Sentimentale,* Gustave Flaubert set a solid mirrored armoire in Madame Arnoux's apartment and a *psyché* in the elegant Rosanette's chambers. Honoré de Balzac, in the novel *Cousine Bette,* also furnished the actress Josepha's sitting room with a *psyché,* but he gave a mirrored armoire to Madame Marneffe, despite all her efforts to climb the social ladder. The mirrored armoire made a name for itself in a "get rich quick" era, and its triumph was such that it incited many controversies. The writer Jules Barbey d'Aurevilly, famed for his novel *Les Diaboliques [The She Devils]* defended it: "The mirrored armoire—I have a weakness, I admit, for this wicked thing. For me it is not just a piece of furniture—it's like a great lake at one end of my bedroom." But the poet, dramatist, and writer Théodore de Banville was indignant: "For imagining and proliferating the mostly flatly hideous, the most crudely stupid, and the most vilely coarse things, a monster has been found—the mirrored armoire!"[54]

A popular housekeeping manual by Madame de Graffigny, initially published in 1910 and reprinted on several occasions, advised newlyweds in getting a start in life, listing indispensable furniture for a new household. The mirrored armoire is near the top of the list: "the door of the armoire, instead of being of painted wood, as in the past, is now covered with a beveled mirror." Advice for arranging the furniture follows: the armoire should be placed across from the fireplace, above which hangs a second mirror, to multiply perspectives.[55] This visual richness thus anticipates the couple's success. Parisian specialty stores, such as Lévitan or the Galéries Barbès, furnished young households at the beginning of the twentieth century with great success. They were not necessarily less expensive, but prospered since they "carried a bourgeois seal of approval." Jean Baudrillard analyzes the success of mirrors in the nineteenth century as follows: "It's an opulent object which affords the self-indulgent bourgeois individual the opportunity to exercise his privilege—to reproduce his own image and revel in his possessions. . . . It is no coincidence that the century of Louis XIV is epitomized by the Hall of Mirrors at Versailles, nor that, in more recent times, the spread of mirrors in apartments coincided with the spread of the triumphal Pharisee-ism of bourgeois consciousness, from Napoleon III to Art Nouveau."[56]

The mirrored armoire even found a place in the bathroom. This chamber, where a woman worked at her grooming in order to perfect her beauty and crown her husband's success, was the object of meticulous description in treatises on household decor and in manuals of social etiquette. The countess of Gencé dedicated an entire volume to it.[57] There are never too many mirrors in a bathroom, she wrote, because "one has to be able to see herself from head to toe, in every direction. . . . The great three-way mirror would be ideal, but one can make do with a single fixed mirror, or even a mirrored armoire that would not be better placed elsewhere." Whether fixed, or better yet, adjustable, mirrors had to allow for a complete scrutiny of one's person, and in that inviolable asylum of the bathroom (sometimes described as a "laboratory," and at other times as a "confessional"), a woman "shouldn't be afraid of making ridiculous gestures. When one is alone, one never has to be shy in front of the mirror!"

The Triumphant Mirror

Ultimately, mirrors conquered urban interiors because they offered what such places lacked most—space: "They brighten up and seem to enlarge small rooms," one observer noted in 1870. "They are the first luxury that frugality will allow itself; placed between two living rooms, they form one of the most gracious arrangements of modern apartments."[58] A few productions pulled from the accounts of the Saint-Gobain Company bear witness, as if any were needed, to the mirror's newfound ubiquitousness: from 1852 to 1862, production grew from about a million to more than two million square feet of cast glass annually. From 1878 to 1898, production doubled once again. These record outputs were made possible through both chemical and technical advancements. After 1850, sodium sulfate was used for making glass and, at the end of the century, silver replaced mercury in the silvering process. With these developments, a mirror could be made and delivered in six days instead of eighteen. As far as the dimensions were concerned, they achieved those of one's wildest dreams: at the Paris Universal Exposition of 1867, Saint-Gobain displayed two mirrors: one twenty by eleven and one-half feet and one eighteen by eleven and one-half feet.

Mirrors were now placed everywhere, in luxury hotels, restaurants, cafés, building entryways, theaters, casinos, and at the opera, where foyer mirrors were as large as twenty-one by ten feet. Construction estimates for the most elegant Parisian houses built in 1857 indicate that spending on mirrored objects grew to 3 percent of the total cost. In the famous Lapérouse restaurant on the quai des Grands-Augustins, the mirrors found in private rooms were still those of the previous century, "covered with grooves traced by courtesans who scratched the mirrors to verify the authenticity of diamonds given to them by their patrons!"[59]

During the Second Empire (1848–1871), a preference for mirrored glass in window casements developed. Soon thereafter the creation of special insurance against mirror breakage allowed department stores to transform their appearance and those of surrounding streets.[60] Boutiques resembled vast greenhouses inundated with light. Merchandise was multiplied by mirrored reflections so as to incite desire. Mirrors ensure the brilliant success of Émile Zola's Octave Mouret, hero of the novel *Au Bonheur des dames* [*The Ladies' Paradise*] who opened his department store of novelties, outshining dark boutiques in which a sad salesperson vegetated behind small, yellowed window panes. Mouret's cathedral of commerce, based on Boucicaut's real department store, offers a parade of mannequins for his clients to admire "whilst the mirrors, cleverly arranged on each side of the windows, reflected and multiplied the forms without end, peopling the street with these beautiful women for sale, each bearing a price in big figures in the place of a head."[61]

Today we live with mirrors. They are no longer noted for their frames or borders that isolate and imprison the reflection, like magical parentheses in the real world. Naked, flat, implacable, and perfect, they return images of the interior to the exterior and those of the exterior to the interior, making a spectacle of everything. Seeing one's face in the mirror each morning is as obvious to us as the act of breathing. Not only does the mirror belong to closed spaces of intimacy, it also occupies the street, the glass walls of apartment buildings, the general space of the city, which inspired this wry comment from the British-born painter and photographer David Hockney: "If we consider life without the mirror, we are only considering it half-way."[62] Playing with Hockney's statement, we might complete his thought: "If we consider ourselves without the mirror, we are only considering ourselves half-way." We must remain before our mirror to discover our dual self.

Part Two

THE MAGIC OF RESEMBLANCE

O sweet mirror, invented in order to know that which our own gaze cannot see.

—Bérenger de la Tour d'Albenas, *The Mirror*

4

In the Semblance of God

Despite its irregularities and imperfections, the mirror was considered a wondrous instrument by our ancestors, allowing man not only to discover his own image and know himself better, but also, by means of the visible, to perceive the invisible. In the conceptual system of the Middle Ages, which was strongly influenced by Platonism, sight was the favored means of acquiring knowledge; through it one could experience the beautiful. The mirror was invested with exceptional symbolic importance because of its capacity to enhance visual acuity and to radiate light, the source of all beauty.

Nonetheless this marvelous object was also a disturbing one. Because it does not duplicate reality exactly—in the mirror the right hand becomes the left—the reflection poses questions about image and resemblance; it returns an image that closely relates to, yet differs from, the reflected object itself. And just where does the image reside? At the same time both present and elsewhere, the perceived image has an unsettling ubiquity and depth, located at an uncertain distance. Looking into a mirror, an image for the most part seems to appear behind a solid screen, so that the observer may wonder if he is seeing the surface of the mirror or looking through it. The reflection creates the sensation of an ethereal world looming beyond the mirror, inviting the eye to cross through to it. Like a prism, the mirror can disrupt the field of vision because it hides as much as it shows.

These baffling questions suggest that the mirror offers an enigmatic and divergent way of knowing. Before it helps to put the world in order and maintain the conscious self, looking into the mirror leads one's gaze on an indirect course marked by echos and analogies, a course that seems to attest to an invisible "elsewhere" in the heart of the visible. Form without substance, subtle and impalpable, the mirror image manifests a diaphanous purity, a revelation of the divine source, from which all likeness emanates.

Antiquity and the Mirror's Image

The World of Images

The source of philosophical meditation on the mirror image in Western culture is Plato. Before him, the reflection was an animated and living form, a double luring Narcissus from the bottom of a pool.[1] At its origin, this myth can be read as an archaic belief in the existence of a double, or of a soul taking on substance, a concept that ethnology has found in many "primitive" cultures and even among cultures in our own era. Homer attributed a double existence to man, one in his perceptible, physical being, the other in an invisible semblance unleashed only at his death (*Odyssey* XI, 495, XII, 222). Narcissus was capable of believing in the presence of a living being at the bottom of the pool, a sudden emergence of his spirit or double. His confusion is not as strange as it may appear to us, as numerous folklore traditions contain similar stories. In ancient Greece, looking at one's reflection could invite death because the reflection captured the soul.[2] It was not until later in the classical period in Greece that the reflected image lost its magical aspect and acquired its status as mere replica or semblance.

The ancients put forward all sorts of hypotheses concerning the formation of images and reflections, including schemes of both direct and reflected vision. According to Euclidian theory, the eye emitted rectilinear visual rays that would extend toward an object and bring back from it shape and color; this theory was reprised by Ptolemy and remained the most widely accepted for quite some time.[3] For the Greek philosopher Democritus and the Roman philosopher Lucretius, on the contrary, the image stemmed from the object itself, which emits very fine corpuscles called *simulacra*, appearances, or forms (*eidola*), which issue forth in all directions and then pull together at the moment they meet up with the eye: "In mirrors, in water and any polished surface, we see simulacra that resemble the reflected objects perfectly and can therefore be formed only by images emanating from them." If an image appeared reversed, it was surmised that "after striking the flat surface, the image does not come back the same, for while bounding back, it tumbles over like a plaster facade applied to a structure when still too moist."[4] In a synthesis of these two points of view, Plato insisted on light's mediation in his dialogue *Timaeus*. The eye is a sun that sends out rays, and daylight must encounter these visual streams—like meeting like—so that an image can form. These theories wouldn't be modified until the eleventh century, when the Arab Al Hazen discovered the persistence of retinal images even when the eye is closed.

Whatever they believed, the ancients were certain of one thing: the image originates from physical contact, from an imprint made from the eye to the object, through rays or forms—thus the mythical basilisk could be killed by its own poisonous stare. In his *De Insomnis*, Aristotle explained that sight exercises a certain action on an object, in much the same way that a mirror or a shiny surface has a dizzying effect on anyone who looks upon it, citing as an example the mirror soiled by the gazes of women who look into it while menstruating. For the

Greeks, the world of images had a tangible existence by reproducing and resembling the real; this realm was a precise imitation of the actual one, although of an inferior and altogether different nature.

Specular Illusion

The mirror reflection, however, does not correspond to any reality because, even if it creates an image that appears more faithful than a painted reproduction, this image has neither foundation nor consistency. The reflection escapes every sense but vision, and in particular touch, which forms the basis of our tangible reality. "You can take a mirror and turn it in all directions: from less than nothing you will have the sun and the stars in the sky, yourself and different animals, furniture and plants, and all the objects you just mentioned. Yes, all of these apparent objects, without any reality to them whatsoever." In *The Republic* (X, 596), Plato condemns the reflection's deception by noting the distortion between a being and its unreal, fleeting double.[5]

Even while discrediting specular illusion, which Plato ranked as the lowest degree of knowledge, beneath even painting since it lacks the tangible reality of the image, he admitted that the reflection, by its very immateriality and its resemblance, lent itself well to another analogical and spiritual sort of consciousness. Far beyond just presenting an enactment, the reflection invites the mind to free itself from the tangible and focus on cause rather than effect—in other words, to contemplate the world with the clarity of understanding, returning to the essence. Like the moving shadows that drive the wise man to leave the cave, the reflection is no longer a trompe l'oeil, but an indication, a shell of meaning, a manifestation of something hidden, more of an apparition than a physical appearance. Deprived of reality, the reflection brings us closer to the symbolic.

When the mirror ceases to plagiarize the tangible world and gives up all attempts at furnishing a mimetic equivalent, its shimmering light lends itself instead to a divinatory knowledge, to interpretations and revelations, indeed to enchantment. The sparkle of the reflecting surface, in the bedazzlement that it provokes, incites all sorts of hallucinations. Many ancient texts call to mind the uses of catoptromancy, or divination by mirrors, which unveils, as do dreams, that which escapes the visible. Artemidorus, for example, in his *Treatise on Dreams*, devotes several paragraphs to reading the future with mirror images.[6]

Magic and scientific thought remained intimately linked. In *De Insomnis,* Aristotle explains that the element "air" is responsible for the modification of images on the surface of mirrors. In *Meteorologia* he explains that a man who does not enjoy good eyesight might occasionally see his double flash before his eyes: weak "sight rays" may come up against an obstacle (like misty air) thus reflecting back an image like a mirror.

From the mirror mirage to the mirror of revelation, from the illusory reflection to the visionary symbol, optical metaphors were used so widely as to invert their meanings. Man looks at himself in the mirror in order to see himself, but the mirror in which he sees himself offers him, above and beyond appearances, an enigmatic and transfigured knowledge of himself. Pausanias, a Greek living in Asia Minor in the second century A.D. and author of a guide to Greece, stated that a mirror decorated the entry to the temple of Lycosura in Arcadia and anyone who peered into it discovered an obscured and strange image of himself. The man entering into the sanctuary shed his own appearance in order to reclothe himself in a new identity before the gods.

Know Thyself

To know oneself, as the Delphic principle invites us to do, is to retreat from the sensory appearances of the common mirror—reflection, appearance, shadow, or phantasm—to one's own soul. Man, according to Plato, must care for the soul that constitutes his essence. Like the eye, the soul must have a reflection in order to see itself. Like the eye, the soul cannot see itself unaided. To study himself, Alcibiades couldn't be satisfied with the mirror that Cratylus, the follower of Heracleitus in Plato's dialogues, used, where only a replica appears—a substitute for his forms and colors, but lacking both voice and thought.[7] Thus the true mirror, loyal, constant, alive, is the one presented by the lover or friend who offers his eyes and his own soul as mirrors. Socrates and Alcibiades constitute living mirrors for each other, mirrors in which they discover much more than the mirror image of Cratylus could have told them.

The misfortune of Narcissus, whose story has been retold so often since Ovid, was to have chosen the lowest degree of knowledge, that of his reflection. He was punished by Nemesis for having scorned Echo's love, for having refused the mediation of the other in the construction of the self. There was certainly not yet a psychological implication to the fable in antiquity, but only the passing of a moral judgment on a young man overtaken by madness and excess, confusing illusion with reality and making himself his own aim rather than investing himself in the polis.[8]

If well used, however, the mirror can aid moral mediation between man and himself. Socrates, we are told by Diogenes, urged young people to look at themselves in mirrors so that, if they were beautiful, they would become worthy of their beauty, and if they were ugly, they would know how to hide their disgrace through learning.[9] The mirror, a tool by which to "know thyself," invited man to *not* mistake himself for God, to avoid pride by knowing his limits, and to improve himself. His was thus not a passive mirror of imitation but an active mirror of transformation.

Diogenes added that Socrates offered a mirror to drunkards so that they might see reflected in it their faces disfigured by wine.[10] The mirror therefore reflects not only physical traits but also interior bearing. As a factor in moral life, it must help man conquer his vices. It shows him simultaneously what he is and what he ought to be. Seneca placed a mirror in the hands of the angry man because the growing ugliness of the soul altered physical traits.[11] The same theme was developed and popularized by a character in Plautus's comedy *Epidicus*: an old man reads the mistakes of his past life in a mirror.[12] The mirror of introspection shines light on the past, the present and the future all at once.

The Trial of the Mirror

As a deceiving image, a vain appearance, the likeness offered by the mirror both attracts and misleads when it is not reflecting the divine. Given to man so that he might know his soul and triumph over his vices, the mirror was corrupted and used toward shamefully material ends. Through antiquity onward, the mirror's status was on trial on these moral and religious grounds.

Seneca devoted several pages of his *Natural Questions* (I, 17) to the properties of the mirror and took up Socrates's arguments. Nature itself, with its pools of spring water and brilliant stones, invites man to look at himself so that the capacity of seeing his own visage might guide him through life: in his prime it shows the vigor of a body capable of feats of bravery, and in his old age, the white-haired apparition alerts him to prepare for death. But luxury, debauchery, and the empire of the senses diverted the mirror's use. It became the extravagant tool of women's coquetry and even an instrument of pleasure that certain Roman citizens, like Hostius Quadra, liked to surround themselves with to multiply and increase their lover's sexual attributes. These new tasks weighed heavily on the mirror: in the service of physical appearance, it enhances, by a game of deforming reflections, the deceptions of the senses.

To the contrary, Apuleius placed a defense of the mirror at the heart of his *Apologia* (XIII). He absolved the object of suspicion and revealed his wonder at the exactitude of the image it reproduced. Where Plato saw simulacra and Seneca vanity, Apuleius saw efficient resemblance, the creative power (*opifex*) of an instrument that, better than the most subtle of paintings, was capable of restoring life and movement. Nature itself, in giving children the traits of their parents so that parents might contemplate themselves through their offspring, values the notion of likeness. Like his predecessors, Apuleius invoked Socrates's teaching mirror, noting that Demosthenes practiced his speeches before one. When he himself was accused of practicing magic, his defense of the mirror's place in the natural world became more adamant. He insisted on developing a technical account of the optical mechanism. Thus is the mirror rehabilitated in both its moral and scientific implications. From then on, any encounter with the self must confront this duality of the reflection, at once both a liar and guide.

The Mirror in Medieval Spirituality

The Vision "in the Mirror"

The mirror became part of the religious vocabulary of the Middle Ages, which developed its symbolic meanings from scriptural writings, Neoplatonic texts, and the patristic tradition (the writings of the church fathers). The utilitarian and self-reflexive use of the object is more or less ignored by these texts, as it also was in medieval iconography, both of which envisaged the mirror image as either "an idealized vision or a pejorative projection," either a reflection of God or an instrument of the devil.[13]

As a model of the transformation of matter into form and as instrument of resemblance, the mirror of medieval spirituality bore witness to the presence of an immaterial reality in the visible at the same time that it designated the means and levels of knowledge, from "speculation" to perfect vision: to know is to reflect, to pass from a tangible vision to the contemplation of the invisible.

Genesis says that God created man "in his image and his likeness." The likeness conveys meaning to the image, for the image is nothing by itself. Because sin darkened the mirror, one has to look at the divine model in order to restore the lost resemblance. The Bible is "the unstained mirror" (Prov. 7:27), intended to educate man. In front of this mirror, the subject looks for his only possible identity, his spiritual identity, outside the carnal and contingent envelope of his body.

Two Christian texts frame all medieval understanding of the mirror and establish its ambivalence. The first is the verse in which Saint Paul explains that the knowledge man has of God here on earth is visible "through a glass darkly" (*per speculum in aenigmate*), a mirror that gives only a veiled image or representation of truth (1 Cor., 13:12). And the second is the verse in which Saint James compares the man who does not practice the word of God to he who "looks at himself in a mirror, sees himself as he is, and after having looked, goes away and forgets at once what he is like" (James 1:23).

The partial and indirect knowledge of Paul's mirror marks out the passage from a blurred view of the divine to an unobstructed one, thus forming a model for all analogical knowledge. James's mirror, on the other hand, reminds man of his inconstancy, his fragility, and his foolishness. Saint Paul's gaze pierces the mirror in order to see something beyond its surface, whereas man, according to Saint James, does not get beyond his own image and, neglecting his resemblance to the divine, loses sight of his true self.

Aside from Christian teachings, many ideas of the early Catholic Church were drawn from classical Greek thinkers like Plotinus and Timaeus. From the latter the church fathers derived a whole metaphysics of light and reflection in which the visible world is the image of the invisible, and the soul is the reflection of the divine. Plotinus emphasizes the idea of a universe organized hierarchically as the basis for anagogic reasoning. Just as in the famed banquet of Agathan described in Plato's *Symposium*, where Socrates tells of his teacher, Diotima, inviting him to discover in the beauty of the body a reflection of interior beauty, Plotinus considers the tangible world a reflection emanating from the world of eternal forms, and the body a reflection that the soul makes visible when it encounters matter, exactly in the same way as a human being makes a reflection visible when it meets a polished surface.[14] Rather than lending prestige to mere appearance, man must leave his distinctive form behind to access his interior beauty.

The theme of the chain of reflections became a central motif in the work of Christian thinkers like Gregory of Nyssa, Saint Basil, Saint Ambrose, and Denis the Areopagite. In the latter's work, angels, purely intellectual creatures, are lights that radiate from the divine source, which they reflect like mirrors. While humans, in their turn, become mirrors when they cleanse their souls.

It is especially in the work of Saint Augustine that the spiritual literature of the Middle Ages draws on the semantic richness of the specular image. To Augustine, every man participates in divine resemblance. The human spirit, if it does become lost in the illusion of the mirror image, a false creation of the material world (*Soliloquy* II, 6), is capable of receiving the light of God and of reflecting His beauty (*De Trinitate* XV, 20, 39). At the same time, the true mirror in which man should contemplate himself is that of the Holy Scriptures. He who sees himself in the mirror of the Bible simultaneously realizes the splendor of God and his own wretchedness: "See if you are who He says you are. If you are not yet so, pray that you may be; he will show you his face" (*Ennaratio in Psalms,* 103). This mirror does not flatter; it tells the truth, and whoever sees himself there is already being transformed: "Its shine will show you what you are. If you see yourself besmirched, you displease yourself and already are finding a way to make yourself handsome. By admitting this to yourself, you will learn how to make yourself more attractive." A mirror of revelation and a mirror of introspection are united in a mirror of wisdom.

The Speculum *or "Book-Mirror"*

The spiritual symbolism of the mirror in Saint Augustine's works encompasses three motifs, "the theme of the analogy, the principle of imitation and the search for moral enrichment through knowledge."[15] In the lineage of Neoplatonists and Christian gnostics, and theologians like William of Saint-Thierry (c. 1085–1148), Alain de Lille (1128–1203), and Richard de Saint-Victor (d. 1173), who came to prominence before the rise of Scholasticism, all make use of the mirror as an analogy to express the soul's likeness to God, a reflection that emanates from him and returns to him. Man perceives in himself and in the material world traces or marks of God: "How could the soul perceive its own beauty and not be overcome by the splendor of the one who is reflected from within?" asks Saint-Thierry (*Homily II, Song of Songs*). By a progressive spiritual ascension, man can pass from an animal state to that of reason, and from the state of reason to that of the spiritual.

Alain de Lille also describes a strongly hierarchical world in which man, formed by Nature and gifted with a soul, reunites in his being all the perfections of nature. In order to overcome the reign of evil in the world, Nature receives the aid of Prudence, who holds a wonderful mirror, capable of protecting her eyes from blinding light and of helping her examine the divine mysteries (*Anticlaudianus, VI*). During her ascension toward heaven, she observes the realities of the diverse orders that Reason illuminates for her while holding her three-sided mirror. At first, she sees the causes of physical phenomena, the union of matter and form. Second, spiritual substances without matter appear to her, and last, she sees the source of all things and the way in which ideas are introduced to the world. Using the many diverse symbolic forms of the mirror the allegorical poem *Anticlaudianus* culminates in mystical ecstasy.

It is precisely because there is resemblance or likeness that there is the possibility of knowing oneself.[16] Theologians did not condemn looking upon oneself, regarding it as a legitimate and necessary activity. Knowledge of the self is a step toward the knowledge of God, and whoever doesn't know how to retreat into himself can get among false appearances. William of Saint-Thierry recommends the examination of the soul: "Be wholly present to yourself. Use your whole self to know yourself, you and the one in whose image you are made."[17] To abandon all opportunity to know oneself, to refuse to see the divine in oneself, is to desert oneself and to break the chain of reflections. Man's worth comes from what he contemplates. It is not his self-reflection that confers dignity upon him, but rather his ability to imitate the divine model, attempting to reflect the heavenly light with the tarnished mirror of his being.

To medieval theologians, any representation of man that would ignore his divine aspects is reprehensible and potentially idolatrous. The moral status of imitation and of looking upon oneself is ambiguous due to the sacred character of the likeness. Imitation, when it is not interacting with or related to the divine, reduces itself to trompe l'oeil. Lucifer is the great usurper of likeness, sin being the foremost of false appearances.

As for Narcissus's transgression, which was commented on by thinkers varying from Plotinus, a Greek theologian, Clement of Alexandria (d. 215 A.D.), Italian Platonic philosopher Marsilio Ficino (1433–1499), and in versions of the anonymously composed fourteenth-century French poem *Ovide moralisé*, it stems from the fact that he was ignorant of his soul and its resemblance to God.[18] Flattered by his corporeal form, he neglected true beauty in order to follow a reflection, thereby condemning himself to grasp but a simulacrum that would never fill the aspirations of his soul.

Dante places Narcissus in Purgatory with the counterfeiters, guilty of being content with the false currency of the tangible appearance. All references to the mirror up until the baroque period invite a movement beyond sensory appearances and a discernment of illusions aimed at reaching the light of the pure mirror.

Not that the tangible world was entirely discredited. This world remains the reflection of another reality. All creation has its origin in the mirror of God. In the twelfth century Hildegarde von Bingen imagined God as a mirror containing "all his works beyond age and time," even before they had been created.[19] Meister Eckhart used a similar notion in his Sermon XVI: whereas man's face ceases to be reflected when the mirror disappears, all images exist eternally in God. Microcosm and macrocosm carry the mark of divine wisdom, this wisdom that the Bible says is the "unstained mirror of God's activity" that bathes creation. Thus creation as a whole was intended as a likeness, much the way that books and paintings are for us, as Alain de Lille wrote, and with them we constantly inventory and catalog creation's riches, using these book-mirrors of knowledge to interpret the secrets of the universe.

Whether mirrors of nature or mirrors of history, encyclopedias known as *specula*, like the *Speculum Doctrinal* of the thirteenth-century Dominican, Vincent de Beauvais, brought together all contemporary knowledge, urging man toward "speculation."[20] In the Middle Ages, when the philosophical polarity between subject and object did not exist, "speculation" was a consideration of a relationship between two subjects like that between the mirror and what it reflects. This mode of thought embraces all the visible world in that it resembles the invisible, serving as a testing ground, providing the clues with which man rises beyond the known to the unknown: "That is why," said Suso, the fourteenth-century German mystic Blessed Henry, "this way of knowing is 'speculating'" (*Vita*, 50). Saint Thomas Aquinas thusly linked "speculation" to the speculum: "To see something

Engraving of Saint Thomas Aquinas from a 1488 Venetian edition of *Opusculum Praeclarum*.

by means of a mirror is to see a cause in its effect wherein its likeness is reflected. From this we see that 'speculation' leads back to meditation."[21]

Aside from its theological implications, the medieval mirror offered man a model for governing his outward behavior as well: it showed him what he was and what he ought to be. Thus the mirror legitimately served to qualify the very ancient moral genre wherein clerics would set forth the ideal, admirable model of the perfect Christian prince, in which young people could discover as in a mirror the countenance that ought to be theirs.

A Carolingian noblewoman of the eighth century, Dhuoda of Septimania, wrote an educational guide for her son that she called a "mirror," comparing it to the mirror that women used for beautifying their faces. The mirror tells everyone his flaws and his obligations. Ladies' mirrors, mirrors of princes, mirrors of spirituality, and moral mirrors—books, paintings, and reflections—simultaneously refer back to the ideal model, the only model that man must work to resemble.

Jean de Meung and Dante

As an omnipresent metaphor in all spiritual literature of the Middle Ages, the mirror owed its influence to optical science, which, during this era, rose to the highest rank among sciences and enjoyed, as did the art of glassmaking, an unequaled prestige. From the twelfth to the fourteenth centuries, the optical treatises of Robert Grosseteste (1175–1253), John Peckham (1225–1292), Roger Bacon (1214–1292), Witelo (c. 1250–c. 1275) in Poland, and the Latin translation of the work of Alhazen the Arab's work reinforced the findings of Aristotle and Euclid. With the Franciscan school of Oxford heading the movement, specular vision came to be considered a privileged mode of knowledge.[22]

The well-documented and well-known writings by Jean de Meung (c. 1240–c. 1305) on the varieties and properties of mirrors that enlarge, shrink, or inflame owed much to Grosseteste's treatise. According to Grosseteste, the whole world was of luminous essence, rays of light were the first form of physical matter; thus all activity initially consisted of reflection.[23] Far from being a digression, Jean de Meung's writings on the mirror constitute a cornerstone of the allegorical poem *Roman de la Rose,* in which the excellence of the optical sciences are contrasted with the distortions that mar reflection.[24]

In this work, the figure of Nature, taking up the mechanics of rainbows, draws a parallel between the colored reflections it issues forth through atmospheric turbulence, and the illusions that affect men: just as the rays of the sun produce forms and colors by crossing the water and air of clouds, the same rays of Providence, when they encounter the moods and instincts of man—which often pose considerable resistance to wisdom—produce chaos in the soul, like the pain caused by love. Jean de Meung contrasts the unhappy Narcissus depicted by William of Lorris (who wrote the first part of the *Roman de la Rose*; Jean de Meung wrote the second section), blinded by his passion, with the Narcissus who masters the optical sciences, moved by reason, and obedient to Nature's laws. The first Narcissus looks at himself in the roiled waters of the "perilous fountain"; the second looks into the "fountain of life" in which he sees a three-faceted gemstone, a trinitarian light, that no shadow can dim and that needs no sun to illuminate it since it is itself a resplendent source of light. This fountain is a mirror of revelation in which man will finally enjoy absolute vision and infallible knowledge.

Jean de Meung boldly makes the mirror the reflection of art: not merely an art of illusion that less successfully simulates the beauty of nature, but an art capable of inventing forms and of rediscovering the process of creation. Here he again follows Grosseteste: "When an object plunged into darkness is reflected in a luminous mirror, it is better recognized by its image than by its reality." In aesthetic creation, the model is a spiritual ideal; for Jean de Meung, as for Grosseteste, art sheds light on an obscure reality, bringing "knowledge of what is to be done."[25]

In entitling his work *Miroer aux amoureux* [*Mirror of Lovers*], Jean de Meung is obviously alluding to the deceptions of illusory love, but at the same time, embracing the semantic richness of the word *mirror* that his predecessors bequeathed to him. His work is an exemplary mirror like that in the famous satire *Speculum Stultorum* [*Mirror of Fools*] of Nigel Wireker (c. 1190), where a crazed lover could consider the effects of his madness when no longer governed by reason. It is also a mirror of wisdom like the medieval *speculum*, the encyclopedia collecting all the knowledge of its era; a mirror of self-knowledge with which each man can learn to make use of his free will, thus thwarting the influences of the stars and fortune; and above all, a mirror of myriad phantasmagoria and poetic creation, since, by his art, the writer illuminates reality from numerous perspectives. All of these mirrors reflect each other to make Jean de Meung's work an ode to all levels of knowledge.

In the *Divine Comedy,* Dante also calls upon optical science in order to represent knowledge. He presents the biblical figures of Rachel and Leah, contemplation and action, each holding a mirror. The mirror helps to uncover the theological truth beyond the empirical one. In the second canto of Paradiso, Beatrice proposes an optical experiment to the poet: "Take three mirrors; put two of them at an equal distance from you, and let the last one, farther away, present itself to your eyes between the two others." Then Beatrice arranges a source of light behind the Pilgrim that lights their way.

Light reflected by three surfaces shines with an identical brilliance, regardless of distance, even though the light reflected in the farthest mirror appears smaller. Thus, the Pilgrim's path is illuminated from afar by the light of the first knowledge; the two intermediary mirrors represent the multiplicity of created things, which themselves faithfully reflect the divine rays without diminishing their shine. The Pilgrim's entire voyage consists in moving from one sphere of the heavens to another, from an inferior mirror to a superior one, until he finally encounters the divine light on which he contemplates.

At the end of the poem, instead of seeing the rays of light reflected in Beatrice's eyes, Dante is placed in the presence of the resplendent source itself; the three mirrors of the optical experiment become mirrors of the Trinity and melt into a single one which embraces the Pilgrim. Dante moves from hypotheses of scientific experiment to proof of the revelation, from "speculation" to contemplation, and from partial knowledge to all-seeing vision.

When "speculation" drives contemplation, the mediation of reflection becomes useless, as does self-knowledge. Because contemplating one's creator transforms the contemplator, bringing him closer to the divine, knowledge gives way to love, as the gazes of the self and the creator blend together. Thus when resemblance and sight become identified with each other, the reflected image disappears: "Because we will see God, we will be like unto him," says Saint John (1 John 3:2).

Reliable, yielding, and obedient, the mirror no longer signifies recorded (*différé*) vision, but the receptivity of he who looks at himself there; pure and without blemish, it offers the image of the mystical union. This theme, well-known to Meister Eckhart, is at the center of an entire religious iconography.[26] In this tradition, the Virgin or the divine child, themselves stainless mirrors of the divinity, are represented holding a mirror, offering it to the soul so that it may contemplate itself.[27]

The Humanist: A Self-Portrait of God

Nicholas of Cusa's Specularity

Inherited from medieval mysticism, the theme of the mirror was altered during the Renaissance when man came to believe in the idea of an infinite universe—no longer closed, circular, and susceptible to being deciphered. With a reflective consciousness, man made use of the "sciences of sight" to take a step back and size up the world. Vision was inseparable from the seeing eye, which is to say, from a particular point of view and mental activity.

According to the Platonic tradition, a mirror always plays the role of mediator in a system of analogies and hierarchies, but beginning with the German cardinal and philosopher Nicholas de Cusa (c. 1400–1450), it was no longer considered the only link between the sensory and the intellectual; the mirror's place between God and the world, gives meaning to the cosmos and is shared with man, who is capable of differentiating and opposing. This new philosophical movement sets out to imagine opposites, beyond the network of affinities and correspondences. Integrating his gaze with experience and history, while not making himself a unique point of reference, the humanist effects the union of the sensory and the spiritual.[28]

Specular perception, central to Nicholas de Cusa's thinking, is offered as the place of mediation between the material and the spiritual, between the finite and the infinite, but it no longer implies the idea of an anagogic step in a structured universe by which one could rise from an inferior sphere to a superior one. The mirror imposes distance and separation within a formerly closed system.

Although there is not the slightest similarity between the sensory and the intellectual, between the sphere and its concept, the material world is the primary environment in which the mind operates. Visual acuity offers reason its foundation, and deductions of sight serve as a models for thoughts. Things seen by perception and those "seen" by the mind intersect in the thematic of the mirror, which Michel de Certeau calls the "instrument of passage from one 'seeing' to another, focal point of de Cusa's speculation."[29] To de Cusa, understanding, utilizing information gathered by the senses, imagines the world, and at the same time is capable of grasping itself in the midst of reflection, as long as it relates back to the all-powerful and all-encompassing source and model of the divine mirror.

But how can a limited and finite consciousness grasp the incommensurable, absolute other that is God? God is the infinite model, the perfect, unique mirror without boundaries, containing all faces, all images and joining all opposites, and he alone has the capacity to offer himself up to be seen. A discussion of a painting by Rogier Van der Weyden (c. 1399–1464), opening a section of de Cusa's *The Vision of God*, serves to illustrate an exchange of glances in which, despite their absolute difference, the eye of man and the eye of God intersect and combine in perception of the infinite. According to a well-known portrait mechanism, the gaze of Christ on the painting follows the gaze of the spectator and moves about in a circular motion at the same time as he does: "So God does not abandon you wherever you travel."[30] The singular perspective of the individual gaze intersects with the infinite perspectives of divine sight. And despite his smallness, his singularity, and his otherness, man sees in the eye of God both the transcendent and the immediate, the incommensurable and his own gaze: "Any face that can look upon Thine thus sees no Alterity, no difference in respect to itself, because it sees its own truth." Just as an eye, small as it might be, "can receive the image of a great mountain," the creature that sees himself in God sees himself as a reflection of his power, a finite image that has his features, his qualities, his creative power. According to the beautiful expression of the current-day French philosopher Pierre Magnard, "man is a self-portrait of God."[31]

Dürer's Self-Portrait

The famous *Self-Portrait, 1500,* in which Albrecht Dürer (1471–1528) painted himself frontally with features traditionally associated with Christ, is perhaps the best expression of this philosophical turning point whereby the individual, the reflection and image of God, discovers himself as an active subject, in a representation both historic and transfigured. Christ, mediator between finite and infinite, gives over his human face to the painter: a fusion of the creature and his model that would be sacrilegious if it did not express wonder in the act of faith. In such a portrait, resemblance is not expressed in general or symbolic terms, but through a sensory form and singular traits; it discovers the "I" and enters into a new experience of subjectivity.

The self-portrait emerged from the portrait at a historical moment when the sovereignty of the artist was being affirmed.

Albrecht Dürer, *Self-Portrait* (1500). Bayerische Staatsgemäldesammlungen, Alte Pinakothek, Munich, Germany.

No longer a simple artisan capable of reproducing a repertory of forms inherited from the past, the artist came to be considered a real and true creator and emulator of God. We know that antiquity used to judge severely those who, like the Greek sculptor Phidias (c. 500–432 B.C.), dared to represent themselves. Only much later did notions of signature and authorship arise. In Flanders, Jan Van Eyck (1390–1441) often used the device of the mirror reflection to reveal his own presence.[32] The convex mirror in the famous Arnolfini marriage painting, placed at the center of the composition, like the eye of God over the world, sees what cannot be seen by the spectator—the reflection of the painter himself, accompanied by a child, playing the role of witness in the marriage scene. The artist, simultaneously present and elsewhere, portrays himself in the form of a minuscule silhouette in the divine eye-mirror, precisely at the vanishing point of the painting, thus signifying the infinite. The mirror here is not an instrument of imitation, but rather both microscope and telescope, calling forth another reality within the closed space of the work. The invisible emerges from the visible, the infinitely large into the infinitely small in a *mise en abîme* ["placing in a void"] that reproduces the process of creation in which the painter, through his art, participates.

Cosimo de Médici made the very modern observation that all painters paint themselves. This notion derived from the projection of the humanist artist in his work, or from the emergence of a subject that organizes a space through the invention of perspective, as art historian Erwin Panofsky noted in his celebrated analysis *Perspective as Symbolic Form.* It also may have arisen, as it did with Dürer, from the personal affirmation of the creator crafting his image in an unending dialogue of the self with the self, although one must keep in mind that this dialogue was situated in the context of its era.

Dürer made his first self-portrait at the age of thirteen, in 1484; other examples followed in 1492, 1493, 1498, 1500, and

Jan Van Eyck, *The Arnolfini Portrait* (1434). National Gallery, London, Great Britain/Superstock.

again on numerous other occasions. In a painting from his Weimar period, done between 1500 and 1505, he even depicted himself naked from head to toe, with an audacity entirely new for the period. We would be frustrated in our efforts to look for a psychological significance in these self-portraits—it would be futile to try to discover clues about his private life or the state of his soul. At most one can discern the subject's pensive, saturnine temperament. Although autobiographical elements are found in the diary that he regularly kept and in which he recorded incidents of his daily life, Dürer did not unite these two modes of expressing his being, painting and writing. For him, the lived self is not implicated in the public man, and by the same token, the public man does not take into account the incidents of the lived self. This is much different from introspection; the "I" of "Who am I?" is here the questioning of an artist who evaluates his place in the world through his art and who seeks a way of making sense of the universe in painting.

The dialogue of the self with the self comes to pass through a dialogue with God. Out of the shadow of theology a science of man is born. When Dürer painted himself in the way Christ traditionally was painted in 1499, in a totally frontal and hieratic way, his hand raised in the gesture of the all-governing God, he broke with the artistic traditions of his era, including that of the three-quarters portrait, in order to make tangible, in a literal sense, the identity of the Christian, a reflection of the divine model that must be forged according to the imitation of Jesus Christ.[33] In reproducing the particularities of his own face down to the smallest detail, Dürer wanted to leave no doubt as to his own identity, and thus affirm the powers of the artist capable of producing a likeness. The painting offers both the historical reality of his presence in the world and the reality of mystical fusion, anticipating the body of glory, restored in its likeness on account of the Incarnation. Dürer precisely illustrates these two verses of Saint Paul's: "I live, yet not I, but Christ liveth in me" (Gal. 2:20); "We all, with faces unveiled, reflect, as in a mirror, the glory of the Lord" (2 Cor. 3:18). In the same vein, Martin Luther affirms that all loyal followers can say "I am Christ."

It is thus the face of God that authenticates the face of man. The mark of baptism inscribed divine resemblance on the forehead of the baptized. Henceforth the matter of man's resemblance to Christ came to the fore, emphasizing at least the human commonalities, if not the autobiographical ones: the child of God lost nothing of his unmistakably human face, with its features, its singularity, and its bearing.

A counterpart to Dürer's painting can be found in two poems by Marguerite de Navarre, queen of Navarre and renowned patroness of the arts (1492–1549), *Le Miroir de l'âme pécheresse* [*Mirror of the Sinful Soul*] and *Le Miroir de Jhesus crucifié* [*Mirror of Jesus Crucified*], written toward the end of her life. Instead of becoming a Protestant, she developed a kind of personal mysticism. In an almost obsessive manner, the queen describes her divine resemblance in the precise terms of her filial relationship to God: despite her sins as a prodigal daughter, a poor mother and wife that mar her image, she knows that she is daughter, sister, mother, and spouse of Christ because she hears the "moans" and "sighs" of the divine presence deep inside her heart, much like the indelible marks of her heredity.

Man's relation to the fallen Adam erodes while the specular image discovers a new, inverted identity for him. As for de Cusa or Dürer, Marguerite's false appearances and sins allow her to elevate herself toward God. The thematic of reflection that makes her conversion possible is no longer the traditional one of the medieval mirror, but an internalized movement climbing from the imperfect to the perfect, from moral countenance to absolute beauty, otherness to similarity, as vitalized by existential experience.[34] In contrast to contemplating biblical passages, the mirror becomes for Marguerite a truly spiritual space of intimate self-examination and confession, allowing the filtering of emotions, desires, carnal weaknesses, and inconstancy of the heart.

In Marguerite's *Miroir de Jhesus crucifié,* identity is expressed as a conflict, a paradox, an anxious interrogation lived through blindness: "Seeing myself as such a great darkness/I do not know myself well."[35] She must wait for the clarity of the face-to-face encounter with the mirror to become familiar with herself in the way that she is known to others. And just as Dürer painted himself so as to look at his reflection, in the suffering figure of Christ as *The Man of Sorrows* (1522, Bremen), Marguerite wants to see herself in the Christ of the Passion at the moment of death: "Here I must look at my fragile body/Formed from mud and flimsy clay/From which my Lord, you took on a semblance and shape."[36] In this sorrowful mirror of Christ in agony, the leprous sinner recognizes her own true face.

This troubling quest, experienced by Marguerite in the fading light of Saint Paul's mirror, becomes, in the mystical experience of Saint Theresa of Avila, an affirmation of every being and of radiant transparency. Theresa had the audacity to write her autobiography—a bolder act than Dürer's painting his self-portrait on account of her being a woman—within which she describes this fusion of faces in the mirror: "My soul in its entirety was presented to me in the form of a clear mirror: the back, the top, the bottom, all glowing with light. In the center appeared Our Lord Jesus Christ, as he ordinarily appears to me. In all regions of my soul I saw him reflected as if in a mirror, but at the same time I wouldn't know how to say what sort of mirror it was."[37] The mirror is an intersecting point where the visible face takes hold of its invisible face in love's transposed gaze.

The Mirror of Perspective

In the Renaissance, the mirror henceforth lends itself to self-examination and interior dialogue. The eye-mirror of the humanist presents a new way of looking at the world, but it continues to situate itself at the core of a system of correspondences and analogies akin to the medieval mirror. A theologian, philosopher, and mathematician like Charles de Bovelles (1478–1567), in the tradition of de Cusa, defines the human being by the activity of his mind, capable of recapturing the material world in order to reflect it back to the Creator, relying on his own wits to arrive at his own ideas about the world.[38] Both outside the world and within it, separated and united, he is at the same time the eye that sees everything and the mirror in which everything is reflected. Much like the world's double nature—part matter, part concept—the Bovellian man has a double gaze, one that knows himself and another that knows the world: one part grasps the other. Because of his capacity to bridge these oppositions, man can surpass simple animal, mineral, or vegetable existence and enter the realm of self-consciousness. Thus "the wise man" comes into being, meaning the "man of culture," a double or mirror reflection of the man of nature.

Humanist education engenders in those inclined toward the life of the mind a capacity, like a mirror, to transform the tangible world into image and idea. According to early humanist Giannozzo Manetti (1396–1459), such a man is also the "only true simulacrum of God, in whom divine resemblance deigns to shine and manifest itself."[39] The painter or poet who interprets the world is a mirror of the world, and not in an anonymous hiding behind the reflection of divine creation, but in the pride of individual affirmation. It is deliberately that Joseph de Chesnes entitles his cosmogonic poem *Miroir du Monde*; in doing so he takes advantage of a continuity with the medieval *speculum mundi*, but above all also lays a claim to his artistic legitimacy. Writing is a mirror of "polished crystal of a smooth fluency" in which man projects himself: "If man still wants to see his reflection/If he still wants to admire the grandeur of his mind/He must then take a look in the mirror of the world." But this mirror remains a reflection in the mirror of God because "only God is a gleaming mirror unto himself/In which the contents of the world are present."[40]

The technical advances that enabled the passage from the convex mirror to the plane mirror reflected humanists' new relationship with knowledge. They no longer viewed the visible and invisible as governed by the same laws. The convex mirror concentrated space and offered a global and spherical view of the world, embracing many perspectives, but its roundness distorted the image. The plane mirror, on the other hand, offered an exact but only partial image, a framed vision from a single point of view that controls what is seen like a stage director. A model of a knowledge that is no longer symbolic and analogical but rather critical and discursive, the mirror finds its place in a new philosophy of representation, responding to its own rules, and in addition to its role in organizing space, it revels in the pleasure of the spectacle.

The artist henceforth replaced an aggregate of correspondences with a homogenous, purely mental space, subject to mathematical laws. Ernst Cassirer and Erwin Panofsky have stressed the great evolution brought about by the conquest of artificial perspective, an open window through which a painter defines an angle of view and lets the subject assert itself, while targeting a vanishing point that opens onto an infinite horizon. It is this perspective that Florentine sculptor, painter, and architect Filippo Brunelleschi (1377–1446) used when he painted the Bapistry of St. John on a wooden panel. He demonstrated the painting's veracity by putting a peephole through the panel, and setting up a mirror so that the observer could compare the painting to the original by shifting his perspective.

A tool of reflected knowledge and an instrument of spectacle, the mirror allowed new optical games that definitively separated objects from their image. If Leon Battista Alberti (1404–1472) and Leonardo da Vinci (1452–1519) saw in the mirror their master, the verifier of resemblances, and the educator of the eye, they also recognized it as a master of illusion, illusion being only a manipulation of resemblance. This theme reached a crescendo in the second half of the sixteenth century. French engineer Jacques Besson (1540–1576), who wrote his *Cosmolabe ou Instrument universel* in 1567, studying "the sciences of sight," demonstrates, following numerous treatises on optics published earlier in the sixteenth century, how relationships between objects could be made deceptive by the diversity of points of view and positions that mirrors made possible. Without a fixed, unique, and objective reference point, that embraces the totality of perspectives, the spectator could never verify the preciseness or accuracy of his point of view.

By organizing and breaking up space according to an arbitrary centering, the mirror reveals the relativity of perspectives and thus restores a complexity and mobility to mind play, a mirror-prism in which concepts and images fit into one another, and graft meanings on top of each other in a network of metaphors and references. The Jesuit Tesauro, in the seventeenth century, at the beginning of his work *Cannochiale aristotelica*, likened the human intellect to the purest of mirrors, remarking that the metaphor provided pleasure because "it is a more curious and agreeable thing to look at several objects in perspective than to see the originals pass before the eye."[41] An illusionary version of the original proves more seductive than the original itself, as does variety over sameness. Reference to the unique source of all likeness is lost in the inexhaustible varieties and mutations of reflections that stimulate the mind.

The Optical Revolution of the Seventeenth Century

The ancient epistemology of resemblance was fading away, and with it, the disturbing mystery of the mirror. The burgeoning science of the seventeenth century completely overturned the foundations of optical thinking. Thanks to Johannes Kepler (1571–1630), vision and the effects of reflection and refraction were forever tied to the physical laws pertaining to the propagation of light. With the discovery of the specific components of the eye—the role of the crystalline lens, the concept of convergence, the optical axis, the retinal screen—the relationships between man and the world were in the process of being transformed.[42]

Up until then, when it struck the eye, the light ray was thought to carry only the form and color of the object, provoking ocular sensation. It was then the role of judgment or reason, in the general sense, to measure distance or to estimate the size of the object in relation to other objects. In such a system, the mirror image disturbed knowledge and misled judgment by making one believe in an object's presence when it actually was not there: *deceptio visus* (deceiving to see), the reflection was an optical illusion, a trompe l'oeil. As for oblique rays, which hit the center of the eye only by refraction on the cornea, the information they conveyed was considered false and distorting. These notions naturally had their influence on secular philosophical and moral conceptions of the reflection.

Kepler boldly abandoned the system inherited from the Middle Ages, slightly modifying the experiments of natural philosopher Giambattista della Porta (1535–1615) (Porta, building a darkroom, recognized that objects in light are "introduced into the hole of the pupil" and hit the crystalline lens in darkness). He identified the principle of refraction as the normal mode of vision and defined three phases of sight: an optic phase through which the image is imprinted onto the retina through the aperture of the pupil, a phase of nervous transmission by the optic nerve to the brain, and a cognitive phase in which the mind recognizes the object. The resemblance of the microcosm to the macrocosm and the physical object to the perceiving eye ceased to be necessary; this conception ceded its place to that of the subject.

René Descartes (1596–1650) completed Kepler's work by drawing epistemological conclusions from the optical revolution: the exterior world's intelligibility derived from the one who perceives it. Twentieth-century philosopher Maurice Merleau-Ponty wrote that a Cartesian does not see himself in the mirror: "His image in the mirror is a reflection of the mechanics of things. If he recognizes himself there, if he finds that the image resembles him, it is his thinking that weaves together this conclusion; the specular image is nothing of him."[43] Resemblance is no longer found in the link between two objects, but rather lies in the man who decodes a relationship and articulates it. The reflection suddenly loses its magic. It hardly reveals any kind of iconic reality, distorting the "real" with which it identifies itself. It no longer hides a secret—the secret is henceforth in the mind that perceives and recognizes the resemblance.

Descartes, like Kepler, still ignored the optical notion of the "virtual image," a fictive extension of rays of light received by the eye differing from the real image. He was satisfied with the distinction between *pictura*, a reflection on the retina, and *imago*, an image without physical substance that is seen in the mirror, that was inherited from medieval categorization. Yet Descartes cleared the way for all sorts of optical experiments and calculations that followed. The *chambre noire*, by enabling the facile reproduction of the image of an object inside it, introduced new ways of thinking about optical games, while numerous treatises on catoptrics published during this era recorded different sorts of illusionary phenomena.

The questions asked of the mirror varied throughout the centuries. The mode of knowing depended on the status bestowed on the reflection: icon, imitation, or sign. The field of subjectivity—knowledge and self-consciousness—slowly extricated itself from a religious perspective that created and shaped it, and at the same time, the mastery of reflection and perspective conferred a new power upon man—the power to manipulate his image, to distort it regardless of the divine resemblance contained in it.

In a somewhat similar manner, the first photographic experiments in France three centuries later were perceived by some as sacrilege because, in reproducing and capturing the image, they no longer attempted to capture a resemblance unique to the model: "To claim to capture fugitive mirror images is not only an impossibility, as the work of German science has solidly proved, but the project itself is already blasphemous. Man was created in the image of God and this image cannot be fixed by any human machine."[44] Old condemnation of mimesis and the simulacrum was reawakened by prodigious developments in the technology of the image.[45]

5

The Triumph of Mimesis

At Versailles, the walls have eyes, and the galleries covered in mirrors create a fearsome visibility. Social philosopher Claude Henri de Rouvroy, comte de Saint-Simon (1760–1825) described the court at Versailles as a multitude of voyeurs observing each other's secrets, even as they themselves were watched, and recalled with amusement a companion there caught trying to play a prank on him: "As we were walking in his small hallway, I saw in the mirror at the end of the passage that he was laughing while lowering his eyes, like a man enjoying the conversation he was overhearing."[1] The mirror allows nothing to hide in the shadows, and its indiscreet clarity provides gratification for the curious eye: he who wants to surprise another is himself surprised, all being exposed to all points of view.

In glorifying the mirror and proliferating the *cabinets de glaces* (small, mirrored rooms popular in the seventeenth century), the ancien régime celebrated the reign of light and clarity and the birth of a brilliant, polished world that would eliminate shadows and otherness. The mirror substitutes reality with its own symmetrical replica, a theater of reflection and artifice, and it was to this civilized double that European society entrusted the expression and the expansion of a self constructed under both the eyes of God and of others.

Before it invited introspection, the mirror was used to attend to appearances, acting as an instrument of social adaptation and harmony. One did not look at oneself in the mirror, the mirror that looked at you; the mirror dictated its own laws and served as a normative instrument for measuring conformity to the social code. Self-consciousness coincided first of all with the consciousness of one's reflection, with one's outward representation and visage—I am seen, therefore I am. Identity was created by appearances and by public approbation, leading toward the prominence of subject.

At the same time, symmetry formed the basis for a hope of reciprocal transparency. Ubiquitous, larger in scale, and providing more light, the mirror made a spectacle of life. Society became a display window in which everyone could see and be seen while striving to become copies of an exemplary model—that of a member of the court. "To be a true gentleman [*honnête homme*] is to want to be always exposed to the view of the proper people."[2] For moralist François de La Rochefoucauld (1613–1680), transparency and social integration went hand in hand.

The ideal of *honnêteté*, a notion of social integrity and decency prized in seventeenth-century France, relied on imitation and likeness. It aimed to establish a perfect harmony among men by replacing pride and self-interest with the impersonal face of propriety. In the Hall of Mirrors, where there was "scarcely a place for a shadow to hide,"[3] the burst of lights and reflections of the mirrors are emblematic of the paradox of an all-seeing society in which everyone is exposed to everyone else's gaze, glances intercepting, surrounding, and manipulating each other, striding toward an ideal of visibility and sociability.

The Mirror and Civility

From the Moral Mirror to the Social Mirror

The mirror taught the art of manners. Present in the inventories of the nobility, it took its place in a system of social identifica-

Engraving from *Les Menus propos de Mère Sotte* (1525) by Pierre Gringore.

tion derived from medieval *courtoisie*, or polite sociability, concern for appearance and the code of civility. This theme was already part of the humanist discourse of the Renaissance: allusions to the mirror can be found in literary works—sonnets and heraldry—in moral treatises, in works on medicine, and in treatises on education.

Socrates's warning was often invoked to legitimate the use of the mirror: a loyal witness in which everyone could examine his soul and discern in it an exhortation to virtue. The mirror of "Know thyself" provided a basic code of conduct, and in the tradition of the ancient philosophers, it affirmed a healthy love of the self. A well-known encyclopedia by Domenico Nani Mirabelli, *Polyanthea nova* (1503), praised the mirror under the title "Amor sui [Love of Self]." Nani Mirabelli defended it with Pericles's maxim: *Te ipsum ne negligas* [Do not neglect yourself]. A popular proverb by satirist Pierre Gringore (c. 1475–1538) written in 1525 alluded to the mirror in emphasizing the importance of humility: "He who sees himself in a mirror, sees himself well / He who sees himself well, knows himself well / He who knows himself well takes little pride in himself." The soundness of looking at oneself originates in the demand for good morals and relations with others.

In Cesare Ripa's *Iconologia,* a guide to allegorical symbols used in art, architecture, and books that was first published in 1593, the mirror accompanied allegories of wisdom, prudence, and truth according to customs of usage more than a century old. The personification of sight, the exact perception of reality, also carried a mirror, which was becoming a symbol of the intellect, and sometimes a compass to indicate the operations of geometry.[4] In Italy and in Spain, the figure of Philosophy was represented holding a mirror, an allusion to the Socratic slogan, the reflection of the mirror thus designating the mental process of reflection.

With these justifications, defenders of the mirror granted it an active role as an educator and shaper of beauty. According to Neoplatonism, physical beauty, a reflection of eternal forms, originated in moral beauty: "[Beauty] is nothing other than radiance, the splendor of God's face and of God's light, imprinted on material beings."[5] Since the mirror was thought to externalize an interior reflection, it became more acceptable to maintain and adorn one's body and touch up one's image, the mirror being a useful tool to harmonize the internal and external. The Florentine writer Francesco Filelfo (1398–1481) devoted a chapter of his treatise on education to the mirror, to adornment and to looking at oneself. While warning against "lasciviousness," he allowed that there was a good use for the mirror: "It is hardly objectionable as long as it leads to modesty and health of the eyes," suggesting a subtle condemnation of appearance and image.[6]

The distance from the moral mirror to the mundane one used for daily grooming became so small that an amalgamation of the two often occurred. Parisian bookseller and translator of Aesop, Gilles Corrozet (1510–1568), placed a mirror in the hands of a disciple of Socrates in his emblem book, *Hecatomgraphie*, and made the mirror an essential part of furnishing for the home in his guide to heraldry and noble life, *Blasons domestiques,* published in 1536. Clear and resplendent, it allowed a lady to remove stains and "ugliness" from the soul, to beautify her face and to foster love. Sixteenth-century poet Bérenger de la Tour d'Albenas insisted on self-inspection and grooming as well: "Wise mirror who dictates and polices Beauty."[7] The doctor Jean Liébault, author of *Agriculture et Maison rustique* (1564), before detailing in five hundred pages the methods a woman might use to come to terms with, and then, if needed, forget her loss of grace, reminded her of the necessity of harmonizing her soul with her body.[8]

It is impossible to imagine the "man of the court," who always took care to marry the moral and the aesthetic, without a mirror for studying his mannerisms, reining in his expressions, and governing his body. Soldier, statesman, and author of *The Book of the Courtier,* Baldassare Castiglione (1478–1529), although mentioning it only once, evoked the mirror in his witticism aimed at expressing the only possible praise, indirect praise. His words established the importance of maintaining distance from oneself: a captain was so valorous and so fearsome that he refused to have a mirror in his bedroom because "seeing himself would scare him too much."[9] This anecdote alludes to Plato's Socratic dialogue in which the courageous captain, Laches, was incapable of articulating the meaning of courage. In Castiglione's story, the captain's presumption provoked laughter, but even more humorous was his inability to distance (or distinguish) himself from his reflection. The man of the court was expected to create an ideal and then compare it with his own image.

Facing his reflection, a courtier, or member of the court, contemplated a socialized form of his self. Beauty, grace, and charm—these natural qualities of nobility—were social qualities that the mirror encouraged and maintained by helping the courtier regulate his instincts and his emotions. "Divine mirror, rescuer from vice/Reformer, singular advisor."[10] Society, with its exchanges, its constraints, its game of reputations, acting as the overall source of emulation, was the matrix in which the interior sentiment of self-worth developed. The reflexive delinking of one's self from one's reflection was not sought in and of itself; it drew its value from the comparison that it implied, becoming a matter of attracting the gaze of others, carrying widespread approval, and giving the best impression of the self. Man became aware of himself through the social group, which he came to realize in front of the mirror.

It was the same Socratic mirror that the physiognomists invoked to patiently and passionately study the human face and to invite all people to examine themselves. As with animal morphology, facial characteristics revealed the internal being to anyone who could decipher their clues. Associated with the medicine of humors and astrology, physiognomy sought man in general, in his invariable essence and, with Italian physician Girolamo Cardano (1501–1576), it became more widely developed, examining tensions and expressions of the face. Cardano wrote, "This sort of science could aid us, not only by our inspection of others, but also by our own self-inspection, so much that we will be able to become our own physiognomists."[11] To take possession of one's face, to become one's own physiognomist: such is the true power of the mirror which, according to a sixteenth-century alchemical writer, allowed one to "contemplate one's self entirely and know the inclinations of one's nature."[12]

The aim of the physiognomists should not be thought of as an attempt to initiate some proto-modern introspective process, but rather as an effort to master the uncertainty of human relationships through a better understanding of character and, as etymology (literally "nature interpreter") indicates, of the laws of nature. Physiognomy sought to introduce coherence into social life and to make possible, beyond façades, a fair evaluation of others. It has been noted that the false appearance and the anguish of being misperceived obsessed men of the ancien régime because misrepresentation seriously threatened a system of relations that relied on a village-like interdependence and mutual trust even in city life and business dealings.[13] In most short story collections of the period, people torn between individual urges and group constraints learned to recognize the contours and limits of the self at the juncture of these competing forces.

In Defense of "Appearing"

In the seventeenth century, the ideal of *honnêteté*, an amalgam of integrity, courtesy, and politeness, was built on the dual purpose of the mirror, a tool of social adaptation and a tentative appropriator of the intimate. The two functions were interrelated, and from the tension between them was born one of the first experiences of the self.

The ability to overcome such tension engendered what the ancien régime called *le naturel*, or natural grace, through which each individual expressed his or her specific inclinations. As a concept that embraced both spontaneity and conformity, *le naturel* referred to a person's authenticity and his submission to the social code by imitating good examples. This submission left very little room for individuality or unrestrained behavior. The mirror, a tool of precision and control in the teaching and enforcement of civility, was not yet an instrument of individual rights even if it allowed the possibility of a solitary interaction with the self. The feeling of selfhood that the mirror awakened was a conflictual one of modesty or shame, consciousness of the body and of one's appearance under the watchful eye of another.

Spanish writer and philosopher Balthazar Gracian (1601–1658), a defender of fashion with a great knowledge of matters of the heart, made the mirror his best ally in dissimulation and self-control. To the courtier who regretted that nature did not provide him the means of looking at himself "so that he might carry himself more correctly, better hide and moderate his passions, or remedy the faults of his person," Gracian replied that nature had the wisdom to let him to see only his hands and his feet. Hands act, and man should find himself reflected in his actions, whereas his feet keep him firmly rooted on the ground and remind him of his humility.[14] Nowhere in Gracian's vignette (in which the power of the eyes is discussed at length) was there room for a gaze sensing its reflexivity. The mirror arbitrated between a moral self always suspicious of vanity and a social self formed by education and accomplished through action.

Each era chooses a particular social venue in accordance with its tastes and ways of thinking and feeling. In the seventeenth century, the *cabinet lambrissé*, or paneled study, was the new standard, and the crystal mirror was its crowning adornment. Men and women of means took in games of light reflected in the mirror's brilliant surface and enjoyed seeing their own faces reflected in the portrait gallery of their ancestors.

Many narratives lingered over descriptions of this private, enclosed space conducive to gestures of intimacy, to the pleasure of rest and introspection, where mood and taste are masters. "What was extremely pleasing to the eye," wrote the Abbé de Torche, seventeenth-century author of novels of manners, describing a *cabinet lambrissé*, "is that there were three large, magnificent mirrors that multiplied all beautiful things in this room: the mirror in the middle had a frame made entirely of crystal that resembled an assemblage of a thousand tiny separate pieces of ice."[15] The English heroine of the novel by François Tristan

L'Hermite (1601–1655), *Le Page disgracié*, received her lover in an almost identical room: "In this beautiful tiny room there were still two large mirrors where one could see oneself up close, from head to toe."[16] Up close, from head to toe—these words contain the affirmation of a nascent subjectivity that delighted in discovering new ways of defining the self.

Even in this refuge, however, the gaze of others never abdicated its rights. The mirror was above all welcomed as the emissary of an exterior authority. It introduced a fictive presence, a promise of the other, of conversation, of the world. In a society impassioned by gallantry, it took the place of company—it had eyes, a gaze that was sometimes indiscreet, and it spoke. It was believed to have human qualities, and its personification was not only a rhetorical device but also evidence of an ability to step outside oneself necessary for man to know himself and feel alive. The mirror was an assiduous courtier, the rival of lovers, a fashion advisor to coquettes, a confidante, an accomplice, and the most impartial of judges.[17]

Thanks to the mirror, which kept him in constant conversation with himself, man was never alone, and even an amorous couple in a most intimate moment would not have known how to set aside socially acceptable behavior. The hero and heroine of the Abbé de Torche, Hermione and Alexandre, embracing in their own paneled hideaway, called on the mirror to be a complaisant and silent observer to their dedications of love:

> Although they were alone in this charming place, it seemed nevertheless, when their eyes fell on the mirrors, that an agreeable company surrounded them and that they had as many witnesses to their conversation as reflected images of themselves in the mirrors. In this way, they enjoyed both solitude and a comfortable society [of people] who didn't inconvenience them.[18]

Love no longer granted a privileged status to passion and thus it could be integrated into social life.

Mediating between an essentially relational mode of being and the dawn of the self's dialogue with itself, the mirror facilitated the narcissistic practice of dreamy meditation, without letting go of social control. The walls of the mirrored study were not impenetrable—the gaze upon the self is a monitored gaze, a watched gaze. The shrewd Jansenist writer Pierre Nicole (1625–1695) knew that "the slightest emotion is all it takes so that everything having been kept hidden will burst forth," and that a courtier always lived under the threat of being "discovered."[19] A young princess, surprised by a friend as she looked at herself in the mirror of her small chamber, "abruptly stood up and blushed . . . then she pulled herself together."[20] Blushing is born from the embarrassment of one who feels betrayed by his or her body or face and from an awareness of the separation between the private and public self of appearances. The princess suddenly saw herself both from without and from within, in the doubled mirror of her gaze observed.

The mirror was not consulted in order to scrutinize one's features in a self-hating way, but rather to realize an image others were expecting, sitting at the junction of a truth too crude to be shown publicly and an artifice that could render it presentable. Personified by fairy-tale author Charles Perrault under the name Oronte, the mirror had neither heart nor memory and it immediately forgot those whose company it had just left. Neither indulgence nor tact was to be expected from it. When his beloved was stricken with smallpox, Oronte was forbidden entry to her house. Finally called to her bedside, he forced the spectacle of her misfortune upon her rather than hiding the ravages of her illness, and a quarrel soon followed. The mirror was never supposed to cease to play its regulatory role. In her *Mémoires*, edited at the beginning of the eighteenth century, Marguerite-Jeanne Cordier de Staal-Delaunay (1684–1750), disfigured by smallpox, related that she waited three months before facing the mirror and that she did not recognize herself.[21] An uncommon spiritual strength was necessary to face the mirror's truth because it reveals one's old age and social undesirability: "The lady Sanguin died a heroine, promenading her bare body back and forth before a mirror in her room, looking at herself in order to see naked death reflected in it," Madame de Sévigné noted with admiration (*Lettres*, 1689). The mirror revealed the unmasked face, as death approached.

Le Naturel *and Imitation*

In all sorts of fables and riddles in fashion at the time, the seventeenth-century mirror expressed the ambiguity of the ties between being and seeming, false appearance and truth, and—beyond this opposition—it determined *le naturel*, or natural grace.[22] This theme is found in an anonymously authored dialogue between a large mirror hung on the wall and a small pocket mirror.[23] The fable praised the new charms of the large mirror: this precious ornament, more dazzling than the brightest objects, was able to reproduce the beauty of places. But this large, reflective glass suffered from one handicap caused by the difficulties of early mirror making. Because of its size, its color wasn't clear, and small imperfections in its tain compromised its clarity. The pocket mirror, by contrast, shone like purest water.

Behind this conventional banter regarding the mirror's ambiguities, other more significant issues emerged: nature versus artifice, the body versus the face, and privacy versus social life, for the large mirror surprised Clymene as she awoke, "half-naked, without make-up or adornment, just as nature made her." The large mirror was the friend of simplicity and spontaneity, unlike the "spot counselor," or pocket mirror, which was incessantly consulted in order to see if "the face has all that is necessary to please," and with which the coquette practiced her gestures. The little mirror was left open to accusations of frivolity and lies, whereas the large one was said to speak the truth of a person. When it was inclined, Clymene could discover her entire animated image, right down to the "well-turned and well-shod foot that could inspire as much ardor as the charms of her face." The foot competes against the face for attention. The large mirror announced concern for the body and its form, but in the end, the small mirror prevails over its rival: the face prevails over raw nature of the rest of the body. The self is tolerable only when mediated by artifice.

But at the same time, artifice could never turn into either affectation or peculiarity. The *naturel* demanded a taming of the self, an imitation of good models without jeopardizing spontaneity. Seventeenth-century theorists of *honnêteté* Nicolas Faret and the Chevalier de Méré insisted on the truth of emotions, on ease and grace. This accurate interpretation of the self assumed assiduous contact with the mirror intimated in the question posed by La Fontaine: "Do you believe that a maid is like a flower that knows how to arrange its leaves without a mirror?"[24] It was in front of the mirror that the *honnête homme*, or gentleman, learned how to position his feet and balance his body, how to smile without effrontery or gaze with modesty. All admitted the difficulty of reconciling such contrary demands, and that such a balance could be accomplished only by certain people of quality. For others, said Faret, "this grace they are studying is a lesson that can only be learned from those who appear unaware of it."[25] Creating distance from one's self while remaining true to oneself was the goal; Méré was explicit in stressing the reflexive attitude that the *naturel* implied.

In addition, the mirror was never to be consulted in public, much in the way an actor could never carry one from behind the scenes to monitor his appearance on stage.[26] An anonymous story published by the newspaper *Mercure galant* in 1672 illustrates the miscalculations of anyone who played his role poorly or allowed himself to be discovered rehearsing his lines.[27] Cléante retires to a study decorated with four large mirrors, in order to reflect on which profession he should undertake. He has three borrowed sets of clothing brought to him—a war uniform, a lawyer's robe, and a priest's cassock. Alone, he tries on each of the ensembles one after another, entrusting his choice to the verdict of the mirror. A career as an officer is abandoned because, with a stroke of his sword meant to mimic the soldier's gesture, Cléante breaks the mirror, a sign of bad luck. The young man hesitates between the two other professions, wondering "which looks best on him," when his fiancée and her mother enter surreptitiously and surprise him before the mirror. "He was barely recognizable for he had removed his wig and his hair went only to his ears." The tale concludes: "He was not the least bit attractive to the ladies in such a state," and so the engagement is broken off.

It was neither the young man's hesitations nor the flippancy of his meditation that provoked the rupture, but instead the shameless spectacle of a man stripped of his artifice. The more one hides behind the veils of artifice, the more one fears any glimpse of the truth; the artifice is what makes the unveiling so dangerous. Moments of intimacy between self and self were only nominally tolerated and had to be kept private.

A Collective Narcisssism

The Art of Appeal

One's gaze upon the self was confirmation of the gaze of others. In the intimate space of the private *cabinet*, the *honnête homme* composed an image that he believed advantageous and of which others would approve because he existed to be appealing and display charm. He was a creature of opinion. His own esteem and merit weren't enough if his reputation was not outwardly recognized. "My mirror and my reputation do not lie," wrote soldier and author Roger de Rabutin, comte de Bussy (1618–1693), in a revealing association.[28]

Reputation was a sort of echo, the mirror's reflection reflected back by others, that confirmed the *honnête homme*'s own estimation of himself. Virtue, honor, and valor gave birth to and added luster to one's reputation and, according to Balthazar Gracian, artifice contributed to it as well, because "he who cannot see himself might as well not exist."[29] Reality and reflection supported each other reciprocally. Far from altering the genuine, appearance is the instrument through which it emerges on the surface and interacts with the world. Méré knew that in order to appear an *honnête homme*, one must, in fact, *be* one, while Faret remarked that "industry greatly helps virtue shine."[30] Being was closely identified with manner of being.

Bodily adornment therefore served to establish the reputation of the beautiful soul, just as a rich frame set off the beautiful mirror. The seventeenth century also attached great importance to the first impression; it was important to harness the gaze: "Ribbons, lace and mirrors are three things the French cannot live without," wrote a Sicilian visiting Paris.[31] A man of rank wore clothes as much as the clothes wore the man. Clothing revealed innumerable signs from which the educated eye could recognize rank and circumstance. Above all, the care that a man put into making his appearance shine revealed his esteem for others; clothing helped to unite people whereas the body drove them apart. The act of pleasing others removed from vanity all that made it detestable.

Social interaction depended on adherence to a common system and a social consensus whereby each man offers to the other the mirror that is desired. The ideal of the *honnête homme* was, according to literary critic Jean Starobinski (b. 1920), perfect reciprocity. Civility demanded that men exchange courtesies with the mimetism of a mirror: "The *Lois de la galanterie* [*Laws of Gallantry*] command that you cannot fail to greet those who greet you with a decency as great as their own," admonished a contemporary arbiter of etiquette. "Don't let it be noticed that you are waiting for another to tip his hat first; you yourself should begin the gesture when he is only halfway in front of you."[32] Extraordinary orchestration, a science of imitation and symmetry, and perfect conformity culminated in the well-ordered celebrations of Versailles, organized around the royal actor and model.

Everything at Versailles was specular magic, not only the castle reflected in the water of the canal, nor the symmetry of an unfolding architecture, nor the repetition of gestures in the mirror, but first and foremost all the rules of etiquette by which the audience of the courtiers bowed in unison, exchanging curtsey for curtsey, glance for glance. The court thought itself a spectacle. Each person wanted to see, to see himself and to be seen, to be narcissistically bedazzled as all gazes converged upon the eye of the Sun King, from whom all light radiated. Ostentatious spectacle augmented royal authority and created a theater of reflection bathed in the artificial clarity of footlights:

> By the reflection of a large number of mirrors
> That make beauty visible in various places
> The fire of diamonds worn by the court
> In the middle of the night give birth to a new day.[33]

Conceived to "launch" the French mirror company, the Hall of Mirrors was the appropriate venue for these displays within which the image of a closed, self-admiring society reflected back and forth. By placing both the social group and the individual before the mirror, a sort of osmosis was established between the two: the *honnête homme* was the reflection of the group, and the group the reflection of the *honnête homme*.

The mirror's legitimacy derived from the social other that it represented. It didn't foster introversion, but rather emulation and exchange. Everyone admired the *honnête hommes* because similarity fostered benevolence. An art of appearances, charm was a tangible resonance, a reversible echo rebounding from one to the other, setting into motion understanding between two beings. Everyone either liked or disliked what he saw in the mirror of others. The social concert would not be sustained without this reciprocal attitude, which fed the collective narcissism; civility—as the moralist Pierre Nicole complained—depended on superficial respect and consideration that "gave one occasion to represent oneself as loved and worthy, thus likeable and estimable."[34]

In holding this accommodating mirror up to himself, the *honnête homme* ran the risk of identifying himself with the flatterer. As a kind of reflection, flattery was often likened to a mirror as in this verse by Madeleine de Scudéry (1607–1701):

> I no more flatter kings than shepherds
> I serve to correct the faults of others without knowing them
> I do not speak but I counsel
> Often when I am true, I am not believed
> And when I flatter, I am always believed.[35]

Certainly flattery was recognized as a deceptive illusion bound up with vanity, but it was considered better to please than to alienate in this social setting. The true sin of Narcissus lay in the preference he granted to his own singularity. By challenging social mimicry, he disrupted the party and was more subversive than flatterers because "it is more dangerous to flatter oneself than to flatter others."[36] The mirror, instead of offering him the clarity of reciprocal admiration, reflected his somber double with a single desire: a bubble of solipsistic confinement that Caravaggio's Narcissus so perfectly illustrated, forming with his arms and their reflection a perfect circle excluding the outside world.

From the Mirror to the Art of the Portrait

In a society of reflections, where personal expression was suspect, to exist, the self needed to be visually echoed. The painted

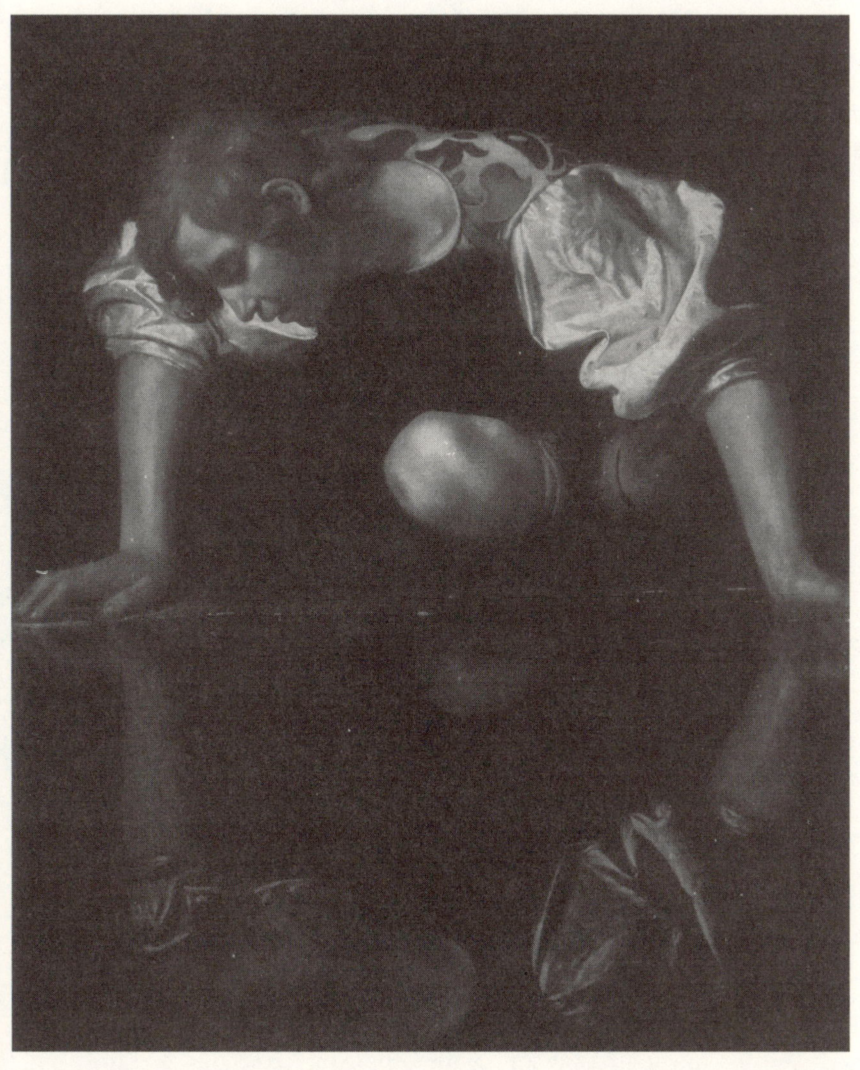

Caravaggio, *Narcissus* (c. 1599–1600). Galleria Nazionale d'Arte Antica (Pal. Barberini-Corsini), Rome, Italy.

portrait and the literary portrait carried out this function in prolonging the pleasure of the mirror. Mirror and painting had the same objective, to increase the value of the image. The lover who wanted to please his lady could attain the same results by offering her either a small painted portrait or a mirror set in a medallion.

The painted portrait was developed beginning in the sixteenth century and met with growing success; before capturing likeness and singular traits, it sought to incorporate signs of social integration. Dress, posture, and face transformed into image or sign, marking adherence to a group. A short story by Charles Sorel (c. 1600–1674), *L'Isle de portraiture*, gaily enumerates the bizarre requests of the innumerable candidates for the portrait, classified according to their fantasies: "All wanted their portrait to be done according to how they seemed and not how they were."[37] Pierre Nicole observed that the portrait was the privileged place of flattery, "a deceptive surface" where the private self is erased behind the vanity of the social man.

By peering into the interior man beneath his deceptive surface, the literary portrait could hope to escape Nicole's reproach and get closer to a psychic truth, one difficult to grasp under the pressures of life at court. Such portraits, made fashionable in aristocratic milieus by Mademoiselle de Scudéry and by Jean Regnault de Segrais (1624-1701), met with immense success in the middle of the seventeenth century. They began an endless debate on whether it was easier to know oneself or to know another, and whether the self-portrait could escape the pitfalls of vanity.

In this context, a *Recueil des portraits* [*Collection of Portraits*] dedicated to Mademoiselle de Scudéry illustrates the limits of this genre and fashion. The work contains a few more portraits than self-portraits, but aside from the fact that some were composed in the first person, while others in the second or third, nothing really distinguishes them. The authors, who all look at themselves attentively in their mirror and through the eyes of others, express their readiness to divulge their secrets in their choice of words, their character, their temperament, or their inclinations, but they emphasize neither their individuality nor the specificity of their experience as having value. In this collection, subjectivity dares to show itself only if someone else has requested it: each author of a self-portrait insists that he is writing at the behest of another. Because these portraits lapse largely into abstraction, the "general" man tending to eclipse the individual, the psychological mechanism of vanity is restrained.

The author of the preface, Segrais, stresses the great diversity of men, but he just as quickly gives a generalist purpose to his enterprise by proclaiming the exemplary worth of his models. Like *Plutarch's Lives*, the chosen portraits offer the court's best examples of virtue, prudence, generosity, honesty; even faults of these individuals serve to enhance their good qualities. The traits that are most often recalled concern sociability, modesty, openness, and friendliness, or their opposites, disdain, coldness, and anger. The protagonists, societal mirrors, can exhibit themselves as spectacle: the secrets of a few are truth for all—or none.

The monotony of these portraits has often been noted, along with the stereotypes they employed: an *honnête homme* is neither tall nor short, possesses a grace neither too proper nor too awkward, and a mind neither too cerebral nor too stupid. That is to say he is "mediocre," a harmonious blend of average qualities. The gaze always has recourse to a symbolic, neutral third party, who serves as a reference point; mediation is ensured by impersonal language, kept independent of the one manipulating it so that the style of portraits or self-portraits is interchangeable. The reader experiences no surprise, and has no doubt about the social identity of the subjects, which certain telltale signs make evident right from the start.

Moral lessons are internalized by even the earliest of ages. A five-year-old girl and an adolescent of twelve created their self-portraits according to the same examples as their elders; however, they are more comfortable with entrusting their images to the gaze of the other. In short, the portrait is a fixed point from which a balance sheet of positive qualities and faults can be established. Court society demanded strict adherence to conventions and proprieties, and did not leave any room for momentary lapses, neglect of details, admissions of preference, or signs of nervousness. How one is known through the mediation of reputation and the mirror comes to replace what one actually is.

Mirrors are described in terms of portraits, and portraits in terms of mirrors.[38] Both communicate obvious signals and elevate the stature of conventional truth. In the eighteenth century, the demand for portraits grew to encompass an even vaster clientele, and painters could surpass the mirror image by adding the glamour of history and mythology, inspiring the following quip by Louis-Sébastien Mercier: "After having looked at oneself in the mirror, one wants to see oneself on canvas." The eighteenth-century art critic La Font de Saint-Yenne, lamenting the decline of "great" painting, echoes Mercier's sentiment: "The science of the paintbrush was forced to cede to the splendor of glass."[39]

The portrait triumphed by confronting the face. The artist complained of having to obey the whims of a crowd that is "obscure, nameless, without talent, reputation or physiognomy . . . beings that have no merit other than that of existing."[40] All of his talent consisted of "flattering the subjects he paints with enough skill to persuade them that he is not flattering them." In short, painters "paint the way wigmakers dress hair."[41] From applying face make-up before the mirror to commissioning a touched-up portrait, it all came down to having a presentable face to show the world. Both the mirror and the portrait allowed people of obscure origins a means of denying their true identity.

The Utopia of Transparency

Instead of trying to express the impenetrable reaches of his inner being, the *honnête homme* utilized a certain number of immediately accessible signs. With the visibility and self-control that this presentation allowed, the mirror became a site to shape one's presence. The reciprocity of manners and propriety put aside pride, while mimicry expressed recognition of likeness, the same in the other. The mirror thus represented the hope for a transparency that would clear the darkness, banish differing perspectives and validate the exemplary nature of a perfectly clear, intelligent order.

But the mirror, a tool of dissimulation, also creates disguises; it generates a superficial being who is satisfied with signs and discards anything strange or foreign. The structure of the other as other is erased, or rather assimilated. In this environment, one can only be certain of the artifice, something the social code considers a lesser evil: "It is even better to be known as a hypocrite than to be known as a bad man."[42] Decorum was meant to be the expression of *le naturel* and of interior sentiment, but it was only the attractive veil of a void: "It is no longer a question of true or false," says Eulalie, one of the fictional *précieuses* in Abbé de Pure's famed satire of society women, "These questions are no longer in fashion. Now it's a question of appearance and attraction."

In the eighteenth century, the utopia of transparency helped to foster the birth of an egalitarian ideology. Unlike the seventeenth century, the transparency of hearts and consciences, not of appearances, mattered most. The philosophy of the Enlightenment believed in man; it rejected masks, or rather the only mask allowed was that of sincerity; the distance of politeness, a "uniform and deceitful veil" that so infuriated Rousseau, only further obscured human relations. Pascal and La Rochefoucauld already recognized that by "covering" pride, one did not remove it. Nostalgic for a mode of communication that would dare to appear as it actually was, Rousseau dreamt of rendering "his heart as transparent as crystal,"[43] founding his hope on the social contract's promise of equality, keeping pride in its place.

The mirror thus becomes the very seal of the human community whose ties of resemblance it brings out. A famous fable by

Jean-Pierre Claris de Florian (1755–1794), *L'Enfant et le Miroir*, explains this reciprocal quality. Addressing a child stamping his feet with rage before her mirror, his mother asks

> Why don't you make this long face
> before the naughty one who causes your vexation?
> Yes, look now, you smile, he smiles
> You hold your arms out to him and he does the same
> You're no longer angry and neither is he
> Here you see the emblem of society
> Good and evil are returned back to us.

Men awake to morality through example. The eye of absolute power yields to an all-seeing social body, united by conforming to the same conventions. The moral aim of solidarity, the social contract of equality and fraternity, justified mimicry. There were certainly always the imitated and the imitators, but the latter could hope one day to become the former. In fact, the end of the eighteenth century saw the proliferation of treatises on civility and mirrors, which allowed everyone a means of learning the gestures of others, of increasing their adaptability, their conformity, and their virtuous sociability.

The mirror that lay at the heart of court life, allowing the valiant knight to learn the gestures of civility, promoted the ideal of the *honnête homme*, or gentleman, refining his image. The mirror was first an instrument of social hierarchy and aristocratic ideal; then, as it became more commonplace, it served as a symbol of the equality among men. Its function was "moralized," as duty and examples of virtue replaced decorum. Everyone became capable of reaching true *honnêteté*. Widespread use of mirrors and the reversibility of their reflections announced the advent of a bourgeois and democratic world.

Changing terms of sociability and exchange in turn fed a narcissistic need for recognition and an overinvestment in the mirror image. Mastery over the reflection was only the first stage of a cultural revolution that influenced the relationship between man and image. With the advent of silhouette artists, and then *physionotracistes* (late-eighteenth-century artists who claimed to be able to draw a person's portrait with a mechanical instrument called a *physionotrace*), the need to have one's image at one's disposal increased, and the right to the portrait, a nascent dimension of the person, would be inscribed as one of the rights of man. The triumph of photography fifty years later would complete the "democratization of narcissism."

6

Staring at the Self in Order to Imagine the Self

The quest for the subject was long and hesitant, limited by all kinds of cultural prohibitions. Initiated by the men of the Renaissance, it had to forge its own path between the suspect moral imperative "Know thyself" and the equalizing rules of life in society. "Pascal," wrote one member of the Jansenist circle known as "The Gentlemen of Port-Royal," "believed that man ought to avoid speaking his own name and even using the words 'I' and 'me.' And he often said that Christian piety destroyed the human self and that civility hid and suppressed it."[1] The mirror was caught up in this double bind. Moralists mistrusted it because vanity "tarnishes the purest mirrors" and deformed the image meant to resemble God.[2] Society men and women idolized it because it was a privileged instrument that helped foster social bonds.

Through this doubled gaze, however, both introspective and mimetic, the individual could define himself as a subject. Examining the self in the mirror of "Know thyself" allows the individual to understand himself through the mastering of his consciousness, whereas by creating his image in the mirror of others, he becomes a spectacle for himself under exterior gazes. To see oneself and to be seen, to know oneself and to be known—these are interdependent acts. On these two levels, the importance of the specular consciousness has been affirmed throughout history.

By consistently reengaging the subject in a dialectic of being and seeming, the mirror appeals to the imagination, introducing new perspectives and anticipating other truths. The face-to-face encounter, a space of intimacy wrested from the gaze of an other, is not only the passive perception of an appearance, but a projection, a circling from desire to reflection and from reflection to desire. To observe oneself, to measure oneself, to dream oneself and to transform oneself: these are the diverse functions brought into play by an encounter with the mirror beyond the cultural stigmas long attached to looking at one's self.

The Renaissance and Looking at the Self

Marvel and Mistrust

In the sixteenth century, praise of the mirror went hand in hand with faith in the eminence of man. The mirror was a precious and noble object invented by "ingenious nature" so that "we may continuously contemplate the dignity of the human form," and it allowed each human being to take account of his strengths.[3] Its precision and limpidity offered a more loyal and exact image than a painting by an ancient Greek painter like Apelles or Zeuxis. Finally and above all, the mirror allowed man to see what nature had hidden from him: "Invented in order to know that which our own gaze cannot see," it showed him his face and his eye, window to the soul.[4]

At the same time, and despite the numerous apologies of the mirror, the right to look at oneself was always subject to strict moral control: the body was excluded from the visual field. An engraving by Andre Andreani (c. 1540–1623) in the style of Giovanni Fortuna (1588) shows a woman craning her neck in order to see her back in a mirror. A skeleton emerges from the darkness to surprise her (Musée des Beaux-Arts, Caen). Only the face and the hands could represent human nobility. For other parts of the body, reserve and discretion were the order of the day: medical doctors and beauty specialists deemed them "nearly all the same in different persons."[5]

Composed of humors that fall prey to illness, the body was above all the prison of the soul and the place and opportunity of sin; its display had to be contained by modesty and temperance. The attention to one's person demanded by courtly life certainly entailed the indiscretion of looking at oneself, but it had to be done with "modesty and shame." Spanish humanist Juan Luis Vives (1492–1540), whose treaty on the education of women guided so many teachers, was specific about use of the mirror: "She will look at herself in the mirror not to comb her hair or to assemble herself in a strange way, but so that nothing in her face nor in all her head might be unbecoming or ridiculous, something she could only notice by use of the mirror."[6] Treatises on cosmetics allowed only three justifications for looking at oneself while grooming: to cover up a spot so as to restore the harmony of body and soul, to please one's husband, and to repair an accident or illness.[7]

Suspicion weighed more and more heavily on gazing at one's self as scientific progress in optics called into question traditional beliefs and certain visions of the world. Historian Carlo Ginzburg points out that sight was slowly emerging as a "privileged erotic sense," behind touch, when the invention of processes like line engraving and etching allowed the production and diffusion of audacious, improper images that managed to reach a wider and wider public.[8] In fact, small engravings of women bathing and grooming themselves abounded, and confessor's manuals of the sixteenth century sternly rebuked the lust these images invoked.[9] Moreover, condemnation of Narcissus, guilty of reveling in the image of his own beauty, increased. Natalis Comes, author of *Mythologiae* (1583), a handbook of symbols, judged him "libidinous," while poet and physician Leo the

Hebrew (c. 1460–1521), without fear of misrepresenting Ovid, spoke of the "carnal delectations" of the one who looked at himself in "a turbid and ugly water,"[10] which did not fail to evoke scenes of steamy public baths with bodies intermingling. Such sharp denunciations heightened the mistrust that the physical world already inspired.

From One Renaissance to the Other

In this ambiguous context of wonder and censure, rare are the texts linking self-affirmation to the pleasure of seeing and feeling, and to the body's sense of comfort with being captured in the mirror. One of the earliest texts of this sort dates back to the first "renaissance" of the twelfth century. An episode of the *Roman de Troie* (1160) by Benoît de Sainte-Maure describes the utopic space of the *chambre de beauté* ("room of beauty"), an enclosed and protected luminous paradise, surrounded by walls of a remarkable alabaster so pure that its properties were like those of modern mirrors. The occupants inside could see the exterior world, "but from the exterior, try as one might to look in, one could see nothing."[11] To see without being seen, this dream is born from an ambiguous desire, affirming the privileged status of the gaze.

In order to access this room, candidates had to cross a vestibule guarded by four statues corresponding to the pleasure of the senses: the first held a mirror set in red gold in which all who claimed to aspire to the ideal of perfect love had to examine themselves. Much more was at stake here than a simple conformation of one's clothes and social graces: an inspection of the body and overall demeanor was followed by the acquisition of a whole new purpose. "Whosoever entered the room could contemplate herself in all of her truth, for the mirror never lied." The mirror monitored appearances, for young girls groomed themselves in it, but it also encouraged a more confident disposition: "They felt more sure of themselves and lost their timidity."

Three other statues completed the specular experience, satisfying the other senses with captivating music and perfumes. Inside the *chambre de beauté* itself was a flaming stone endowed with the magical power to heal any pain or banish any foolish desire. Contrary to the "mortal mirror of Narcissus," to whom Benoît alluded in invoking the impossible love Achilles had for Polyxene (daughter of Priam and Hecuba), the mirror of the *chambre*—at once both a symbol and a visual reality—initiated the reigning in of anarchic impulses, preparing one for perfect pleasure.

The many titled nobleman and poet, René d'Anjou, offered this same mirror, in the service of a sensory paradise, to lovers. When the "Heart enflamed with love," an alter ego of the poet, arrives at the Castle of Pleasure where Love lives, a mythic paradise with crystal walls, he is welcomed in the entryway by a mirror nearly three feet in diameter, sparkling like a sheet of diamonds, "where one could gaze at oneself from the first gate of the castle." The mirror is framed by two figures, Fantasy and Imagination, while, under the portal, an inscription of a few lines invites the Heart to be a good lover: "no one should look at himself in this mirror/Who does not see himself a loyal lover."[12] The mirror, without failing to refer to a symbolism appropriate to the Middle Ages, recenters the notion of the individual around impulses of the body, of the imagination, and of desire. Everything is meant to satisfy the eyes—the brilliance of precious stones, reflections, the sparkling variety of colors. In the middle of the courtyard, a fragrant fountain recalls the enchanted garden of Jean de Meung—the truth of desire expressed through allegory.

Poliphilo's Vision

With regard to the emotion experienced at one's first encounter with the mirror, there exists no definitive text, only some scattered allusions. A few lines from Francesco Colonna's *Hypnerotomachia Poliphili* (1499), the strange romantic tale of Poliphilo's quest for his beloved Polia, incidentally reveal initial reactions to confronting the mirror, and its author already sensed the mirror's significance in the consolidation of identity.

The hero discovers his image as he undertakes an initiatory voyage in search of love and wisdom, and comes upon a preliminary checkpoint that allows him to measure his strengths: before entering the palace of Queen Eleutherilida, Poliphilo passes between two marble walls "in the middle of which, on each side, was a great round jet stone, so black and polished that one could see oneself as in a crystal mirror. I would have gone through without taking much notice, but when I was between the two, I saw my face from one side and the other, and became in no small way frightened, thinking there were two men there."[13] The experience of dividing or splitting in two, and the confrontation with these twin likenesses first incites terror. But terror can include a touch of admiration. Dread emerges when Poliphilo discovers the copy of his twin in the second mirror, in other words, when he catches in his reflection of the reflection another face that he doesn't recognize. This discrepancy provokes such a malaise that the mirror image frees itself and is no longer perceived as a phenomenon of reflection, but as a three-dimensional reality. The phenomenon of copies, or twins, threatens one's identity. Subsequently, when the image is recognized for what it is, Poliphilo discovers in the reflections' reversibility a space of play between what he is and what he is not, a theatrical stage where he can try out several fictional identities. He leaves strengthened and composed.

If Poliphilo so easily overcomes his terror, it is because the test comes just after an initial reassuring experience. Indeed, before the encounter with the mirror, he entered a gigantic hollow bronze statue of a man lying down, and from the orifice of the mouth "through all the other parts of the body to the intestines and the bowels, " he examined human anatomy, "so that one could clearly see bones, arteries, nerves, veins, muscles and intestines." This methodical exploration resembles that of Andreas Vesalius (1514–1564), author of the first complete textbook of human anatomy, whose scalpel sought parts of the body exposed beneath the skin. It also brings to mind the experience of Montaigne, who, after a fall from a horse which left him near death, described the symptoms of his injury and claimed, by the authority of Socrates, the right to examine himself, body and soul: "I am *all* on display, like a mummy in which you can see the veins, the muscles and the tendons in one glance, each piece in its place" (*Essays*, II, 6). This visit to the heart of man gave Poliphilo a familiarity with tactile experience, and taught him good use of the carnal body. Before the "mirror stage," he experienced a group of muddled impressions that the anatomical promenade allowed him to categorize. The doubling of his reflection assured him an overview and visual mastery of the body.

A restored Poliphilo sets off to face the other tests that guard the gate of Mystery. Five nymphs, the five senses, lead him to an octagonal pool so that he can quench his thirst, for the appetites of the body must be satisfied for the voyage to proceed. His gambols among the nymphs take place between walls "of very black and very polished limestone that shines like glass," and statues of small, naked cherubs. Horasia, the nymph of sight, always holds a mirror. Mirror, water, polished glass—here man has nothing to fear from his reflection. The gaze upon the self, as with Benoît de Sainte-Maure, is not that of the imprudent Narcissus, whom Poliphilo encounters during his journey. Instead of dooming man to immobility, the specular encounter multiplies his strength by inviting him to both cast himself upon the world and study himself within it.

The Mirrors of Thélème

In the sixteenth century, with the gradual furnishing of private space out of sight and sheltered from prying eyes, the right to a solitary tête-à-tête was won with the aid of the mirror, but according to estate inventories, the mirror was still rare. It took the audacity of François Rabelais (c. 1494–1553) to put a mirror in every bedroom in his fictional, utopian Abbey of Thélème described near the end of *Gargantua*: "a crystalline mirror set in fine gold, garnished with pearls and so large that it could represent the whole person."[14] There were 9,332 mirrors for 9,332 bedrooms—everyone's privacy was respected. As much care was taken to protect the intimacy of private life as to safeguard collective happiness.

Within Thélème, the gaze upon the self was authorized and encouraged, but with restrictions, for a strict selection process governed entry into Thélème. Only "well-educated men, conversant in honest company," and "women as beautiful as they are charming"—only "well-formed and good-natured" people—gained entry. Valiant, handsome, and virtuous, those elected had no vocation other than to develop their talents and to reflect in the mirror visible evidence of human excellence. Far from finding pleasure in love of self and the narcissistic gaze, the Thelemites lived in "praiseworthy emulation," offering themselves to one another in harmonious spectacle. The gaze of others disrupted the confusion of self-love, while the bedroom mirrors encouraged self-knowledge.

The Thelemites also developed an art of living that refused to dissociate the body from the soul. Rabelais imagined mirrors the size of man, anticipating an invention that would arrive one hundred and fifty years later, in which an entire person could be reflected from head to toe, but also metaphorically, inside and out. The abbey was furnished for the pleasure of the senses—mirrors, perfumes, exquisite food—and praise of the moral doctrine was not at odds with the joy of laughing and eating. This trust in the powers of sight and the senses to shed light on the opaqueness of existence forced man to relinquish the notion of thinking of the outside and the inside, or the top and the bottom, separately, allowing a certain interpenetration of body and soul through experience.

The duality of man was called into question by Montaigne as well, but in a much different way. He knew how much the self experienced through the body, not only because the body was the vessel of the soul, but because its constraints influence internal impulses. Montaigne preferred the polarities of outside and inside and seeing and feeling to that of being and seeming. He certainly looked at himself—he described himself as having a full face, medium build, and a sturdy constitution. He knew that appearance served as a reference, allowing a certain porousness from the exterior to the interior, much as "the shoe shows the interior form of the foot. . . . My face and my eyes reveal me unbound. All my changes begin there."[15] But he also knew that distorting mirrors, deceiving expressions, and manipulations of appearances shroud the reflection of the true self in ambiguity, and he adjusted what he saw with what he felt. Significantly, his "true mirror," in which man sees himself in a good light, is "the world" and "the course of our lives" (*Essays*, I, 26).

But the Abbey of Thélème and Montaigne's gaze would not be capable of rendering a discourse on sight and the mirror that is still marked by a religious language and by a dualist philosophy, that is hardly concerned with experience and the lived.[16] Moralists thought that man could only achieve his unity by freeing himself from the constraints of the body, and thus they continued to censor the gaze upon the self.

Self-Reflection in the Seventeenth Century

Identity and Vanity

By extending the field of sight and revealing images that would be impossible to view directly, the mirror questioned the visible, the appearance, and the real, and thereby demanded a critical mind. An instrument of reflection, it also offered itself as a model of reflection. In the seventeenth century, the experience of the self was rooted in a clear-sighted gaze sharpened by the mirror and the exercise of reflective thought.

The mirror sustained the effort at introspection imposed by the moral code and reinforced self-awareness. The study of passions and the description of their organic states and manifestations owed their precision to the lucid gaze the mirror cast on appearances. Descartes's treatise *Des Passions de l'âme* [*On the Passions of the Soul*], found its plastic equivalent in the physiognomic studies by the painter Le Brun. Roger de Piles advised his pupils to complete philosophical reflection by putting themselves in the shoes of an impassioned person, and by "warming up the imagination after really entering into it, really feeling it." For this the mirror was a tremendous aid.[17] It reflected the agitations of the soul and supported or verified inferences of logic.

But this experience of the self that the mirror developed was immediately destroyed by meditation on the vanities. Site of the ephemeral, the impalpable, and the precarious, the reflection is a photographic negative that always lets the very thing it is supposed to ward off slip through—the worst aspect of narcissism: "Man wishes to see himself because he is vain," said Nicole, "and he's afraid to see himself since, being vain, he cannot tolerate the sight of his flaws."[18] Unclouded truth is the truth of vanity, a truth of nothing. "A captain looking at himself saw a ghost on horseback commanding his soldiers," wrote Nicole.[19] The reflection mimics a derisory identity.

The motif of vanity itself functions as a mirror in which the essence of man is reflected.[20] Writers of the seventeenth century dreamed in vain of a "mirror in which the soul could contemplate itself freely."[21] But in the image of the mirror in La Rochefoucauld's *Maximes* contemporaries saw only optical illusions, transience, and inconstancy. This book-mirror, in exposing the mystifications of vanity and the contradictions of existence, ends up devaluing even the powers of reflection. The *honnête homme*, or gentleman, is never sure to break free of his own strategies because "the mind is always the dupe of the heart" (Maxime 102). Obsessed with psychology, the moralists demonstrate the mirror's lack of power when God's grace does not bring its light. Self-knowledge recedes into an inaccessible darkness, a failure of intelligence before the opacity of appearances and the deceptions of vanity: "The more one looks at oneself the less one sees of oneself."[22]

Thus La Fontaine's character flees the water of the canal and gives up on searching for his image in the mirror, for fear of encountering his own vanity.[23] Invited to see himself reflected in the *Maximes*, he discovers enough dissimilarity and falsehood to give him vertigo. La Rochefoucauld, in order to get around psychological illusion, makes disillusionment his way of being because only negation has a chance at reaching truth. When he questions his mirror and touches his chin in order to describe his appearance, he undoubtedly hopes to give a faithful physical portrait of himself, as a sort of model for the internal portrait (*Portrait de La Rochefoucauld fait par lui-même* [*Portrait of La Rochefoucauld by Himself*]). But the mirror, a simple acknowledgment of surface, refuses to anticipate any such truth. On the contrary, it flaunts its secret and returns only questions by offering a melancholy spectacle of division and doubt. The suspicion engendered by *Réflexions ou Maximes morales* hangs over La Rochefoucauld's self portrait just as a trails its owner. While identity is still an obvious social fact tied to the reflection, as yet unshaken by later doubts, on the other hand, it was felt that the reflection concealed the individual, making him appear more indistinct and far away.

Identity can therefore only be grasped through vanity. A self-portrait by Austrian Johannes Gumpp in 1646 illustrates the means by which identity is delegated from its subject to a reflection, then recedes from the reflection to a painted image, in other words, to a fiction (Florence, Uffizi Museum). Triply visi-

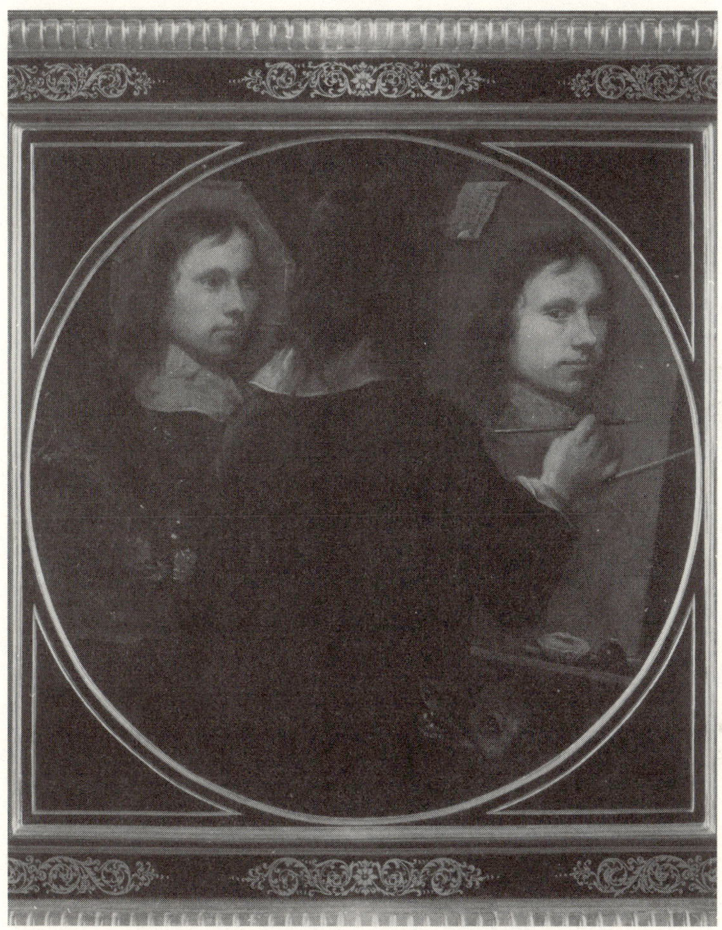

Johannes Gumpp, *Self-Portrait* (1646). Uffizi, Florence, Italy.

ble, the artist painted himself from the back: his face appears in profile in a mirror, his gaze oriented toward his own three-quarter-length portrait on the easel from which he stares out at the spectator. The tools of his trade are conspicuous: they underline the gap between the subject and its representation, "between the

I, the me and the self."[24] By entrusting his full face to a fiction, the painter reflects on the nature of illusion, suggesting the precariousness and the uncertainty of the real. By manipulating various angles and perspectives, he recalls that all identity is at first an abstraction derived from one's spiritual essence, a relative "point of view" within a certain context.

Deprived of its cognitive worth, the defective reflection does not cease to refer to a reflexive mechanism and affirms the value of all thought that imagines itself. By putting various pieces of information in perspective, the reflection participates in a work of knowledge. Gumpp, like many other artists of the seventeenth century, utilizes the image of the mirror and of the painting within a painting to designate both his critical activity as a subject in the process of painting himself and his vanity, in a *mise-en-abîme* (roughly "story-within-a-story," like Achilles's shield) that reflects these contradictions indefinitely. He puts himself before his mirror as a witness to himself. While the reflective glass helps to demystify illusion and artifice, the effectiveness of this "visual rhetoric" gives these qualities a certain validity. The painter and the moralist recognize a common denominator in their efforts to show that all is conjecture and subjectivity.

Painting and Specularity

The pictoral process of *mise-en-abîme* was closely linked to the production of mirrors. Mirrors, optical lenses, and the darkroom offered new instruments of learning and of understanding of the real, thanks to which the gaze could discern both the inside and the outside and juxtapose several fields of vision simultaneously so as to compare them. Many painters were sons of glassblowers; some even made and sold mirrors themselves.[25] Velasquez possessed, according to his estate inventory, more than ten mirrors.

Among several works that present specularity within the scene they depict, the celebrated *Las Meninas* [*Maids of Honor*] (Madrid, Prado Museum) pushes optical subtleties to their limits

Diego Rodríguez da Silva Velásquez, *Las Meninas* (1655). Museo del Prado, Madrid, Spain.

by telescoping together different planes of both the real and the reflection in order to enlarge space and to simulate depth and expose the heterogeneous nature of reality.[26] The hidden architecture of the work, which above all celebrates the powers of painting, describes a historical situation accessible only by indirect representation. The complex network of gazes exchanged between the protagonists gives a special position to the spectator who, like the painter, is ushered into the scene and encouraged to enter this dance of specularity. The interior and the exterior, the mirror play that invites what has escaped one's eyes back into the painting, the overall view and a particular point of view are part of the same space, but their margins are blurred: the work exposes the illusion of an objective gaze, the prerogative of the single divine gaze, and the limitations of knowledge. Reality is confirmed by its reflection, just as the identity of a character is revealed by its refraction in the gaze of other characters.

The genius of Northern European artists was their ability to express the subject reflecting upon himself, creating a paradox of a sufficiently "present" interiority emerging on the surface, yet maintaining enough distance so as not to degenerate or destroy this subtle quality. The portrait, even while seeking to faithfully capture individual characteristics of the subject, refused to reveal anything beyond appearances, and yet it became the stage for a secret consciousness. One thinks of Vermeer's *Young Girl Reading a Letter* (1657), for example, in which a young girl with an indecipherable expression is seen in profile absorbed in reading a letter while a three-quarter-length image of her downturned face is reflected in the window panes. A curtain draped behind the window marks the boundary of the space of private life. The letter, illegible to the spectator, is a symbol of inaccessible interiority. Together with the reflection, an image of concentration and reflexivity, the letter makes palpable the impenetrability of the secret: a mystery redoubling the mystery of yet another.[27]

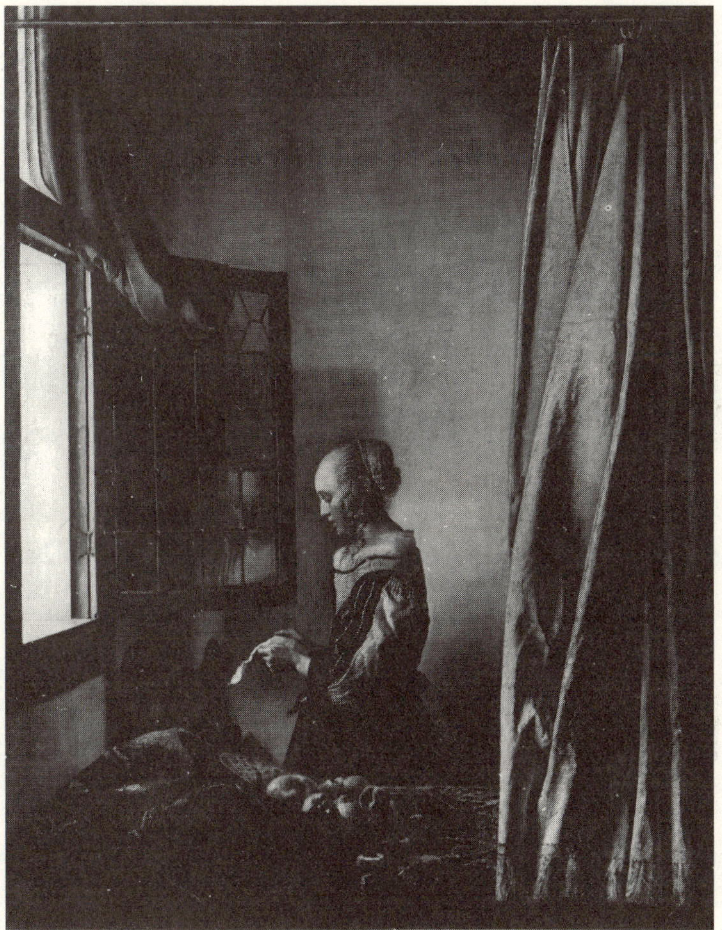

Jan Vermeer, *Young Girl Reading a Letter* (1657). Staatliche Kunstsammlungen, Dresden, Germany.

Vermeer also succeeds in conveying the presence of the unknowable through showing a juxtaposition of points of view in one of his rare self-portraits, *The Allegory of Painting*. He represents himself from the back, working at his easel and painting a young girl holding a trumpet and a book. Two mirrors probably

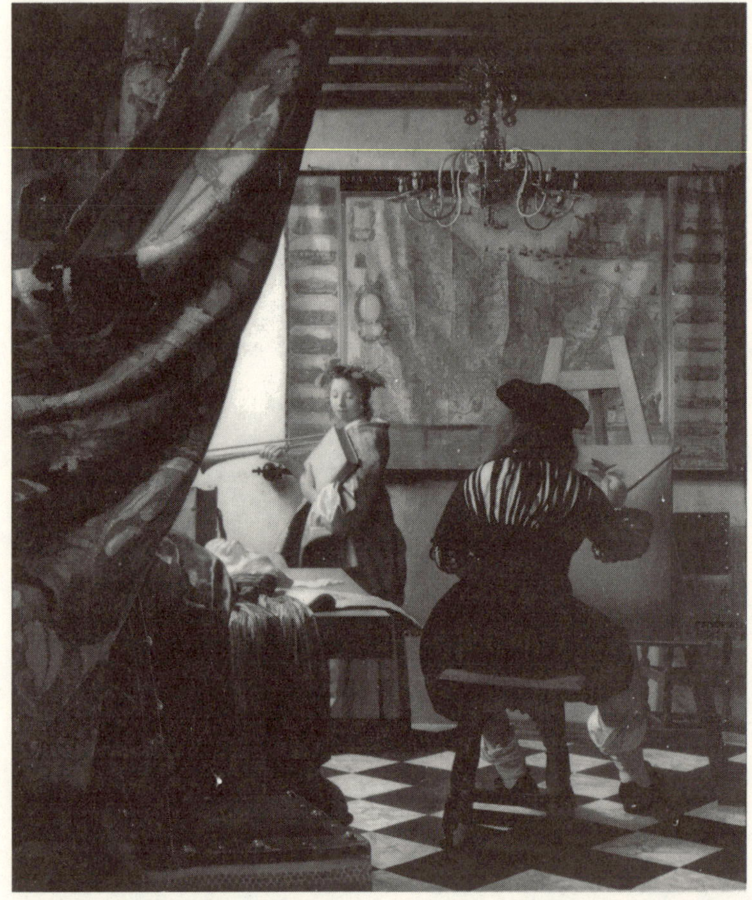

Jan Vermeer, *The Allegory of Painting* (1666–1667). Kunsthistoriches Museum, Vienna, Austria.

aided the execution of the work: one large one was placed at the back of the painting to enlarge the dimensions of the workshop, and the other, a small one, was attached to the easel to serve as a rearview mirror.[28] The subject at the focus of the mirror is distanced by a sort of optical illusion of angles making the painter visible only from behind, voluntarily concealing himself behind the luminous young girl with the trumpet, toward whom the lines of perspective converge. The optical montage has disappeared from the work. Vermeer does not take as his object the exercise of painting, but the artist himself, hidden and mysterious, is overshadowed by a goal that surpasses him.

Most authors of self-portraits are content with referring to their profession by the presence of a paintbrush, a book, or a patron's coat of arms; others fail even to allude to it, choosing instead to expose themselves as subjects rather than as painters. With a bust visible at a slight angle, a paintbrush (if there is one) held in the left hand (the image is reversed by the mirror), or a gaze that intensely engages the eye of the spectator, the painter affirms his presence and his subjectivity.

This is how Rembrandt interrogates his own face in approximately sixty self-portraits done over the course of his life. He sought to unearth the psychological content of his being and, moreover, to probe the enigma of interiority and make it felt through the thickness of surfaces. The white glare of a turban, of a piece of silk or armor, dazzles the eye of the onlooker and dissuades him from penetrating any further in such a way that the painter's eye—all the while questioning his own presence—seems to stare at and interrogate the spectator: Why look at me? And what meaning does this face convey?

Rembrandt plays with the mirror's capacity for illusion. It is widely known how much he liked to paint the shimmering light of swords, helmets, and jewelry, vacillating reflections of vanity and of passing time, but also the trembling of perceptions and sensations. In the guise of self-portraits, he painted himself as all sorts of fictive identities, giving himself, for example, the characteristics of a beggar or the visage of a biblical king. The variety of faces plays hide-and-seek with truth and fiction, just like the magic lantern projections to which art historian Svetlana Alpers rightly compares them.[29] The mystification of the magic lantern is not in its capacity to disguise, but to transfigure. Even while recalling the fragility, the uncertainty, and the capriciousness of the human condition, the play of projections suggests possibilities of the human being's transformation in accordance with the different effects of light, thus implementing another truth.

Performances of the Mirror

From the Seventeenth to the Eighteenth Century

The mirror acts more or less as a theatrical stage on which each person creates himself from an imaginary projection, from social and aesthetic models and from an appearance that all reciprocally sustain each other. Without this counterbalance, the image of the self grows unchecked. It founders in the unreality of the dream or becomes the pure surface that the playwright Pierre de Marivaux (1688–1763) mocked incessantly, ridiculing coquettish women, the vain, and all those "carriers of faces" who identify themselves by their reflection.

The theme of vanities developed by the seventeenth century denounced illusion in all its forms: the illusion of an introspection obscured by pride, of a self that is nothing but dust, of a painting that exposes itself as illusory. The eighteenth century discovered, on the contrary, that there is a power of creative illusion capable of opening a theatrical space of play between the too-real and the not-real-enough, and that the glistening of reflections, ruses, and the disguises of "appearing," or even the work of imitation, can inform the human being about what he is just as much as three-dimensional representation.[30]

Just as identity defined itself as a gradual evolution, the mirror image became identity incarnate. This relationship did not remain entirely superficial because it brought about an awareness of organic fluctuations like gaining weight, losing weight, standing up straight, and transforming one's silhouette. As they became larger and more broadly available, mirrors wrought a new consciousness of the body, as documented by the sensualist philosophy of the Enlightenment.

Sensory information played the driving role in the elaboration of the subject. The body was not a mute thickness, a mechanistic construction; it was composed of organs endowed with life and sensitivity, to which the circulation of blood gave color and vigor. The body was the vessel of each person's singularity, which fashion, with its new aesthetic example, expressed in its own way. Sexual differentiation became more pronounced. Women wore tight-fitting clothing and abandoned whalebone corsets and hoops—at least for a few decades until the corset of bourgeois respectability constrained them once more. "They obey[ed] their contours," according to the eighteenth-century expression, and "the figure [was] the mirror's outline."[31] It was up to each person to uncover his personality: "O sex that desires beauty, seek what suits each of you, uniformity is unpleasant. Why renounce your charms only to be ridiculous copies of an imaginary model?"[32] These new developments in the consciousness of the body are echoed in medical discourse and in a pedagogy of hygiene and physical exercise. They promote an aesthetic of ease, animation, and naturalness expressed in the key words of "confidence," a "steady gait," "candor," and a "welcoming mien." Due to the mirror, a human being's singularity and sincerity became part of his overall appearance.

Marivaux expressed this osmosis between body and image, between interiority and the outward gaze of the world. His work is a hall of mirrors in which eyes and mirrors exchange reflections. The image gives birth to the being: the heroine of *La Dispute*, Eglée, comes to life when she first sees herself in the water of a brook, then in a mirror. She is in all innocence thrilled by this spectacle: "I could spend my life contemplating myself. How I am going to love myself now!" The mechanism of appearances conditions the feeling of existence itself; in her image and in the interest that it awakens, Marivaux's character seeks not only the truth of her own emotions, but the source of her desires. Identity takes a step from the outside to the inside, a gleam with possibilities, supporting intimate feelings only previously revealed through the gazes of others.

Thanks to the mirror, the protagonist of Marivaux's *Paysan Parvenu* can dress fashionably and copy the gestures of the great. He loses his weather-beaten complexion, changes his name, and suddenly discovers a certain credibility to others and to himself: "The joy of seeing myself in such a good position gave me a more lively countenance and I myself felt as though I had more spirit than ordinarily."[33] The character of Marianne, for her part, complains of having only one small mirror when she tries on a new outfit given to her by her protector. But by the strength of depicting herself as beautiful and virtuous in front of Madame de Miran, she convinces herself that she is of noble lineage and models her behavior on this basis. The image in the mirror that Marianne and the *"Paysan parvenu"* compose with so much care serves to further improve on their current situation; it is projection, anticipation, exhilarating assumption.

Certainly all such facades and lies do not foster a blossoming of truth. Deception often leads to being deceived; the trickster is duped because his own reflection blurs: "I had a mask that hid my face and I no longer knew who I was when I looked at myself in the mirror," admitted the character Brideron.[34] Marivaux repeatedly and mercilessly presents the coquette absorbed in her own expressions, always ready to deceive men. He tells of a young man who returns unexpectedly to his lover and catches her before the mirror practicing the gestures and expressions she had used an instant earlier in his company and decides to break off their relationship. "I had thought her natural and I had loved her only as such, so that my love suddenly ceased."[35] In order for the reflection to become true, several conditions must be met—

sincerity of the heart, youth, verve, and quality, as well as an attractive appearance, for the body and its appeal do not lie. Finally, the approving gaze of an outside witness is necessary to guarantee the metamorphosis.

Man's gaze upon himself was no longer only that of God upon his conscience, nor society's demand for the conformity of appearances: it was that of self-consciousness. The seventeenth century deemed it necessary to "return to one's character." The following generation flaunted its inner secrets and proclaimed the irreducible singularity of each personality, and thus the right to ostentation and affectation; for "a shortcoming all one's own is worth more than a good quality that is shared."[36]

The tragic poet Crébillon (pen name for Prosper Jolyot, 1674–1762) in a text on the education of young men, justifies "a bold and singular smugness," an insolence through which he flaunts his artifices. Affectation is the double studied in the mirror, which masks one's shortcomings. The subject interprets his own role, and in acting it, overcomes his self-consciousness. Louis-Antoine de Caraccioli (1719–1803), Neapolitan ambassador and observer of French mores, thus described the portrait of the eighteenth-century man: "He trains his eyes to become faithful interpreters of his impertinence and of interior life, the mirror being where he looks so as to use them to the best advantage."[37] The subject musters his strengths so as to live within his reflection, but the reflection doesn't necessarily become more real. On the contrary, it is the subject that becomes artificial by overinvesting in the image: the subject disappears behind the character he produces and takes pleasure from himself as he would from a realized fiction.

The Dandy

With the new notion of coenaesthesia that emerged at the end of the eighteenth century that recentered the idea of the self around a neurological structure capable of coordinating the impulses of the body, it seemed that sight, creator of illusions, would lose its privileged position and yield to the perceptions of the "interior senses" governing the psyche.[38] The intimate gained a new importance, supported by the evidence that *sentiment* served as the foundation of the self, whereas the exterior image always exposed it to being denatured or disguised.

In fact, the harnessing of the reflection and the rise of a specular consciousness together created a new desire and unleashed a new sensibility—a cult of form—that of the aesthete. Elegant finery, grooming, and hours spent before the mirror were inseparable from notions of luxury, leisure, and seduction. They restored an "aristocratic code" within reach of the idle rich, in which beauty and fragility triumphed. The mirror defended an art of living that was delicate and free from the social contingencies of work. Unable to expel illusion, the mirror offered it as spectacle.

The recurrence of the figure of the dandy, son of the eighteenth-century *petit-maître*, or fop, reveals the subject's need to become his own spectator, transcending himself by constructing a harmonious image with the aid of artifice. Consciousness of the self and subjectivity are found in the spectacle of dividing the self with the mirror image. According to philosopher Gaston Bachelard (1884–1962), the reflexive mechanism of the mirror offers each person an image of his own creativity, in an "idealizing narcissism," according to which the subject says not "I like myself as I am," but "I am or I should be as I love myself. . . . I want to appear this way, so I must better my appearance."[39]

Egotistical aspirations and the cult of the self feed themselves on this encounter between the intimate gaze and the exterior image. From the outset both consist of never losing sight of oneself and in revealing only those innermost secrets that one chooses to reveal. Stendhal's novels rely on this dialectic in which the subject constructs and takes pleasure from himself in an endless exchange between the experienced self and the represented self. It matters little that he gives preeminence to the interior world or that appearances impose their omnipotence on him; the hero is a "hypocrite by condition" who chooses not to leave the theater's stage but rather to make controlled illusion his mode of being.

There is no successful or mastered artifice without the mirror. In *The Red and the Black,* opposite the young and innocent Julien Sorel still entangled in his own duality and confronted with the duplicity of the world, Stendhal places the bishop of Agde, barely older than Julien, who in order to prepare the next day's services, practices his role by solemnly giving blessings before a full-length mirror.[40] Julien and the bishop represent, to a certain extent, the same character at different moments in his life, and his success is attached to the same mirror. Julien is initiated into impassivity, and soon, in Paris, he will learn to put on "that cold face a thousand leagues away from present sensation." The bishop so perfectly manipulates the distance of the reflection that he forgets its existence.

Before this episode emblematic of egotism's nuances, the true and the artificial constantly cross paths. The rehearsal of the blessing before the mirror is meaningless as long as Julien seeks its explanation in the context of genuine behavior; the distress he feels while watching this mime makes the ease with which the bishop inhabits his role stand out. The embarrassment is paradoxically on the part of the one who sees and not the one who is seen, for the bishop really has nothing to hide. His understanding of himself is constructed from the outside by the mirror and the eyes of others. He disposes of all transcendence and all interiority, whereas Julien, the indiscreet spectator, is invited to participate in the game as a partner or accomplice.

The play is presented as real—even the visible fatigue on the bishop's face is the real effect of a mime. If the prelate tries so hard to seem real, he must surely be fake, and much more so because he is challenged by his true double, Julien, the innocent and sincere young man. And yet, truth is on the side of the bishop, transparent and fully present in his simulacrum, whereas his counterpart Julien experiences only doubt and confusion.

From the irreducible distance between the outside and the inside, and from their connection and their struggle, Baudelaire creates the condition of self-consciousness itself: "To live and sleep before a mirror," such is the wish expressed by the dandy, a sort of aesthetic and moral ideal by which the subject never ceases to be painfully conscious of his duality and performance.[41] This heroic mastery expresses nostalgia for a world that no longer exists and a revolt against the mediocrity of bourgeois values. It is this sketch of the dandy he presents in his semi-autobiographical novella, *La Fanfarlo,* through the contradictions in the character of Samuel Cramer, the "great idler," "the ambitious failure," "the notorious wretch." He cannot even miss a crumb of himself as spectacle; when a tear comes to his eye, he runs "to the mirror to watch himself cry."[42]

The dandy lives in front of the mirror because he monitors his appearance, cultivates his singularity, and seeks only references to himself. He never imitates anyone but rather incarnates the cult of the self, reveling in his difference. Contrary to Narcissus, he is not a lover seduced by his own reflection: "I stare at myself for hours with steadiness and an unimaginable attention, in order to see if there has not been some improvement in my face," confesses the hero of Théophile Gautier's novel *Mademoiselle de Maupin*.[43] He observes his image in order to modify it. He preserves his distance from it and never stops looking for it in the gaze of others reified in the mirror.

The costume of the dandy is his second skin; thus he makes it the object of loving composition, in search of either, as for Baudelaire, the beauty of absolute simplicity, or, for Jules Barbey d'Aurevilly (1808–1889), author of *The Anatomy of Dandyism*, the pleasures of eccentricity. Louis-Sébastien Mercier took a swipe at the elegant man of the end of the eighteenth century who "placed himself between four mirrors in order to see if his breeches were tight against his skin."[44] The ultimate dandy, Beau Brummell (1778–1840), needed two hours in front of the mirror to tie the tails of his white tie, while the characters Gautier satirizes in the stories of *Les Jeunes-France* carefully monitored the creases of their pants. Appearance had to be impeccable, the face smooth, the silhouette corseted, because the vanity of appearance was dictated thusly. The dandy, this "sitting room stoic,"[45] constantly exercised an ascetic self-control. He allowed himself no spontaneity, passion, conviction, or manifestation of nature if it was not reified by artifice.

As much as nature, with its stenches and its untidiness, repelled the dandy, the enclosed, artificial environment of the interior appealed to him. Edgar Allan Poe's essay "The Philosophy of Furniture" takes interior decor very seriously, paying particular attention to the role of the mirror. He advises deep sofas, wall hangings, soft, filtered lights; all is orchestrated so that one may find pleasure in himself. If he does away with glass gas lamps and the exaggerated use of mirrors, it is because they reproduce the raw light of day, incompatible with the nuances of opalescent reflections: "We line our dwellings with great British plates, and then imagine we have done a fine thing. Now the slightest inkling will be sufficient to convince anyone who has an eye at all of the ill effect of numerous looking glasses, and especially of large ones."[46]

Colorless, dull, and flat, whereas the sensitive being seeks the rare, the singular, and the intimate, a multiplicity of mirrors signifies for Poe the "odious uniformity" of the democratic spirit, the fresh fortune of the American upstarts, "the frothing of mediocrities": "A room with four or five mirrors arranged at random, is, from an artistic point of view, a room of no shape at all. If we add to this evil the attendant glitter upon glitter, we have a perfect farrago of discordant and displeasing effects." Reflections disperse attention instead of focusing it on one subject. A single beautiful mirror—Gautier and Mallarmé liked only Venetian ones—is sufficient to create the precious decor to keep life's distresses at a distance. Moreover it is hardly necessary to see oneself from every angle because "a dandy may take ten hours to groom himself, but once it is done, he forgets it" so as to devote himself to internal contemplation.[47]

First born on the social scene and then later cropping up in literary life, the dandy appeared to struggle against ennui and moral hypocrisy. His grandeur was constructed on the fixedness of his gaze that never turned away from his self, and on this subtle mockery of appearances that would, at the end of the century, turn into a decadent and sterile game.[48] The mirror is the space of the ephemeral, the instantaneous, favoring artifice and illusion, and loosening the subject's bonds to reality until they are cut altogether.

Baudelaire, even while viewing the dandy as exclusively masculine, bestows this title on Madame Bovary. Emma, dreaming of Paris, imagines the capital as a salon decorated with mirrors in which ambassadors flit around. She constantly interrupts her gestures in order to look at herself in the mirror. She believes she can glimpse her soul reflected in the glass, an appearance of depth that seduces and captivates her. The reflection reinforces her determination to escape her mediocre reality and challenges her to maintain her fictive self, more beautiful than reality, against all odds. It is this mirage that leads her to a double life in which each transgression of bourgeois morality renders her slightly more like her image until, riveted to an empty mirror, having deserted life, she can love herself only in death. Between Emma and reality, Flaubert-Bovary places the shimmering prism of the mirror: "Do you know how I spent my whole afternoon the day before yesterday? Looking at the countryside through colored panes of glass. I needed to for a page of my Bovary."[49]

Mirror and Transfer

Consciousness of the reflection, and reflection of the consciousness, the mirror image never ceases to be an illusion. Yet the illusion is not always deceptive. It can even provide a useful moment of psychic reality. The mirror is the place of transfer, a space of imagination in which the subject disguises his self and makes contact with his fantasies. The fiction of the mirror refuses the rigid distinction between real and imaginary and allows a more subtle dialectic of the subject.

It is this transformation or magical transfer that a writer like Théophile Gautier, fascinated by the specular experience and by travesty or exaggeration, put at the heart of his work, rediscovering the foundations of the psychology of the subconscious through an aesthetic truth. Sometimes the reflection is plunged into darkness by an autonomous and menacing double, sometimes it becomes a luminous anticipation of the subject. *Le Capitaine Fracasse*, which critics have recognized as autobiographical, opens with this theme: a magnificent Venetian mirror in a tortoiseshell frame lords over a table in the room of the château where the baron de Sigognac is stranded with the troupe of actors that he decided to join. Poor, his clothing tattered, his face pale with hunger, the young man considers his haggard expression in the mirror before donning the theater costume that his partner, Blasius, brings him. Then, dressed in velvet and silk, he turns around to look at himself and suddenly sees himself "as he had sometimes imagined himself in a dream."[50] The resplendent reflection of the disguised actor acquires an authentic power of metamorphosis.

The image might certainly have remained a fictive double, preserving illusion or delirium. If the image takes on substance, it is through the demands of the dramatic play, the imagination stimulating the real and the real in turn replacing the imaginary, largely due to the agent of the loving gaze of the young actress Isabelle. The real is certainly present when the theater troupe together confronts the ups and downs of daily life. The theater stage, with its amalgam of real and imaginary relationships, offers a space of transition where dream and reality, the psychic world and the exterior world, cross paths. The well-heeled character Fracasse is Sigognac's compensation for the hardships he has suffered, transposed onto the stage. But in order for the "transfer" to function well, when the theater vanishes, the real must reassert its rights. It is from Sigognac, the man and not the actor, that his very real rival, the duke de Vallombreuse, attempts to steal Isabelle's hand.

Gautier, over the course of a first version of the novel written in his youth, reportedly would have liked to conclude his story with downfall of his hero, illusion giving way to disillusion. But in 1865, a mature Gautier modified the denouement to satisfy his readers and recognized another truth: that life resembles theater and nature resembles art like "an original resembles its portrait."[51] The narrative, the materialization of a painful experience, creates a new mediating space. The mirror of writing successfully achieves the exact same metamorphosis experienced by Fracasse disguising himself before his mirror: Gautier frees himself from a past that he reconstructs, just as Fracasse-Sigognac relives, in the last lines of the work, "his first childhood impressions," but henceforth "stripped of their misery and sadness."

Man relies on the reflection to construct his own truth. The mirror opens up a space of play between the visible and the invisible, between dream and reality, with which the subject takes account of himself by projecting himself into images and fictions, having mastered their unfolding. "It is only shallow people who do not judge by appearances," said Oscar Wilde ironically.[52] The old devaluation of the image, or of the surface, always suspected of lacking depth, is erased before the truth of desire and the reality of artifice. The terms of Platonist condemnation are reversed, phenomenology renouncing the illusion of a world behind the scenes.

The effect of shimmering can, however, verge on mirage, and the reflection can be frozen in a refusal of reality. "Vanity" always awaits the one who looks at and disguises himself. This "other" of the mirror, endowed with a fleeting life, is a volatile and capricious reflection. Sometimes it seems ready to melt into the original, for lack of sufficient distance; at other times it appears dangerously liberated from its source, endowed with a troubling strangeness.

Part Three

TROUBLING STRANGENESS

Likeness does not make things "one" as much as unlikeness makes them "other."

—Montaigne, *Essays*, III, 13

7

The Devil's Distorted Faces

"Whereas certain items highly suspected of being kept by her for the casting of evil spells were found among her belongings, which she admitted were hers: two umbilical cords, some sheets soiled with menstrual blood, grains of incense, a mirror and a small knife wrapped in a linen cloth, written formulas . . . "[1]

Thus begins, in early 1321, the trial of Béatrice de Planissoles, arrested for heresy and adultery and accused of witchcraft. The possession of a mirror, a tool of the devil, is included in the charges against her. The young woman appeared before the bishop of Pamiers and was condemned to the "wall" (life in prison).

With the emergence of the mirror, a fantasy world of fears and desires is born. For the preacher, mirrors were the paraphernalia of witches who lock demons inside them, but they were also dangerous objects for any Christian because they attracted "crazed stares." When the mirror was not reflecting the spotless divine model, it was the seat of lies and seductions, used by a cunning Satan to deceive men. As an instrument of both simulation and lust, the mirror fed illusions of the mind and cupidity of the flesh, and thus was tied to numerous allegorical representations of sin.

As advances in optical science were gradually able to explain the mirror's magical or distorting effects, the archaic belief in the

Mirror of Hell. Engraving from *Der Selen Wurczart* (1483). Ulm.

devil's spell on the mirror yielded to psychic reality. However, the reflection still managed to incite other fears. Johannes Hartlieb, the author of *Buch aller verbotenen Kunst* [*Book of Forbidden Arts*] (1456) and medical advisor to Duke Albert III of Bavaria, recounted its bewitching power as a mediator of desire: "I have seen masters who claim to prepare mirrors in such a way that anybody, man or woman, might see in them what he desires."[2] Once an emblem of the fear of supernatural forces, the mirror now reflected an image of interior demons and of a threatening otherness that blurred identity.

Satan's Mirror

Magical Practices

In antiquity, mirrors were among the instruments of soothsayers and sorcerers, along with shields, bowls of water, and polished objects—all reflected and made visible hidden portents. They were present in all sorts of rites of initiation. In the Middle Ages, their convex shape and their somber color created strange effects, thus earning them the moniker "mirrors of sorceresses" and a reputation for occult powers. Behind these magic arts were the silhouettes of Lucifer and his diabolical pact, popularized in various versions of the Faust story.

From the twelfth to the seventeenth century, most treatises of demonology condemned the reprehensible practices of men and women who sought the support of the devil through hydromancy (divination by water), catoptromancy (by mirrors) or crystallomancy (by crystal balls). In his *Polycratius* (1159), John of Salisbury (c. 1115–1180) attacked all polished and brilliant objects: from the blades of daggers to polished fingernails and metal. Mathematician, philosopher, and scholar Michael Scotus (c. 1175–1234) described fortunes told in pools of water. Around this time, the bishop of Paris, William of Auvergne (d. 1249), evoked the magical practices of catoptromancy on many different occasions.[3] The explanation was always the same, confirmed by present-day inquiries: the mirror's reflection can trigger a hypnosis or trance state. The brilliance of the instrument prevents the onlooker from fixing his gaze on anything else, and with his attention captured, blinded, and turned inward, he begins to perceive supernatural communications, sometimes from God, but more often from the devil.

The Church opposed all experiments with mirrors. Curiosity, unlike faith, sought to pierce the secrets of God and to seek out that which was supposed to stay hidden from man, most especially the future. Saint Bernard (778–842) and Saint Thomas Aquinas (c. 1225–1274) denounced the *libido sciendi*, an unchecked appetite for learning, as the first degree of pride. In their eyes, curiosity led to lust, ushered in dissipation and a desire for the unusual. The Inquisition relentlessly pursued those adept in the "specular" arts, and one of the questions of the *Summa de Officio inquisitorii* of 1270 was put as follows: "Have you conducted experiments with mirrors, swords, fingernails, spheres or ivory handles?"[4] In 1326 Pope John XXII excommunicated those who "make a pact with hell, offer sacrifices to demons, worship them, produce or have others produce an image, a small ring, a mirror or some other thing to which demons might attach themselves."[5] Condemnation was renewed in the following centuries because occult practices continued, and Jean-Baptiste Thiers (1636–1703), the seventeenth-century author of the widely read *Traité des superstitions* [*Treatise on Superstitions*], referred to a judgment by the French Faculty of Theology, concluding that "it is idolatry to invoke demons and to lock them up in a mirror."[6]

Undoubtedly, at the beginning of the Renaissance people no longer believed in the possibility of keeping the devil in a bottle or a mirror, but allusions to magic practices based on scintillating objects were still often made. A poem by Pierre de Ronsard (1524–1585) evokes those "who imprison demons within mirrors."[7] This superstition apparently was still hardy enough to generate words of protest by Girolamo Cardano against those who "by skillful mirror games reveal supernatural and secret things."[8] Poet Théodore Agrippa d'Aubigné (1552–1630) was suspicious of those who "make use of abstruse sciences, pharmacopoeia and the subterfuge of shadows and mirrors" to take advantage of people.[9]

Even if scientists knew how to distinguish diabolical magic composed of "vile spirits," from natural magic, and even if they studied the laws of catoptrics like Cardano and Porta, they still believed in a mystical connection between the mirror and its subject. In the chapter of his work *Magia Naturalis* [*Natural Magic*] entitled "On the Mutual Communication of Things," Porta adopts a *topos* of the time by which "any person who looks at himself in the mirror of a whore will resemble her in impudence and bawdiness." His explanation is that the mirror acts like a magnet that attracts iron shards.[10] Porta, Cardano, and many of their contemporaries also said that a woman "with flowers," menstruating, "tarnishes the mirror," or that a basilisk that looks at itself kills itself.

Divinations by mirror did not end with the advent of the scientific age, and are evoked in numerous texts well into the modern period. Among the most famous are the visions (recounted by the Genevan Calvinist Simon Goulart) of Catherine de Médicis (1519–1589), queen of France, who saw the future of the kingdom in her mirror, and those of the occultist duc de Saint Germain (c. 1707–1784), adviser to Louis XV.[11] The looking glass continued to fascinate credulous minds and to seduce visionary souls: history provides numerous anecdotes relating the misadventures of unfortunates seeking advice from and being deceived by so-called magi.

At the beginning of the nineteenth century the famous clairvoyant Mademoiselle Le Normand, passionate about physiognomy, claimed to have rediscovered the mirror of Luc Gauric, a famed sixteenth-century astrologist whose works were republished in the middle of the eighteenth century. She placed her illustrious clientele of politicians before a polished surface in order to induce a sort of hypnosis. She was arrested for her activities in 1809; she reportedly carried her mirror with her to prison. Jacques-Albin-Simon Collin de Plancy (1794–1881), author of the *Dictionnaire infernal* (1863), writes that in the nineteenth century, soothsayers using catoptromancy were still numerous in rural areas, and that villagers came to consult them in order to recover lost or stolen objects: the consultant was blindfolded and placed in a dimly lighted room in front of a mirror in which the devil appeared.[12] At the end of the century, followers of the neurologist Jean-Martin Charcot (1825–1893) tied the phenomenon of witches to hysteria and mirror apparitions to hypnosis and the workings of dreams. Nietzsche opens the second part of *Thus Spake Zarathustra* with a prophetic dream in which a young child, the token of innocence, hands him a mirror in which the hideous face of the devil appears, an image of the demonic effects of his doctrine.

But beginning at the end of the sixteenth century, the charms of magic and the science of catoptromancy allowed themselves to be exploited by art, and their aesthetic effects served to emphasize a moral lesson. The *Crystal Gazer* by Titian (c. 1490–1576, located in the Louvre) teaches that it is better to trust oneself in the theological virtues than in the mirror or the crystal ball. The bishop of Belley, Jean-Pierre Camus de Point-Carré (1584–1652), an author of instructive tales, denounces the effects of vanity using a series of enchanted mirrors in *La tour des miroirs* (1631). The poet Jean de Caen Bertaut (1552–1611), bishop of Séez, makes them the driving force of his *Timandre* — when a lover discovers his beloved's face in the mirror of a sorcerer, a wise man warns him against "the mute lies of bewitching mirrors": "Do you not recognize the error you fall into / By consulting the father of lies?"[13] Whether the reflection is magic or ordinary, whether the devil uses natural illusions or supernatural enchantments, he is the master of duplicity and the deception of man.

Speculum Fallax

Father of lies! The first and greatest sin of the mirror is that of fabricating mirages and providing a simulacrum of Creation. For the Fathers of the Church and the Church Doctors of the Middle Ages, the mirror replaces divine reality with a deceptive world. The almost perfect resemblance of reflection opens it up to the same condemnation as a painting: superficial imitation representing a plagiarism instead of a truth. Lucifer, the great usurper of resemblance, pushes man, idolatrous of his own effigy, to lose sight of the divine model. A common iconographical image of the mirror from the Middle Ages to the Renaissance is that of a monkey who copies and ridicules everything he sees.

This negative symbolism of the mirror is inseparable from and begins with the exultation in seeing oneself. But reflection inverts these positive properties: the imperative "Know thyself" turns to pride, madness, and melancholy. In sermons from the fourteenth and fifteenth centuries, the convex mirror that disperses the rays of the sun symbolizes fashionable men and women of society, pawns of illusion and vanity, while the concave mirror concentrates the rays and thus represents spiritual light.[14]

The theology of sin, at the heart of the Christian doctrine of salvation, made the "mad stare" its centerpiece. All things visual, including seeing and thus knowing oneself, were linked together through sin. Most sins, pride or arrogance first and foremost, derive from sight. The mirror served as an attribute of sin because it is the emblem of the powers of sight, whose perverse effects it increases.

The list of the seven deadly sins was classified and codified from the fifth century onward and only slightly modified by Pope Saint Gregory I (c. 540–604, also known as "The Great") according to changes in societal mores. Sins are like iron shackles, every link engendering new sorrows and tightening the noose a little more around the neck of the unfortunate man held captive by his senses. In his *Speculum doctrinale*, Vincent de Beauvais makes a significant addition to the list of sins with a chapter on "the vices of the gaze." For him, the eyes are doors through which vices can enter and contaminate the soul. Because of our eyes, we cannot tolerate our poverty or mediocrity. They incite envy and push us headlong into the dissolute ways of passion and lust. Ultimately, only those who have lost their sight are truly free.[15]

Pride, the foremost of deadly sins, leads man to turn his gaze away from God and to make himself his own master. Pride is often likened to vainglory, the dissolute impulse of the soul that makes man want to outdo himself. Alain de Lille gives Pride ten daughters, several of whom represent sight's improper use: ostentation, pride, arrogance, jealousy, and presumption. Saint Thomas Aquinas, borrowing his nomenclature from Gregory the Great, makes a shrewd analysis of vainglory, in which he sets forth all accusations against the mirror. Something vain has no reality; it is therefore false. It is inconsistent and has no solidity. Anything "in vain" is powerless and cannot reach its aim.

Pride is surrounded by a rich retinue that clerics endowed with an incontestable psychological meaning: "I will glorify myself by looking at my arms, my legs, my robes, my castles, my land, my possessions, my horses, and I will not value my neighbors at all," writes Jean Dupin (1302–1374), author of the *Roman de Mandevie*, in a famous psychomachia, or allegorical battle of virtues and vices.[16] Jean Gerson (1363–1429), fifty years after Dupin, gives Pride three daughters, also sins of sight—"curiosity, singularity and envy," from whom "is born a deadly race—rivalry, dispute, impudence, obstinacy, immoderation, self-love, confidence in one's own opinion and contempt for others."[17]

One of the oldest representations of Vanity at the mirror, according to art historian Raimond Van Marle (1888–1936), is that of a 1330 chancel sculpture in the Cologne cathedral.[18] At the end of the Middle Ages and during the Renaissance, self-indulgence took the form of a beautiful lady looking at herself in the mirror, a peacock at her feet, with its feathers displaying innumerable eyes, reflections of her vanity. Even at the beginning of the seventeenth century, Comenius describes "the peacock who fills with pride, and makes his display, unfurling a tail strewn with eyes and mirrors."[19] In a painting by Hugo van der Goes (c. 1440–1482) (Kunsthistoriches Museum of Vienna) and in the Limbourg Brother's famous book of hours, miniature in the *Très riches heures du Duc de Berry*, the vain Eve is tempted by a serpent who reproduces her own features so that she sees and listens only to her own image. The *Seven Deadly Sins* by Hieronymous Bosch in the Prado depicts a woman looking at herself in the mirror to represent Pride. In the sixteenth century, the enormous production and distribution of engravings and the spread of printing shops further popularized the image of the woman in the mirror to represent Vanity: according to the *Liber Emblemata* [*Emblem Book*] (1531) of Andreas Alciat, "woman's vice is pride."[20]

The Mirror and Imagination

Beyond these codified representations, men of the Renaissance also made the mirror a metaphorical prism of the imagination. Vanity was but a mirror's reflection, an illusion caused by an imagination amenable to its pompous and fanciful nature: "For how long, my soul, will you contemplate things in a mirror ensconced in vanity?" asked poet Jean de Sponde (1557–1595).[21] Humanists presented the imagination as "a hollow mirror," with distorting effects. Imagination was less a faculty informing the subject of his identity than an external prompting, a foreign agent causing turmoil, profiting from the weakness of the senses and the fragility of reason. The mirror-imagination had the capacity to feed creative intuition and poetic inspiration by presenting the soul with "the best, most gracious and beautiful images or appearances of things according to their truth," but it often also came up with repugnant figures that troubled one's thoughts and unsettled the course of life.[22]

Associated with the saturnine temperament that often signals genius, imagination combined with pride to become a bittersweet madness of melancholy reflecting upon itself. It is known that, for the men of the Middle Ages, Accidia, or spiritual sloth and morbid introspection, derived from the devil. During the Renaissance, Accidia was sometimes personified by a woman holding a mirror. In a tapestry of the seven deadly sins (c. 1500) at Hampton Court, Accidia sits astride a pig (symbolizing the bestial appetites) while gazing at her face in the mirror.[23] The melancholic gaze tries to convince itself of its lucidity, but when confronted with a knowledge that eludes it, it is tormented by doubt, caught in a diabolical irony of negation. By turning back upon itself, the gaze reveals precisely that which it tried to avert:

the reverse of prudence, the fear of what lies ahead, a wavering faith. Alluding to the unicorn who turns its horn upon itself, the doctor André Du Laurens (1558–1609) describes the melancholic person as "being afraid of everything, frightening even himself like an animal who sees itself in the mirror: "Of myself I am fearful."[24] This defiant and antisocial gaze is often associated with the theme of pride.

Magic, image, and imagination are all closely linked. One of the texts consulted by soothsayers was *De Operatione daemonorum*, translated by Marsillo Ficino in 1497. The devils in the work take on many forms; "aerial" ones simulate all sorts of "shapes, colors and likenesses meant to please our taste for the fantastic," just as the air or a cloud is shaped by the rays of the sun, "as we can see and practice with in mirrors."[25] To do his work, the devil uses the imagination and manipulates his victims by presenting them with ghosts and images, or by frightening them with dreams and hallucinations. Both the dream and the mirror, which the ancients already associated with a power of divination or prophecy, share the capacity to make visions suddenly appear.

It was in this way that the poet Jean Molinet (1435–1507) transformed the medieval theme of the moral mirror into a veritable tragedy of the human heart, depicting an unquiet mind yielding to the phantasms of the imagination. With his "eye disturbed by anguished wakefulness," the poet is led into a nightmare and finds himself trembling with pain, before a mirror of death:

O murky, terrifying mirror
Pride's proclaimer, meant to displease worldly society
Horrible spectacle, detestable image
Proud vision, fearsome object
Mortal spectacle, o very brilliant example
You are an impossible and contrary monster.[26]

The dream tells of the adventure of man since his creation, when in the Garden of Eden, Adam and Eve had at their disposal a glorious mirror in which the portrait of God shone brightly up until the moment they tasted the forbidden fruit. Then "looking at themselves in the mirror, said mirror split completely in two." From then on the tarnished mirror reflected only sadness, envy, jealousy, greed, bitterness, lust, curiosity, and obscenity—all the evil desires. God, however, did not abandon his people for whom their good angel held out the mirror of the saints.

The Ship of Fools

The expression *la folle du logis,* literally "the madwoman of the house," came to personify the unfettered imagination, a form of madness: both the mirror and madness offer an inverted version of the world, prey to the irrational and to confusion. Ghosts, spectres, and apparitions could be explained by optical illusions or by "nature's hidden chambers," but they nonetheless undermined the scientific view of the world, alienating weak minds from this outlook.[27] The theme of the madman manipulated by the devil was widely used at the end of the Middle Ages to signify the instability of the world, the subversion of truth and the reality of sin.

In *Das Narren Schiff (The Ship of Fools)*, the German humanist Sebastian Brandt (c.1458–1521) gives the mirror a special place next to a few of the 112 categories of madmen he lists that roam the world. The king's fool often mirrors himself with his dummy-headed staff. Another capricious young man, slave to new fashions, changes his clothes before a mirror. A conceited old man consults his mirror and believes he sees a wise man in it. A lady contemplates her beauty while seated at one end of a bench which the devil sets on fire. *La Nef des Folles* by Josse Bade (1498) is in the same vein. A mirror is set on the prow of the head ship leading a flotilla of five vessels, each representing the five senses: sight is the first of the senses, and the madwoman

Engravings from *Ship of Fools* (1494) by Sebastian Brandt.

who holds the mirror invites her companions to join her. The sins of the "mad gaze" from the Bible until Roman antiquity pass before them in review. Bade then offers a tirade against the mirror, an exhortation to abandon its deceptive charms. Old age has a ponderous perspective: "With oneself, one is never content," because one's gaze sees death.[28]

The mirror and madness share the same ability to mystify. The madman does not retain what he sees any more than the mirror does, and he does not recall his own madness, although he is knowledgeable of madness in others. He has philautia, or self-love, at the head of his retinue, a purveyor of illusions who takes his desires for realities. And although he looks at himself incessantly, a madman does not truly know his own face because if he saw himself as mad, he would be wise. The mirror of madness is the place of absolute contradiction. By blurring the boundaries of reason, however, the eccentricities of the madman bring forth another reflexivity: just as the power of the image comes from its dissimilarity rather than from its likeness, the wisdom of the madman stems from the fact that he does not claim to tell the truth. Freely expressing himself outside the realm of social norms, he exposes the madness of wisdom and proclaims the wisdom of folly.

Eulenspiegel, the mischievous character of German literature at the end of the fifteenth century, plays on this ambiguity: holding a mirror in one hand and an owl in the other, he places himself at the fringes of a society whose order he refuses, proclaiming its lunacies and injustices. Some have tried to see him as a mirror of illusion in which men, seeking to view their own splendor, see only a blind owl (as in the version by Johann Fischart [1546–1590] toward the end of the sixteenth century). But for humanists, steeped in antiquity's symbols, the owl, blind by day, becomes clear-sighted at night and, like the mirror, is turned into a positive symbol.[29] The sin of the mirror becomes the mirror of the sinner.

The Devil's Accomplice

Eve at the Mirror

The Christian perspective, according to which the only pure mirror is the divine one, never ceases to bring to mind both the eye's lust and the taboo on looking at oneself. Moreover, the woman who stokes desire is the devil's accomplice. Eve, a naturally libidinous seductress, looks at herself in the mirror in order to see her beauty and exercise her power, her curiosity leading man toward evil. These associations were so strong that early Christian texts and iconography often represented sin in feminine forms.[30] More susceptible than man to illusions, she maintains a specular relationship with the devil, and the mirror, sometimes depicted at the foot of the deceiving siren, is the site where they commune to hatch their schemes.

Lust is associated with Vanity, both metaphorical daughters of Eve. From the thirteenth century onward, Eve is depicted brandishing a mirror.[31] The rose window of Notre-Dame de Paris presents her as a beautiful courtesan who holds a mirror in one hand and a sceptre in the other, emblems of her seduction and power. At Chartres and at Amiens, she is accompanied by a young man embracing her. In the cathedral windows of Auxerre and Lyon, the mirror is all that distinguished her. The text of *Somme le Roi*, a moral treatise composed in about 1280 that aimed to make an examination of the conscience easier, is illustrated by a miniature representing her in the same way: young, beautiful, pleasing, the idleness of the thirteenth century still resplendent with the light of the courtly age. But in other representations, she is accompanied by a monkey carrying a mirror, an incarnation of the bestial impulses of sensuality, of imitation, and of inconstancy.

Among the old tapestries of the *Apocalypse* at Angers, the Whore of Babylon holds a mirror. The theme is highlighted in

The Ship of Fools and in other illustrations of the same era: the female monkey pleasuring itself. A German wood engraving shows a woman who caresses a man's penis with one hand and steals his money with the other; above the man, a monkey holds up a mirror. The monkey, fascinated with its reflection, becomes an image of one who is a slave to his own sensuality.[32]

The chain of sins led by the vain and luxurious woman carries with it coquetry, laziness, envy, greed, untruthfulness, which are all riveted to the mirror. A drawing by Antonio Pisanello (1395–c. 1455) depicts vanity adorned with jewelry, surrounded by demons, looking at herself naked in the mirror (British Museum, London); her provocative feminity is concentrated in her long, ringed hair draped loosely across her shoulders. *Vanity* by Hans Memling (c. 1430–1494) (Musée des Beaux-Arts, Strasbourg) and another by Giovanni Bellini (c. 1430–1516) (Academy of Venice) hold round, convex mirrors in their hands, but the latter is so sure of her seduction that she does not look at herself. People have surmised that she might represent Prudence since she appears capable of turning away from the mirror and looking at reality rather than fiction. Memling's *Vanity*, on the other hand, with her flat feet, short legs, and imperfect but enticing nudity, suggests a diffuse eroticism that contrasts with the innocent and paradisiacal decor of the flowers and fields. Memling's painting is part of a polyptych of five works representing, around an image of Christ in all his glory, a skull, a skeleton, and hell.

Vain and sensuous, Eve plays the role of coquette. She neglects domestic tasks, leaves the unfortunate father to care for her children, and forgets the hour of the divine office. "The Lady who looks at herself spins little" goes the saying. The distaff for spinning wool confiicted with the mirror, modesty and care for the home contrasting with coquetry and a lady's idleness, "because her hands, instead of spinning wool, know only how to comb, put on make-up and hold a mirror."[33] Guillaume de Lorris (c. 1215–c. 1278), author of the first part of *Le*

Hans Memling, studio of, *Vanity*, from a polyptych (c. 1500). Musée des Beaux-Arts, Strasbourg, France.

Roman de la Rose, named her Lady Idleness and described her adjusting "a crown of roses" in her hair. In his description, she wears white gloves to protect her hands and certainly does not ruin them with work: "When she was combed, adorned and well arrayed/Her daily task was done."[34] Beautiful and passive, she took as her role to invite a man into the garden and to prepare him for the contemplation of love. Lazy and neglectful, the idle woman ruined her husband and fed masculine resentment with her incessant demands for "scarves, ribbons and earrings, comb and mirror."[35] She combed her long hair for hours before the mirror as in *Vanity* by Pier Bissolo (1470–1554). Even to church, she wore mirrors at her waist and fluttered her eyes all about, an action vigorously condemned by cleric Jean de Caures who raged against the decadence of his century: "O God, alas, into what unhappy kingdom have we fallen to see such depravity on earth as we see when stained mirrors hanging at the waist are worn even to church."[36] Finally, lust was greedy. An engraving from the end of the sixteenth century by Philippe Galle, *Divitiae,* shows Cupidity covered in jewelry, while her little sister comes toward her equipped with a mirror.[37] Around them, couples are making love; greed, lust, and vanity all have the same face.

To these faults were added cunning, inconstancy, and envy, for the coquette who made herself up used veritable cosmetic magic so as to ensure her power. Numerous engravings from the sixteenth century in France and Italy depict women's grooming rituals in front of their mirrors, surrounded by small vials coating their faces with makeup in fashion boutiques (the antechambers of hell). Cosmetics, tools of the devil, strip the soul of all its beauty. "The greatest extravagance," noted Clément of Alexandria,"is to have invented mirrors for that artifical beauty that is theirs, when really a veil should be thrown over this imposture."[38] Ecclesiastical writer Tertullian (c. 155–c. 220 A.D.) was similarly scandalized: "If the mirror was already able to lie so well, and if Eve really invented all this, it had to be after she was chased out of paradise and already dead."[39] A cosmetically made-up Eve presented the mask of infidelity.

This panoply of corsets, yokes, and wigs, this shrewd strategy employed before the mirror that distorted the work of God and unraveled his greatest accomplishments, had but one goal: to catch man in beauty's trap. Therein lay the true crime: the heart of the woman is a "net," and her hands are "chains" that stoke the flames of hell for Adam. In a series of proverbs published in 1529, the German Protestant moralist Johann Agricola (1494–1566) developed this theme with an avenging pen; his aggressiveness, common at the time, betrayed his fear but also the acuity of his insistent gaze:

> Women never act except under the influence of the mirror. . . . They have no greater joy than that of adorning themselves. This is why they have a counselor named mirror who teaches them to adjust their veils, to whitewash their mugs, to look at themselves frontwards and sideways, to turn their heads, to laugh and to banter, to walk and to sit still.[40]

The woman who awakens the lust of men assumes all of the fantasies of a repressive society. She's the one responsible for the madness of the world, according to Sebastian Brandt, who condemned even the heroines of the Bible who were nonetheless adorned for a worthy purpose:

> She is the decoy, the owl
> the lure with which the devil flatters himself
> She was able to lead minds that thought themselves lucid
> into the abyss.[41]

The daughter of unsatisfied Pride, Envy is also a sin of the gaze (*in-vidia*), personified by an old, dried up, wrinkled woman with flaccid breasts and hair in disarray. Diabolical sin par excellence, the mother of murders, the rust of virtues, the ringworm eating at the soul, Envy follows the virtue she denigrates everywhere: her malicious and deceitful gaze corrupts what she sees. Worse than death, said Saint Thomas Aquinas, Envy is damnation on earth.

A famous text of the fourteenth century from the Cistercian monk Guillaume de Deguilleville, *Le Pèlerinage de l'âme sur terre* [*The Pilgrimage of the Soul on Earth*], places Envy in the pilgrim's path: dry and thin, she shoots arrows from her eyes and slithers like a serpent. On her back is a masked woman named Betrayal. Flattery serves as a mount for Pride looking at herself in a mirror with its horn, gusset, and spurs. The inverted double of Envy, Flattery reassures, cajoles, and puts the pilgrim's vigilance to sleep. Weapon of the seductor, she keeps her victim in a state of deceptive security by feeding his vanity. A miniature engraving from the Bibliothèque de Lyon gives Envy the grimacing face of an old woman facing a beautiful young girl looking at herself in the mirror. The old woman ardently desires the girl's youth and beauty, but the girl pushes her away. In the work of Guillaume de Lorris, Envy squints and looks askance—she cannot look the other in the face. Dante punishes the envious by sewing their eyelids shut.[42] An engraving by Andrea Mantegna (c. 1431–1506) represents Envy holding a mirror.

In the fourteenth century, Envy often appeared with the repulsive face of Medusa. A powerful painting by Dutch artist Jacques de Gheyn II (c. 1565–1629) presents her with hair twisting into snakes, in the middle of a rural countryside in which fire is destroying all greenery.[43] Duplicity and envy bring only ruin and chaos. Perfidious Eve, the woman reptile, allied herself with the serpent in order to deceive humans. Incarnating fraud and lies, intimating a social disorder and world turned upside down, she carries a mask and sows ruin.

The Devil's Ass

Woman thus personified the disorders of the soul, and by looking at herself in the mirror, she always played the devil's game:

either she gave in to his temptations or, possessed, she sheltered a demon in her heart. The old woman, part healer, part go-between, part abortionist, and the young woman whose beauty holds a trap for men were equally suspected of serving evil spirits, inciting the anguished interrogations of the preacher: "Is this occasional foolishness brought on by the actions of these so-called fateful women possessed by the devil's spirit?"[44] Popular imagery is filled with moralizing topoi of the devil lurking behind the woman looking at herself in the mirror. The mirror, says the proverb, is the real ass of the devil.

A treatise entitled *L'Education des filles*, written by the Chevalier de La Tour-Landry in the fourteenth century and widely read after that time, tells the story of a young lady who "spent a quarter of her day getting dressed. Everyone waited for her saying 'What! Will this woman ever finish her combing and looking at herself today?'" And when the lady gazed at herself she saw, "turned around, the enemy in the mirror showing her his derriere; it was so ugly and horrible that she fainted and remained ill for a long while."[45] The German translation of the treatise was published in Basel in 1493 as *Der Rittur vom Turn;* the scene is depicted in one of its woodcut illustrations.[46] The young girl, comb in hand, admires her hair before the mirror; behind her, the devil contorts himself and presents his posterior to the mirror instead of her beautiful face. At her feet, a coffer full of jewelry suggests the vanity of terrestrial goods. This topos is present in hagiography throughout Europe. An Italian woman from the fourteenth century, Villana della Botti, accustomed to spending hours before the mirror, saw one day, instead of her face, her soul in the form of a hideous demon. Thus forewarned, she joined a Dominican Third Order.[47] In Brittany, an old proverb depicts a young girl who looks at herself in the mirror and sees a werewolf, another form of the devil.

By reflecting the soul sullied by sin, the mirror inverts the relationship between reality and appearances, unveiling the truth

Albrecht Dürer, *Diabolique Coquetterie*.

of the being according to faith. The brutal reversal of the illustration from the *Rittur vom Turn* states another truth, of the psychological variety: by flipping the top and bottom, the mirror reflects a sex that shows its true face, one of unbridled and obscene desire. The beauty turned beast discovers her threatening double, an other inseparable from the self, a witness who looks and sneers, created by the guilty conscience. In his essay "The Double," psychotherapist Otto Rank (1884–1939) recalls a court case reported in the news from London in 1913 in which a young lord whose mistress was unfaithful to him imprisoned her for eight days in a room with walls covered entirely by mirrors so that she might contemplate herself and mend her ways. The young woman could not bear this constant confrontation with her accusing gaze and lost her mind, desire having turned into culpability and revulsion.[48]

The girl in the engraving from the *Rittur vom Turn* does not seem to be afraid of the horrible vision, almost as if she were familiar with this image of herself. Perhaps a witch, she holds the mirror aloft while waiting for the sabbath dance of spirits to begin again, a mobile and inconstant figure of an unstable world. The engraving plays with the effectiveness of the devil's gesticulations in order to introduce the idea of disorder and insecurity. The mirror offers only a derisory and fleeting appearance. A parallel and profane iconography makes the mirror's reflection the sign of fortune's instability. Fortune is a smooth mirror without a handle, to which nothing, not even a fly, can cling. Foolish is anyone who would entrust himself to it. The world of illusions belongs to Satan while the only consistency belongs to the eternal kingdom.

The woman in the mirror also appears in the famous *Garden of Delights* by Hieronymus Bosch (Prado Museum). In the middle of a sterile landscape of dead trees, a negative double of paradise, a woman seated on the ground looks at herself in a mirror installed in the posterior of a demon, while another demon grasps her from behind. The work obviously denounces lust and arrogance but also the sterility of the narcissistic woman who refuses the legitimate love of man, incarnated by Adam, turning his gaze toward her in the window of paradise. Proudly contemplating her beauty, the woman is incapable of engendering life. Sterile like her, the mirror imitates forms rather than creating them, thus taking its place among other human inventions, many of which are useless and dangerous.

The Mirror and the Hourglass

Death also lurks behind the devil's mirror. The sudden entry of death adds a tragic dimension to the spectacle of the beautiful woman contemplating herself in the mirror. Represented by a skeleton or skull in the Middle Ages, death was the ally of the demon for whom it labored. On one level of meaning, death reminds the vain woman that her beauty is nothing but "dressed up manure," "a bag of excrement," and "a pile of worms," according to the preacher's preferred vocabulary, and that she will burn in the fires of hell. This theme is frequently exploited in Germanic countries: as accomplices, the cadaver and the devil dance around Vanity. The cadaver itself is a mirror in which man sees the reality of his sin, a motif that dates back to monastic writings and echoes the didactic works of the Middle Ages. A skull appears in the mirror instead of the face of the onlooker: "Death in whose mirror the soul gazes."[49]

Representation eventually evolves and becomes more secular. A copper engraving by Daniel Höpfer (c. 1470–1536) shows a bourgeoise woman, no longer very young, whose portliness is a reminder of successive pregnancies. Adorned with jewelry, she looks at herself in a mirror held by a servant. A skeleton holding up an hourglass surprises her from behind, while a devil approaches her to seize her body.[50] The lesson offered is the culmination of a multi-secular tradition. Its outrageousness—a second devil comedically stands on top of the first—makes the meaning evident: the woman, marked by age, comes to realize both time's passage and fear of death, while the stereotypical devils, grotesque and equivocal figures, mock her. The mirror punctuates the hours much like the hourglass, so that man becomes aware of his mortality. The link to vanity is still there, with its moral resonance, but beyond that any further meaning is lost. The irreversible degradation to which beauty is destined is full of nostalgia: "Thy glass will show thee how thy beauties wear/Thy dial how thy precious minutes waste/The vacant leaves thy mind's imprint will bear."[51] Death invites man to look at it, to live with it, and even to keep it at a distance through laughter and irony, represented by the buffoonery of the devils.

Engraving from *Ship of Fools* (1494) by Sebastian Brandt.

Aside from the theme of natural decline, the mirror also appears in relation to that of unexpected death. A celebrated tableau of Hans Baldung Grün (1484–1545), painted in about 1510, which is sometimes referred to as *Vanity*, but also known as *The Three Ages and Death* (Vienna), confirms the alliance of beauty, the mirror, and death. A young nude girl with rosy cheeks stands before a mirror arranging her long, wavy hair. Her body is barely hidden by a scarf held up on one side by a cherub-like infant, and on the other by a skeleton with sparkling eyes, brandishing a half-empty hourglass. The child, his eyes veiled by inexperience, tries to hide himself from death, to which he is linked by the scarf. Next to the young girl, behind the mirror, an old woman acts as her double. Both the child and the old woman see the skeleton emerging, but the beautiful girl continues to consider herself in the mirror. Premature death grabs her unawares. One should be ready for death at any moment.

Grün comes back to this theme on several occasions: death brusquely grabs the young woman by the waist, by the hair, by the arm, and embraces her. Yet, despite death's sudden grasp, the victim never lets the mirror fall from her hands. Whatever the

Hans Baldung Grün, *The Three Ages and Death* (c. 1509–1510).

interpretation, the painter is clearly an innovator in German iconographic tradition: the naked body full of vitality has nothing of an abstract and idealized nudity about it, and what's more, the devil is absent, but in his place lingers a perfume of eroticism that heightens emotion and distress, to the point of eclipsing the moral message.[52] Only the keen perception of time and carnal reality seem to persist. The devil and the terror of the eternal don't have much business in these desacralized representations where the embrace of love and death express the mournful sound of human experience.

Feminine Mystery

Through the edifying theme of the woman, the mirror, and death, sensuality earned the right to be expressed. Nudity was considered a mark of moral deprivation and impotence in the Middle Ages and was thus rarely represented. As an object of shame and humiliation ever since the original sin, the body had stopped reflecting divine perfection, and painters strove to erase sexual attributes. The medieval body was a body lived in rather than one to be looked at—doctors were unlearned in physiology, and dissection was considered a diabolical and sacrilegious curiosity.

It was not until the dawn of the Renaissance that artists, through an ever more realistic representation of cadavers, revealed their interest in anatomy. The unveiling of femininity, surrounded by taboos, first occurred in descriptions of obscene witches possessed by the devil. Scenes of such women bathing and holding a mirror are numerous. A large painting by Jan Van Eyck (that has unfortunately been lost) depicted a history of magical practices. At its center, a mirror reflected a nude woman bather from behind. This work, admired by Van Eyck's contemporaries for its "optical refinements," inspired many others like it.[53] A menacing devil is sometimes seen hiding in Hans Sebald Beham's sixteenth-century engravings depicting the woman at her toilette, but here the mirror no longer has any function other than to represent and reinforce beauty under the guise of the allegory of Vanity.

Through their mythological or biblical scenes, Italian painters and the artists of the Fontainebleau school placed even more emphasis on women bathing: Venus or Diane, Suzanne and the old men, and Bathsheba. But these motifs did not deliver any moral message; they no longer had anything to do with the threat of the devil. Instead they served as a pretext for iconographic boldness that still delights present-day spectators. The idealized bodies reflected perfect harmony; the shame of the forbidden gaze is transformed into the pleasure of an indiscreet gaze. Guilt disappears behind a cloak of aesthetic magic: associated with light and feminine mystery, the mirror becomes a necessary attribute of beauty, held out to Venus by Cupid or a lover.[54]

Venus is born in the water, her first mirror. Woman awakens to life when she has access to her image.[55] Enamored of her reflection, she wields the power of seduction heralded by the poets of the Renaissance, even as they bemoaned it at the same time: "Damned be the mirror that reflects you," protests Pierre Ronsard, following in Petrarch's poetic tradition by endlessly embellishing the theme of the lady who prefers her mirror to her lover's eye. The mirror and women together, as a repository of beauty, guide the poet's aspirations toward the sacred, pointing toward a celestial reality. The woman and the mirror become an absolute end, more goddess than woman, an inaccessible idol.[56]

> Let only the beautiful face
> Be your mirror and our heaven
> because it attracts to itself such light
> that your mirror looks at itself in it
> And for the mirror itself is the mirror

sings the Italian poet Giambattista Marino (1569–1625) in a few "precious" lines.[57]

Man is the one who invented the seductive and "fatal" sorceress, because the idealization of the "Lady," impassive and riveted to her mirror, kindled his desire. Gilles Corrozet evokes her narcissistic gaze: "The fair and pleasing beauty/Sees, reflects and considers herself/By gazing at her countenance," while Bérenger de la Tour combined simultaneously the glamours of both the mirror and the woman, bathing each other in light in a reciprocal reflection.[58] An expert in beauty, Agnolo Firenzuola (1493–1543), recommended that the lady maintain her grace by "inducing the desire in others to have themselves looked upon and to take pleasure in it."[59] As a result, the poet fears that she might meet the unfortunate fate of Narcissus. The woman at her toilette represents far more than just herself: she incarnates controlled nature, the mystery of seduction, and the epitome of beauty freed from the contingencies of work.

Between the Lady, object of a cult, and the passionate lover, enamored of a myth, the mirror reflects an impossible reciprocity. Torquato Tasso (1544–1595) lends moving accents to this doomed duet in his famous story of Rinaldo and Armida (*Gerusalemme libertata* [*Jerusalem Delivered*], Canto XVI), a drama of the First Crusade. Armida, a sorceress, wants to keep her resistant lover, the crusader Rinaldo, at her side, so she hands him an enchanted crystal mirror, calling it "this confidant of love's mysteries": "Armida then made herself a mirror of the same glass, but for Rinaldo the eyes of his beloved were his only mirror. One takes pride in enslaving him, the other glorifies in his empire. She only sees her in her being and in himself he sees only her." Rinaldo succumbs to Armida's enchantments, losing his powers of conquest until he discovers his face, racked by shame, in the reflection of his shield. With impossible symmetry the bewitching mirror of desire is inverted to become the disenchanted mirror of introspection.

Femininity is a creation of the mirror. When she is not this concupiscent monster, vilified by clerics and depicted from the

Middle Ages to the nineteenth century as an old hag busy before her mirror with the obscene gestures of a macabre coquetry, the lady is herself "a brilliant and polished crystal mirror that the slightest breath darkens and tarnishes. She should be treated like a relic, adored but not touched."[60] Goddess or concubine, she consents to this double role when she carries out the magic ceremony that is beauty's due, priestess of a mystery that surpasses her. This ambivalent status is precisely that of the mirror. Beauty, wisdom, and vanity are reduced to a single symbol, for the same mirror that unveils beauty and incites desire also warns of the fragility of the qualities, and thus needs to be handled with care.

Forbidden Gazes: The Sins of the *Grand Siècle*

Vanity, Curiosity, Lust

Although in the seventeenth century the mirror was an object of daily usage, preachers continued to condemn it, making it the emblem of a guilty society, founded on the false values of ostentation: "Those who minister to vainglory and to appearance with the aid of a mirror fuel a malady of the soul."[61]

Classical morality is built on the omnipresent theme of the vanities and reflection. Mary Magdalene, the repentant sinner before the mirror, incarnates both vanity and lust; the mirror goes hand in hand with the candle, the hourglass, and the skull: interchangeable symbols of the passage of time. Of all the vanities, that of the reflection, of the image or the painted thing that "attracts admiration through a resemblance to things that are hardly admired in reality," best emblematizes the ambiguity of a century always ready to denounce self-esteem, even while indulging in a tireless collective autoscopia through mirrors and portrait galleries.

Self-love inherits traits that Erasmus granted to Philautia, the seductive and cajoling woman who holds a mirror, mocks reason, and veils the world in illusion. A veritable malady of the soul, moralists represent self-esteem with the image of a distorting mirror that alters perspectives of the gaze and upholds vain desires with the imagination. Self-love is nothing other than lust, said the famed seventeenth-century French preacher François Sénault, and his term was divided into the "love of pleasure, honor and knowledge."[62] The eyes open the door to all desires, thieves who deliver the soul to its pillaging. "One looks, one admires, one loves, one attaches oneself, one sullies oneself." Such is the merciless spiral of the sins of the gaze.[63]

Curiosity, the lust of the eyes, is the object of numerous sermons and occupies a long section of the *Bibliothèque des prédicateurs* [*A Library for Preachers*] (1718), a collection of material for sermons assembled by the Catholic preacher Vincent Houdry (1631–1729), serving as a prime example of argumentation for all pastoral literature. Worried, inconstant, and never satisfied, the curious person seeks out the singular, the rare object, the superfluous. His passion pushes him toward dissipation and intemperance; it leads to idleness, despair, and even disbelief. The rationalist who demands a reason for everything is impious because God does not reveal his mysteries. Even when ordered and subdued, curiosity remains vain, for he who acquires knowledge wants to make known what he knows. The curious gaze is always the indiscreet gaze, and often the shameless gaze. In a word, Houdry concludes, the curious man empties himself of himself, like "a spirit that is spread through the eyes."[64]

The gaze upon the self, upon one's body, is the guiltiest of all, the fermentation of all vanities. The celebrated Catholic mystic Madame Guyon (1648–1717) admits that she gave up putting on makeup and curling her hair, but that she still looked at herself a bit in the mirror![65] Revealing the suspicions of an era, pedagogical literature marked the strict limits of attention to the self and accompanied step by step a young pupil's daily activities, along with those of his master. Thus the *Examens particuliers* by Father

Tronson, written for seminarians, devotes several chapters to "modesty." So pure that it's horrified by the slightest nudity, modesty "treats the body with so much respect that it fears its own gaze."[66] The same strict beliefs held true for religious women: mirrors were prohibited in convents, and the nuns had to learn to put on their habits without them.[67] One must deny one's image and forbid oneself those emotions fatefully born from the gaze upon the self. The nun learned to walk with her eyes lowered. If man closed his eyes, said the famed French bishop and orator Jean-Benigne Bossuet (1627–1704), his form would certainly escape him, but his being would remain: "What is this image of myself that I see more deliberately still, this lively apparition in this running water? It disappears when the water is disturbed. What have I lost? Nothing at all" (*Discours de la vie cachée en Dieu*).

Educators subjected children and young adults to the same discipline. When dressing themselves, little girls were expected to keep their eyes raised toward heaven, because removal of their clothes brought to mind the shame of original sin.[68] Mirrors were forbidden in many boarding schools, and each girl styled the hair of her peer "without vanity or curiosity." In the evening as they undressed, they had to take care to be modest and to cover their breasts. Even at Saint-Cyr, the school where young girls were trained to take part in life at the Royal court, mirrors were strictly controlled. One account mentions only one mirror in the chambers of Madame de Maintenon (1636–1719), who taught there in the later years of her life. A century later, inventories indicate that there was one mirror for the red class (ten-year-olds) and the green class (eleven to thirteen years old), three for the yellow class (fourteen to sixteen years old), and five for the blue class (seventeen to twenty years old).[69]

Treatises on civility distributed by the *Bibliothèque bleue* prescribed the same rigorous level of modesty. Among many similar items, the following warning is addressed to young girls: "When they put on their blouses, they will do it so that no-one sees them naked. . . . They will not look at themselves in the mirror with affectation, but only out of necessity and without making faces."[70] These exhortations had their parallel in Protestant countries, where young girls were advised to say a special prayer before grooming themselves. The prayer, entitled "When you gaze upon yourself in the mirror," was meant to remind them of original sin.[71]

Pretense, Idolatry, Envy

Three major grievances come up again and again in the numerous sermons that seventeenth-century moralists devote to appearances and the excesses of grooming, and their invective is of course first addressed to women. The first reproach only reiterates traditional diatribes against cosmetics, the imposture of coquetry that usurps the colors of virtue: "Do not make yourself mistress of your own face, otherwise you should expect from it nothing but false appearance," writes Nicolas Pasquier to his daughters.[72] The mirror takes modesty away from women. Their beauty, explains the moralist, excites in men "criminal desires and dirty thoughts,"[73] and therefore should be tempered, held in check by the discreet veil of modesty. "You will be accountable for your beauties at the judgment of the Most High," intones the Jesuit preacher Nicolas Caussin (1583–1651). "If you consult your mirrors so often, you will confront the ire and the vengeance of God."[74] Frequent encounters with the mirror ruin this modest grace and delicate blushing caused by the emotion of the gaze, creating an unseemly boldness incompatible with the attractions of the weaker sex. A short piece by eighteenth-century playwright Antoine Petit relies on the argument that the only woman worthy of being loved by the noble Lord Almoradin will be the one whose face, put before a mirror, covers itself with "a bright rosiness, the secret guarantor of a sensitive and delicate heart."[75]

Pride lies in wait for the woman who has a habit of looking herself; she becomes "idolatrous of herself," according to expression of Bishop Fenelon (1651–1715). Her beauty not only provokes the desire of the other, but it deceives she who possesses it. There are just a few years separating the woman who is beautiful and the one who no longer is: "What sorrow, then, when a mirror that doesn't know how to lie tells her that she is aging, past her prime or plagued with red and blotchy skin."[76] The mirror is to women what travel, business, and conversation are to men, a diversion that discourages them from knowing themselves that can take the place of everything else:

> They find in it the art of keeping themselves company with little inconvenience by the multiplication of their own face and image. With these images, they have a sort of conversation to which approval, accommodation and flattery always have the upper hand. Through the intervention of the mirror, women pay homage to these emotions. Finally, they do so much that the impious cult of profane, counterfeit and plastered images becomes an occupation on its own, and in relating to these phantoms, women find the art of hiding from themselves the sight of themselves.[77]

Coquetry, lies, laziness, insouciance, and pride: all of these old demons of the mirror are present at the grooming table.

If vanity reflects a double that is satisfied and full of itself, envy, on the contrary, is the negative reflection of a depraved duplicity. In a hierarchical society founded on appearances, envy wreaks havoc with a coterie of servants: jealousy, hypocrisy, and gossip. Looking at oneself forces a comparison with others, thus creating envy. Seventeenth- and eighteenth-century preachers placed envy right behind lust and greed in their hierarchy of sins.[78] Moralists viewed it as one of the most perverse passions, for it rots one from the inside, refusing to be acknowledged, like the metaphorical pocket of venom that a hunchback carries in his hump. Sin of the reflexive gaze, envy reminds everyone of what they lack. The envious person attaches his unfulfilled desires to the mirror of the other. His eyes dart between the spectacle of the one who enjoys something that he desires—beauty, social rank, fortune—and the spectacle of himself tormented by his own impotence.

The seventeenth century frequently paired jealousy and envy, which fueled the plots of many a "precious" novel. The mirror, a space of comparison, allows no rest for the envious coquette whom it attracts and enslaves like a magnet: "She pulled her mirror from her pocket a hundred times in order to compare the charms of her face with those of her unknown rival and closed it a hundred times in vexation."[79] A mocking presence, it switches from friend to enemy, irritating the wound to such an extent that Iriane, the heroine of Theodose Valentinian's novel *Amant ressuscité* is "greatly vexed at having received so many affronts," and drops her mirror on purpose, smashing it "into a thousand pieces. When we began to bemoan the loss of the mirror and wanted to pick up the pieces, Iriane did not want to at all."

Anger and resentment are born from envy. Spite, which Furetière's *Dictionnaire universel* (1690) defines as "an anger that yields disgust," figures prominently in novels and plays in which the evaluation of rank and beauty establish rivalries. In another seventeenth-century narrative, Bélise, a jilted lover consumed by curiosity, cannot refrain from going to see the one who has supplanted her. The beauty of her rival causes her great pain: "I found something so humiliating for me in the comparison I made between her person and mine that I spent almost a month unable to look at myself in the mirror."[80] Disgust, humiliation, and the interior presence of a malicious double: envy can only disappear with the death of the person envied.[81]

The symbolic representation of Envy synthesizes centuries of some of the most repulsive fantasies of the subconscious. If vanity inflates the self by removing all obstacles to lust, envy disfigures desire, the negative mirror of life. Iconography describes Envy as old, sterile, melancholy, and masked—a carrier of terror and death. In the work of Rubens and Poussin, she takes on the frightening traits of the Medusa with bulging eyes. Envy has a Medusa-like gaze because the contemplation of the other reactivates old frustrations and fantasies. In folklore it also takes on the grimacing face of Snow White's stepmother: "Mirror, mirror on the wall, who's the fairest of them all?" This image, pregnant throughout the centuries with sterility and hate, is like the anamorphosis of the face of man.

The mirror is the space of inversion from which the strangeness of an unknown face emerges. To the one who looks straight ahead, the game of reflections reveals what is behind, the shameful hump full of malice. Narcissus with his infected, fixed gaze can no longer hope to contemplate himself in a clear mirror. Always guilty and divided, he begins to project the devil in the mirror, that archaic double of forbidden desires, and then reintegrates into the real what had been considered fantastic. The mirror thus reflects the facial contortions of daily life: passions and repressions.

8

Oblique Mirrors and Specular Trickery

In a tale from the end of the sixteenth century, the author Étienne Tabourot mocks the simpleness and ignorance of a poor man, incapable of distinguishing reality from its representation or reflection. This man placed a mirror at the end of his bed "to see if he looked well as he slept."[1] This comical anecdote has a serious side: the mirror hides something absolutely essential, the face of the man sleeping. This is the limit of the experience of the mirror—the impossibility of seeing oneself with eyes closed, or the impossibility, even with the artifice of several mirrors, of meeting a darting glance. At this unreachable point, this void, everything that escapes comes creeping back and is reconstitued as a whole—the unknown part of the self. Shielded from consciousness, this invisible presence is sensed by each of us.

It happens that this emptiness etches its fleeting trail on the mirror. Who hasn't been surprised at least once by seeing his reflection in a mirror he happened across? This "strange and merciless" mirror Proust spoke of, describing his room at Balbec, eyed him with hostility and "obliquely close[d] off" the room.[2] His emotion is evidence that the encounter with the mirror touched a sensitive nerve by capturing the inexpressible in a fraction of a moment. Once the awkwardness has passed, the image is reconstituted, identical and familiar, and the anxiety dissipates. The famous text in which Freud recounts how he thought he saw a stranger enter his train compartment just as a violent jolt suddenly opened the door to the lavatory has familiarized us with this "uncanny" feeling, the face of the intruder, not of an other, but of the other in one's self: "I hurried to help him, but was quickly taken aback when I realized that the intruder was none other than my own image reflected in the mirror of the connecting door. And I remember that this apparition gave me profound displeasure."[3] If Socrates's mirror is the instrument of self-construction, the revelation of otherness occurs in the flash of the chance reflection and the sideways glance. It is in the unexpected encounter or brief trespass in which the unknown self emerges. In the sudden interruption and in dissonance, what is missing or repressed carves out its disconcerting face.

The Mirror and Alterity

Sideways Glances

In order to get the mirror to admit to its falsehoods, the onlooker must not fall prey to its steady, straightforward reflection. Just as an echo abbreviates and alters the direction of a sound, the reflection caught in the corner of the eye offers an alternate path of vision, revealing new angles while at the same time ensuring a kind of symmetry, albeit an imperfect one. The object and its reflection cannot be superimposed onto each other since in the mirror the left hand becomes the right hand. A dissemblance slips into duplication, and maybe some duplicity as well. The comments on the mirror of the Italian humanist and architect Leon Battista Alberti (1404–1472) in his *Della Pittura* [*On Painting*] (1436) are well known: "I do not know how it happens that painted objects have grace in the mirror; it is a wonderful thing to see how any fault appears deformed in the mirror."[4] The reflection creates a tiny gap in the heart of resemblance; it adds grace, this *je ne sais quoi* of beauty, irreducible to the rule of proportions. Its unsymmetrical qualities overpower the ugly and border on the monstruous. In order for there to be congruence, there would have to be a series of mirrors in which the object and the image of its image would coincide, but with this arrangement, the distortion caused by this optical assembly would cause the image to lose any link to reality. By simulating resemblance, the mirror dissimulates another truth, one that can emerge only surreptitiously, in a fearsome difference and obliquity: "dubious resemblance" or troubling strangeness, the mirror is a mirror of otherness.

"Likeness does not make things 'one' as much as unlikeness makes them 'other.'"[5] As much as the efforts of classical psychology, from Aristotle to the seventeenth century, sought a stable and like image of the individual in the inventory of his humors and the observation of his physiognomy, they were able to shed light only on the traits of the universal man in his generality and abstraction. It took the imagination of the artist, the intuition of certain spiritual people, the very oblique gaze of Montaigne to discover the hidden profile. It was by renouncing the reproduction, by refusing the frontal, fixed mirror (the verifier of identity) that singularity affirmed itself.

It is in "the great mirror of the world," that Montaigne observes himself, not in an attempt at introspection, but obliquely, in the reflection of circumstances and occasions: "I do not find myself where I look for myself, and find myself more often by accident than through the exercise of my reason."[6] The self-portrait does not attempt to grasp something within or repressed waiting to be revealed; rather, it is slowly developed from a fortuitous encounter between two "selves," the familiar face and the unknown one that unexpectedly bursts forth. In the same way, "the sun and wind beat down more heavily on us when deflected than when they come down directly."[7] Obliquity is feared because it takes one by surprise, as a thief does, and its "larceny" reveals a hidden truth.

Rousseau often reproached Montaigne for having painted himself in profile. But it is only in a succession of lateral points of view, by a circumspect approach, that the gaze can apprehend alterity while avoiding petrified fascination. A painting by Giorgione, lost but described by Vasari, could emblematize this peripheral knowledge which refuses frontality: it is a representation of Saint George, seen simultaneously from all sides thanks to all his reflections. He is shown from the back, his feet submerged in clear water in which the front of his body is reflected, whereas his left profile is reverberated in a polished breastplate and the right profile in the mirror. The artist circles around his body, capturing its contours from multiple perspectives worthy of a Cubist painter. He unfurls the facets of the man like the many forms of his presence in the world.

Mirrored funhouses and mirror games, upon which playful visual experimentation (specific to the sixteenth and seventeenth centuries) thrived, expressed the hope of domesticating strangeness through an ideal panoptic vision. But they also taught the relativity of all points of view and fed skepticism. The multiplication of incompatible gazes divides representation into smaller pieces, and the cohesion of the subject is sacrificed to the aggregate of disparate images.[8] Man gets a piecemeal understanding of himself, he knows only bits of his singular experience and, as a fragment or shrunken image of a shattered mosaic, he loses his central and privileged position.

The theme of the blurry mirror, present in Montaigne's *Essays* on both ontological and epistemological levels, takes on a spiritual and religious resonance in other authors. With this challenge to its status as an instrument of mediation, the mirror ceases to reflect the analogy of the cosmos and no longer serves as an intermediary between heaven and earth since the two are mutually exclusive. This is the theme of a poem by Jean-Baptist Chassignet (1570–1635) who "adjusts his mirror," turning from one to the other, the victim of a merciless dilemma: "If you love heaven, in heaven you will be/If you love earth, to earth you will fall."[9]

The chain of reflections is broken and this gap condemns man, this hybrid monster, to live in contradiction. Original sin, shattering initial unity, was a chink in the armor though which dissonance could pass. At the same time, the notion of the subject was being developed through reflexive writing and the self-portrait, and an awareness of its mutilation and its intermittent nature emerged. The mirror abandoned its clarity; an emblem of fragility and falsity, its cracked surface cast doubt on the unifying power of consciousness.[10]

Mannerist Mirrors

At about the same time that Dürer was painting himself as Christ in agony, thereby seeking resemblance in substance, Francesco Mazzola, known as Parmigianino (1503–1540), created his *Self-Portrait in a Convex Mirror* (1524) and played on the deformation caused by the mirror's rounded shape to create effects of distortion. In one way this hand—stretched out by the curvature of the mirror, immense, independent, and megalomaniacal, and leaning on the edge of the painting like an allegory of the creative act — is testimony to the virtuosity of the painter demanding his liberty. But one might also view the mirror's optical illusion as a corrosive acid. The arbitrariness of the game borders on madness. Ontological resemblance, fundamental to the notion of man as image of God, is broken by the painter's whim and identity, which is reduced to an anguished question instead of becoming clearer in the mirror. The hand introduces monstrosity, the part representing the whole. The self-portrait becomes a troubling tête-à-tête, in which seeing means giving oneself over to hallucinations. In fact, Vasari called Parmigianino, who died a madman, a "wild and melancholic mind."

Alterations, irregularities, unsymmetrical qualities—these distortions of reflecting surfaces reveal what the classification of

Parmigianino, *Self-Portrait in a Convex Mirror* (1524). Kunsthistoriches Museum, Vienna, Austria.

psychology and the typology of personalities keep from view: discordance and change. The mannerist suspects his own gaze and suspends his judgment, listening to his emotions. Thus a "psychology of discontinuity"[11] takes shape, whose keywords are instability, inconstancy, and division. This psychology attaches itself to the less visible layers of the personality; it prefers the singular to the general, the provisional and the accidental to the invariable, the irregular to the symmetrical, and the transient to the permanent. Neither personality nor mood can help give shape to this singular being made from "patches" or "snippets," modified incessantly by experience and opportunity. This mirror is no longer reliable for looking at oneself; its agitated surface forms and deforms the image. It is Montaigne painting "the passages," and Tabourot painting the "colored patterns" (*les bigarrures*); La Rochefoucauld tracking "the obscure, tucked away things," and Pascal seeking to understand the contents of this self that "is neither in the body or in the soul"; it is Pierre Nicole probing the impenetrable depths of the heart, and François de Sales exploring "the human labyrinth."

Thus the vacillating reflections of mirrors momentarily become, like nature's turbulent and retreating waters with the crackling, foamy remnants of waves, tormented by crises of consciousness, the symbol of indecision. Mirrors in seventeenth-century French poetry, like that of Théophile de Viau (1591–c. 1626) and Saint-Amant (1594–c. 1661), blur reflections and reverse the top with the bottom. The inconstant mirror of the Abbé Cerisy de Malleville, the sonnet of Etelan called "Mirror," and the crystal of Jean-François Sarrasin all seem to address the fantastic and capricious part of man, the fleetingness of his passions and desires. "Brilliant painter of an inimitable art/You create without any effort an inconstant work/That always resembles and is never like."[12] Proof of existence is found in instability and the swift passage of time. "Water, by receding, makes us see our fleeting nature."[13] The subject is resigned to the ephemeral, to scattered points of view, to virtualities, and finally taking pleasure in the mirages of brilliant surfaces that have ceased to retain any meaning for him.

In this world of contradictions and optical illusion, whose "harmony consists of dissonances," human motives and resilience are capricious and impenetrable. Reason loses its powers under the force of desires and affects. An irruption of the strange, passion is a distorting mirror with multiple powers of metamorphosis, and it unsettles perspectives. The subject no longer knows who or where he is. The myth of Actaeon, the hunter who happened upon Artemis bathing and was punished by being transformed into a stag, was often retold by the moralists. It describes the upheaval of the reflected face by the catoptric prism of a violent desire: "A secret hand changes his face/Obscures his reason and fills it with clouds," and when Actaeon sees himself in the river, "at first terrified of this savage object, . . . he takes himself for another and cannot judge/From whence comes this strange monster."[14] Moving water captures his astonishment for an instant, but already Actaeon no longer recognizes himself because his reason faltered in the bedazzlement of his glimpsed strangeness.

Mannerism has a taste for glasses, prisms, and enlarging and distorting mirrors; all of this optical machinery aims to blur dimensions and distances, to change perspectives and scales, while allowing one to traverse through the oddities and incoherencies of the world.[15] The protagonist of Comenius's *Labyrinth of the World and Paradise of the Heart* wears special glasses to explore and decode what he encounters, just as the hero of Balthazar Gracian's *El Criticon* does to discover the reverse side of a deceptive reality.[16] Initiators of surprise and instruments of a doubling game, these glasses destabilize the gaze, but also act as a protective screen that, unable to unveil an objective truth, guide the melancholy pilgrim though a world of appearances.

The Mirror as Go-Between

The Eye-Mirror or the Restored Reflection

In order to restore the broken and troubling image of an "I" that discovers itself as other in the oblique and cruel mirror, the intersection of gaze and desire are necessary mediation. As projections of the self into the other and of the other into the self, friendship and love offer these lateral mirrors in which a person can view a tolerable self-image, at once familiar and different. There would be no Socratic wisdom of "Know thyself" without a dialogue between the philosopher and the beautiful young people of Athens, says Nietzsche. Love is the encounter with the self by way of alterity, the successful integration of narcissistic impulses.

In the gaze of the alter ego, the lover discerns his tastes and his differences, and perceives himself as a unique individual, "reflected in a mirror," says Plato. "Have you already noticed that the face of one looking in the eye appears there as though in a mirror? Thus we call it our pupil (*pupille*), that is to say small doll (*poupée*), because on it there is an image of the one who looks into it. When the eye looks into another eye . . . it recognizes itself."[17] In antiquity, the eye served precisely to characterize one's beloved: *ocule mi*, my little eye. Reciprocal transparency, the eye-mirror achieves both fusion and separation, identity and difference.

On this theme of the eye-mirror that begins with Plato, love poetry—and, in particular the poetry of the Renaissance—offers all possible figures of exchange, projection, reciprocity, fascination, and alienation. It was in Eve's eye that Adam learned to know himself. From the meeting of their gazes, reflection, concentration, self-construction, and reproduction were born:

> And me in astonishment that in such a small place
> I can be seen to shrink as large as a point in the middle
> In the round, blue-gray azure of two white eyes
> Doubly shortened and yet fully doubled in her
> A sign that in a short while I will be in her
> Of two multiples in which I will see myself.[18]

All of the operations of the mirror are contained in this mirror of love evoked by sixteenth-century poet Maurice Scève. Recentered by and within the gaze of the other, Adam began by losing himself, then seeing himself split and multiplied in his work and in his children. A related image appears in the work of Scève's contemporary Claude de Taillemont, whose motto was "One's duty is to see": "The pupil of the eye transports me to itself/So that I enter in the center/Where I see myself clearly."[19] Although the reflection remains clear and well centered, here the idea of fascination prevails since the lover allows himself to be ravished, absorbed in the furthest depths of the lady's pupil.

The eye-mirror reciprocity is rarely reached—and then only temporarily. Poets have more often sounded the distressing theme of alienation, when love becomes the capturing of the other in his own narcissistic field, a loss of identity and madness. A courtly poet of the thirteenth century, Bernard de Ventadour, chose the image of the eye-mirror to describe the fascination his lady incites:

> Mirror that has pleased me so well
> Mirror ever since I have seen myself in you
> Deep sighs have killed me
> And I am lost myself
> Just as handsome Narcissus became lost.[20]

Here the lover is stupefied, "petrified" by the eye of the beloved; his gaze merges with the object upon which he looks and which engulfs him because he cannot escape the omnipotence of his desire. The theme of the lover petrified by too much contemplation of his beloved is superimposed on the theme of Narcissus: for Ronsard, the woman becomes this "strange Gorgon"; for Pontus de Tyard she becomes this "gentle, cruel Medusa," whose eye has the power to transform the poet into a "cold image" or to render him silent and incapable of writing: "She turns me to stone, mute before her eyes."[21]

The force of desire and fascination wielded by the other can upset the field of perception and take away the subject's ability to be an introspective consciousness. For Scève, Délie is this "murderous mirror of my dying life," from which he cannot "unglue" his eyes.[22] Four centuries later, surrealist Louis Aragon (1897–1982), the mad lover of Elsa, describes this painful tension using the same mirror:

I am this unfortunate wretch comparable to mirrors
Which can reflect but cannot see
Like them my eye is empty and like them inhabited
By your absence which makes it blind.[23]

But Scève does not stop seeing himself, for if the heart of man serves as a mirror to his lady, desire is itself "the mirror of the heart." This desire-mirror that reflects Délie remains his, always ready to be revived by memory and imagination and to feed itself through writing. As the memory slips away—"more swiftly than a deer"—the untouchable lady becomes a projection of the poet, a fantasy, a representation devoid of its real weight, but also deprived of its menacing alterity. For Scève, Délie is woman and poetry, desire for the other and desire for the self: the latter offers its "specular" ruses—anagrams, oxymorons, and metaphors—by which it can make the former come alive again.[24] But the transference toward poetic creation does not exactly fill the desire. By deriving it, it deceives and exasperates it in a frustrating race so that the exhausting struggle remains unresolved—trapped between the real and the imaginary.

Love's mirror maintains a constant relationship with emptiness and absence; this void, or blind and scintillating stain that distracts the eye, is the very condition of a dream. The image of the lady takes form when the lover, a victim of his obsession, loses interest in the present, something that's ordinarily the case when the loved one is physically absent. The introspective conscience, no longer prisoner of the real, becomes prisoner of his thought and desire and the subject creates the spectacle that he wants to see, just as the mirror can ignite fire by reflecting the blazing rays of the sun. The magical mirror is thus the mirror of efficacious desire. This theme was already present in the poetry of the Middle Ages (as in the fourteenth-century work of Jean Froissart, who, for example, gives a lover a mirror, a reservoir of all possible images) and runs throughout the following centuries of romantic literature.[25]

Games of the Mirror and of Love

The mirror mediates between the dream and the real. It offers a virtual space for the encounter with the other—a fictive space in which an imaginary scenario is played out. It can be the mirror of the shy person, of the voyeur, or even of the spy: those who observe with the aid of a mirror a secret that is not meant for them. The frontal encounter is eluded or deferred, while the mirror frees up a margin of interpretation in the face of a truth that cannot be told face to face. It can also be the seductive mirror of catoptric games; the luminous and reflecting surface tames the strange and transfigures the scene in order to adorn it with a grace and beauty that the real does not have.

The reflection de-realizes the spectacle, and through it, desire is given the legitimacy to express itself since it no longer fears the sanction of the real. It creates a truth unburdened by the weight of its consequences. Critic Jean Starobinski has said it all about the scene in which Rousseau surprises Madame Basile, his hostess, at the half-open door (*Confessions*, L.2).[26] Believing himself to be sheltered from her gaze, he falls to his knees at the entrance to her room, "holding out my arms in a passionate embrace, well sure that she couldn't hear me and not thinking that she could see me. But there above the fireplace was a mirror that betrayed me. She hardly looked at me, hardly spoke to me, but turning her head halfway, with one simple finger, she showed me the braid at her feet." On the lover's journey to his beloved, the mirror serves both timid and exhibitionist tendencies. The joy of seeing without being seen is replaced by the thrill of being discovered peeking. Once they have found refuge in the imaginary field of the reflection, Rousseau and Madame Basile can love each other guiltlessly.

Starobinski confers the status of archetype on this short scene, because it is useful for representing the act of writing itself. The *Confessions* are certainly this oblique reflection by which Rousseau watches himself and reveals himself with impunity, with an immodesty that takes the reader as its accomplice just as Madame Basile had consented to the role that her partner assigned her and allowed herself to be stared at in the mirror, renouncing all Medusa-like power of petrification and punishment. The *Confessions* are meant to exorcise, or to seduce, the face of the Medusa that a "virtuous self" represses—Perseus triumphs obliquely. Afterward, the fatal trophy, represented on the shield or aegis, makes its holder invincible because it deflects the impulses of those who wish to judge him.

Stendhal, particularly sensitive to the mediating powers of the mirror that the novelist carries along with him in his wanderings, said that, in certain cities of Prussia, all of the distinguished houses have near their windows mirrors a foot high attached to an iron stand and inclined toward the interior.[27] Thanks to these mirrors, young women observe their suitors in the street, but the suitors cannot see the interior of the apartment — nor that of the heart. Here the mirror is an instrument of dissimulation and of an oblique power: while the lover abandons himself to the gaze of the young girl and accepts his subjection, she exercises the only right conceded to her by society, that of indirectly observing, without lowering her eyes. The mirror confers impunity on the one who sees and on the one who is seen, but only reciprocity and the exchange of glances can stabilize the image.

It is this perfect reciprocity, in which the love of self and the love of the other intersect, and where fantasy joins the real in the fulfillment of desire that Goethe presented before us in his *Wilhelm Meister's Travels*. The catoptric novelistic exploitation that writers made of "mirror staging" is well known. It was aimed at expanding a narrative by grafting a second narrative onto it.

The mirror, at once metaphor and object, carves out a potential space and imposes a shift in time that function as a parenthetical aside. The mirror calls forth time, space, and the imaginary, and thus plays the role of projecting an "other" truth, a truth which the characters have not understood or of which they are unaware.[28]

This is how Goethe uses it, inserting a short story on the theme of the mirror within his *Wilhelm Meister's Travels*. Two young people, Lucidor and Lucinde—two mirror names—discover that they love each other, and before abandoning themselves in an embrace, Lucidor frees himself from Lucinde's arms and pulls her before a mirror: "Then he saw her in his arms and saw himself wrapped in hers; he lowered his eyes and then raised them again and again."[29] Reality and the world of fantasy meet in the mirror, intensifying the gestures of love and trumping reality, each lover drawing happiness from the spectacle of the other. But the goal of the writer is even more to illuminate a trivial little love story by the grace of the reflection. All of the narrative takes place in effect under the magic of the large mirror placed in the entryway of the house, a mirror reflecting the love scene onto an immense backdrop of wooded countryside: "No one could grow tired of turning from the mirror toward nature and from nature toward the mirror." The telescopic mirror, reverberating the distances beneath the rays of the sun, is useful as a metaphor for the passage from the tangible world to the poetic one: it encourages the couple to not remain prisoners of narcissistic love and the comfort of the home, and, as an emblem for the whole work, it offers a cosmic tableau whereby the union of man and nature is sealed.

Playing with Monsters

The Seduction of the Anamorphosis

By attempting to surprise the alterity of desire and love in the oblique mirror, however, one risks setting the deceptive forces of the imagination in motion and causing the unexpected to appear—one's own face disfigured by emotions, passion, and repression. How can one know that the mirror won't reflect some horrifying trait? The oblique mirror disconcerts; it is sly and deviant. Therefore, rather than allow himself to be taken by surprise, the man who masters optical games prefers to organize the spectacle himself, to make strangeness trivial and to trap this fear of mirrors (specular fear) by diverting its insidious or seductive effects onto the other.

Fioravanti, the sixteenth-century alchemist, who devoted several pages of his *Miroir des arts et des sciences* to the miraculous workings of mirrors, tells of Italian princes and noblemen who decorated their palaces with mirrors in order to better enjoy the distress of their guests: "I remember having seen once in Naples a knight with a mirror made with such ingenuity that when a person would present himself before it, that person would see more than a dozen figures or shadows come out of it, terrifying those looking into it."[30] With their illusions and shimmering surfaces, mirror games offered endless possibilities for producing bizarre and distorted images and for taming monsters: the mystifying powers of reflections were thus deliberately sought, exploited, and implored with willing fascination.

To represent a monster is to tame him. Leonardo da Vinci enjoyed creating monstrous forms and constructing optical chambers in which the disturbances of the images and the explosions of space lent themselves to dreaming. Like the painter, the Renaissance scientist took pleasure in multiplying experiments of this "natural magic" of optical manipulations. Cardano devoted fourteen chapters of his treatise to the miracles of catoptrics, describing in precise detail the types of mirrors that make it possible to invert, multiply, make distant, draw near, or fragment an object in space. A man can be made to appear to fly in the air, appear upside down, or become suddenly obese. His nose or hand can be isolated and distant parts can be joined "so that a monstrous spectacle will appear before you."[31] One can also "see in secret, without alarming anyone, what is happening afar." Horror before the monstrous is transformed into exultation, which is not wholly exempt from fright because it consists of a secret, and thus provides guilty pleasures: those of surreptitiously wielding hidden information, being found out, and manipulating others.

Anamorphosis, a calculated distortion characterized by art critic Jurgis Baltrusaïtis in his study of anamorphic art as "a rebus of monster and marvel," relies on a subversion of the image and a "teratology of perspective." [32] By substituting the reflected angle in place of the visual angle, by adding a lateral point of view to a frontal one, anamorphosis breaks up the coherence of space: seen from a certain angle, a portrait is only pieces—deformity, dislocation—but from another, unity is reconstituted and the initiated spectator recognizes the laws of a rigorous science behind the optical aberrations. On account of these laws, confusion and the irrational are resolved.

These games that deconstruct similitude present new content. A famous painting by Hans Holbein the Younger (c. 1497–1543), *The Ambassadors* (1533), displays power, wealth, glory, and knowledge from the front, but the lateral gaze reveals, in the unusual and distorted object at the foot of the two dignitaries, the contours of a skull. To the viewer who knows how to take the right point of view, in this case the point of view of Christian faith, anamorphosis unveils a hidden reality, the instability of the world and the necessity of abandoning vainglory. Such is the moral lesson of anamorphosis which forces one to admit that reality must be interpreted and that what appears proper is exactly that which is deceiving. In his *Sermon de carême* [*Lent Sermon*], Bossuet uses the figure of anamorphosis when he compares certain paintings, the meaning undecipherable at first sight, to "a certain natural image of the world and its hidden justice, that we can only acknowledge by looking from a certain point of view that faith reveals to us."

Hans Holbein the Younger, *The French Ambassadors* (1533). National Gallery, London, Great Britain.

A Hallucinatory Technique

Most optical manipulations are presented as hallucinatory techniques, or devices for escaping reality. Their hidden rationality sets off a defensive reaction and constitutes a challenge to skepticism and dreams of dismemberment.[33] This reaction signifies that amusement is possible at the site where monsters and anxieties once prowled, like a child who plays at frightening himself. Like Perseus decapitating Medusa, the ingenious man evades being spellbound by employing lateral vision, through which one can make sense of chaos. Although these refracted glances are comprehensible through the laws of reflection, shifted and blurry, these constructions generate no less anxiety and vertigo because the gaze is nonetheless still subject to enchantment by incoherent forms; seduction, based on strangeness, unhinges familiarity and preserves ambiguity. The spectator's ambiguous pleasure, caught between the fantastic and the logical, comes from a lingering doubt, and perhaps a secret desire, that the magic be real. Lurking inside the desire to delude one also finds a desire to be deluded.

Above all, the space broken by anamorphosis is, before being rectified, the space of the schizophrenic. A threat stems from the fact that at any moment the spectator can tip the scales on the side of reason or on the side of fantasy, on the side of knowledge of optical phenomena or on the side of unbridled illusion. The rationalist project overtakes its goal and is reversed: deceived here, disabused there, the spectator is ensnared by the manipulator and never feels safeguarded from illusion. If the secret and the illusion are too easily discovered, achieved through a mere turn of cleverness or aesthetic feat, the game loses its resiliency and causes frustration. Moreover, if an illusion reveals its key and is to still maintain its fascination, it should hint at another, deeper secret layer, like a false-bottomed drawer. Holbein's painting reveals the value of such phenomena: once the anamorphosis is decoded, the spectator contemplates death, not only the death of traditional, moralizing representations of a skull in a mirror, but insecurity, misunderstanding, and dissonance. Worse than the fear of the final end is the process of decomposition, vertigo, and anxiety. The perception of dissolving illusion establishes a being's negative intuition. Try as he might to justify himself by putting forward a moral alibi, the painter offers his spectator the impious angle of a theatrical artifice, and his indirectness undermines the moral rectitude of the representation. Thus Baltrusaïtis correctly labeled these games born from an optical perversion as "depraved."

Mannerist sensitivity, ceding to the overtures of a sparkling imagination and playing on the distortion or the perversion of forms, is certainly conscious that beyond a lesson on the vanities and on the deception of the real, it brings to light an intimate and deviant experience for the one who systematically chooses to abandon himself to the arbitrary, who, at the risk of drowning himself in subtleties or of being engulfed by his dream, delights in his capacities of invention. The artist who engenders new meaning by twisting images and words sees the world through a prismatic mirror, in which mirages of analogy become more attractive than what is real.

Among scientists, there is a certain exultation in mastering the laws of reflection by producing artificial images, just as the artist struggles against a rational hardness through metaphor or anamorphosis. Daniello Barbaro (1514–1570) perfected a camera obscura in 1559, and Cardano imagined a device that made it possible to project landscapes and animals painted on a plate of glass. This optical research culminated in the scientific explosion of the seventeenth century. Famous treatises on catoptrics such as *Perspective avec la raison des ombres et des miroirs* (1614) by the exiled engineer Salomon de Caus (1576–1626) or *Perspective curieuse* by Jean-François Nicéron (1613–1646) offered "productions so admirable or rather effects so prodigious" that they rivaled magic and, with the multiplication of mirrors, made "an army appear there where only one man might be, or a long row of columns and a well-ordered edifice, by placing a single column across from the mirror."[34] The German Jesuit Athanasius Kircher (1601–1680), in his *Physiologia* (1669), described the functioning of the magic lantern and invented a sort of "metamorphosis machine" in which a man looking at himself in the mirror sees a row of bull's heads—or deer's heads or donkeys' heads—instead of his own face. The slightly inclined mirror is placed on an axis where the reflections of the human face and of bizarre animals painted on an octagonal wheel converge. The creator of this dream machine wrote, "From nothing a complete image is born."[35] In the same vein, transposed to the literary narrative, lies the "temple of laziness" anonymously invented in 1667 and described as a "cave decorated with large, crystal mirrors cut into different sides." All sorts of fantastic images decorate the walls of the cave and are reflected there. Through the prisms, the fragmented images are randomly juxtaposed, so that one can simultaneously see "a bit of landscape, a small part of a château, the face of a beautiful lady, the wings of a cupid or the ruins of an old palace—all in the mirror."[36] Man voluntarily sacrifices the rational to taste "the confusion of dreams."

Hallucinatory techniques were therefore used to serve magic and mark an evolution from a scientific and curious conception of catoptrics to its agreeable and worldly utilization. The deceptive effects of mirrors were sought to stimulate dulled imaginations. With reduced production costs and better distribution, Saint-Gobain mirrors took up residence in galleries, alcoves, and hideaways, on ceilings and on doors; placed across from windows, they opened up oblique and mysterious perspectives, camouflaging passageways. "Mistresses of sweet impostures" that "sweetly amuse the imagination," according to Mademoiselle de Scudéry, mirrors enlivened the walls. The vertigo and impression of emptiness brought about by the mirror's ubiquity was no longer considered troubling, these labyrinths creating a space of marvel.

Court society resembled Psyche transported into a palace of mirrors: in order to take pleasure in her happiness, Psyche must allow herself to delight in a universe of enchantments and metamorphoses without seeking to pierce their mystery, otherwise she will discover only empty simulacra. According to Starobinski, "there is a correlation between a moment of society and an aesthetic climate."[37] If the seventeenth century relished the *cabinets de glaces*, it was because by magnifying splendor, their symmetry offered the court the brilliant symbol of its power and the joys of a collective narcissism. But as twentieth-century philosopher

Gaston Bachelard elegantly put it, "symmetry is a mediocre source of dreams." Rococo art, with its scrolls, its decorative excess, and its profusion of mirrors, aims less for the symbolic prestige of authority than for the reality of luxury, pleasure, or the image of pleasure, and the stimulation of the senses. For an aristocracy dispossessed of its political functions and partying with abandon in the *fêtes galantes*—the costumed parties of young men and women illustrated by Jean Antoine Watteau (1684– 1721), the fictive series of corridors simulated by the reflection of mirrors offered up a theater of illusions that disguised—behind a proliferation of images—the loss of power, the emptiness, and, all too soon, death.[38]

The Libertine Mirror

The value that a libertine society eager for pleasure put on agreeable taste and sensation is well known. Pleasure must incessantly be renewed and excited by new impressions. In the eighteenth century, the effects of mirrors, from which surprises and seductions are born, become the indispensable element of all settings for games of love. For the architect Nicolas Le Camus de Mézières (1721–1789), it was the boudoir that constituted the temple of pleasure, "the sojourn of sensual delight." He devoted more than twenty pages of his *Génie de l'architecture* (1780) to the arrangement of mirrors in these spaces.[39] The boudoir must be an octagonal or circular space of variety and sensuality, where mirrors alternate with solid walls to leave the eye spaces of rest and to create soothing perspectives. Behind the meticulous description of the perfect house, Le Camus pursued his quest for a way of life that combined the serenity of the soul and the gratification of the senses. The use of mirrors reinforces both because in hedonistic self-contemplation "the soul finds delight in itself." So all that frustrates this intention must be carefully avoided: boredom, monotony, worry, and fatigue always lurk near pleasure. When they are too numerous or badly positioned, "mirrors render a space sad and invite melancholy." Narcissus wore himself out by staring at his reflection in the water.

Since it links privacy and disorientation, the desire for pleasure, and the pleasure of desire, the boudoir decorated with mirrors is at the center of the erotic strategies that make visual possession precede the embrace. Sight, said physician and philosopher Julien Offroy de La Mettrie (1709–1751) in his *L'Art de jouir*, establishes charms and excites the senses: "The shepherdess is also curious about herself for the first time. She had already seen her pretty, fresh face in the clear spring water. Now the mirror will help her contemplate the secret charms unknown to her. She then discovers the difference between her and her shepherd . . . and she returns the surprise."[40] Desire that feeds on difference needs to defer its satisfaction in order to sustain itself. The mirror shows "to the eye," without giving, and it offers this untouchable part in which fantasy is separated from reality. Distance and indirectness control the spectacle. The mirror displays the scene desired by the autoerotic imagination, where the other counts less as a person than as the role that he agrees to play. This indirect optical use in which everyone uses the gaze of the other as an instrument, in which the pleasure of the intellect and of the imagination extends beyond the body, somewhat resembles the perverse reflection of anamorphosis, the imaginary capturing of a gaze that delights in disconcerting the spectator by first dissimulating, then by revealing what is hidden from him.

For the libertine, love is certainly neither a gift nor a renunciation, but an ordered, theatrical scenario that demands self-control, duplicity, and the dividing of oneself in two (actor/spectator). Repetition or the miming of desire, for which the mirror offers infinite possibilities, replaces the spontaneity of instinct and the transport of passion. Illustrator and government official Dominique-Vivant Denon (1747–1825) beautifully described "the vast cage of mirrors," decorated with birds and flowers, where lovers meet and see their gestures infinitely repeated. "I see this island inhabited by happy lovers," where "desires are reproduced by their image."[41] Casanova, leading his new conquest into an octagonal room "hung, tiled and covered with mirrors," less subtly explained that mirrors constantly enlivened the sense of spectacles and especially fed the narcissism of a woman accustomed to being seen by dozens of eyes, "by presenting her with a new vision of herself, causing her to fall in love with herself."[42]

The mirrored boudoir serves as a theater stage upon which, in a dual narcissism, each of the lovers is both voyeur and exhibitionist and tries to attract the gaze of the other, as though this gaze could restore an identity forced to retreat by uncertainty or by a deficiency of the senses, and as though the fantasy of the other was intended to revive one's own desire.[43] The blasé imagination of the libertine incessantly demands the rapid change of the spectacle, its brevity assuring him of its intensity. By a sort of anamorphic decomposition of desire, the spectacle's destructuring of space promises him vertigo and disorientation. The terror of fully facing one's troubling impulses is transformed into hedonist contemplation seeking surprise and reintegrating transgression, and, when all is said and done, as with all anamorphoses it rationalizes its pleasure.

There is no objective mirror. The subject is inhabited by a desire that emerges just when he's least expecting it, in such a way that the spectacle of his reflection, by unearthing buried images, shows him a strange and often disquieting alterity. The shadow of sin, of the irrational, and of the mysterious impulse threatens identity and the face-to-face encounter with a forbidden desire that runs the risk of madness or death.

Thus it is by mirror trickery that Perseus is able to neutralize the eye of the Gorgon. Only the indirect gaze can glimpse the sudden flash of strangeness while escaping its blinding fascination. Due to all kinds of specular trickery that introduce a space of play and interpretation, the subject no longer gets lost in the reflection, and the reflection regains its formative function. The parallel universe of the mirror offers its mediation, and by this mediation desire can be converted into beautiful forms, always peculiar but somehow deprived of their malevolence. The lover who looks at himself in the eyes of the other and the artist who portrays himself in words or colors discover a deferred (*différé*) reflection of their face, in which the "I" takes pleasure in knowing itself as other.

9

Mirror Fragments

The novelist Nicolas-Edme Restif (1734–1806), known as Rétif de Bretonne, relates that at the age of two, since no one was in a hurry to dress him in the morning, he was often left—much to his dismay and fury—stark naked. At such times his sister brought him a mirror to show him his grimaces. He grabbed the mirror and tried to break it in rage: "The cracks made me even uglier and in the fragments that multiplied objects, I believed I'd found a world behind the mirror. This phenomenon stopped my tears and I felt my first astonishment, my first admiration, my first reflection."[1] This episode would find its place in a Lacanian scenario: the development of consciousness of the mirror image is integrated in the progress of symbolic activity. For the child who anticipates his unity by the mediation of the mirror, the kaleidoscopic fragments of the broken mirror reveal a protean self, with infinite virtualities. The unordinary world behind the mirror becomes the prism of the imagination and the dream.

As it so happens, however, this dynamic function of reflection is held in check. The image sets into motion too many affects, and the mirror, instead of anticipating unity, breaks into pieces. As a powerful vehicle of the imagination, it is also an agent of dissociation and illusion that threatens the integrity of the self. If romantic sublimation and mastery of games of anamorphosis provide an inkling of otherness without harm, a confrontation with one's double can also lead the subject, a narcissistic or sadistic spectator of himself, to the edge of delirium.

The mirror is not a neutral, equitable, passive witness. It attacks and betrays its subject when it is not held up lovingly. Psychoanalysts express this phenomenon as follows: if the first mirror, that is to say the mother's gaze, did not respond, the mirror becomes a threatening object that one does not dare to look at, like the "the baby afraid of his mother's face, putting aside his own needs."[2] This deficiency or primordial frustration obscures all mirrors and distorts the face-to-face encounter. The mirror image becomes a source of fear and anxiety.[3] Sometimes, through defensive reaction, the image is overestimated and feeds a narcissistic impulse that nourishes grandiose dreams but fears the gaze of others. Sometimes it becomes a terrifying and aggressive image and loses its symbolic status, to such an extent that it emancipates itself and takes on the attributes of the real in order to persecute the subject. At still other times, refusing all fantastical projection, it disintegrates or disappears. The mirror of dream and of doubt, the mirror of madness, and the empty mirror of insignificance all open the door to monsters, and the fragile bridge linking the inner and exterior worlds is thus broken.

Reflection and Identity

A Fragile Image

Man's relationship with his reflection is conflicted. Forced to let his image enter the mirror, he is revealed—visible, naked, vulnerable, subject to the sight of himself as others see him. He has to control his face, adjust his behavior, hide his secrets. Whether he embraces or rejects this image, he exposes himself to the anguish of being misperceived. Furthermore, the reflection is fragile, ephemeral, and inconsistent—a mere weakening of consciousness or the cruelty of a sideways glance might cause it to lose its familiar conformity. Worse yet, by revealing the image of the body to consciousness, the mirror becomes a screen for many imaginary projections and identifications. "One no longer belongs to oneself, what a frightening thought," exclaims the protagonist of Pär Lagerkvist's 1944 novel, *The Dwarf*, after consenting to have his portrait made.[4] Something from inside becomes fixed and is lost in the image that anyone can capture.

Of all the faces we come across, our own is the one that we know the least. Contemporary psychologists have emphasized the constantly changing nature of the self image; their studies have allowed them to measure the degree of imprecision normal adult subjects can have with regard to knowledge of their appearance, and this despite the large amount of information—photography and video footage—available to them. Memorization remains vague and incomplete, threatened by emotions and subject to all sorts of pathologies. And this was even more the case in other eras, in times when mirrors were rare, small, and dark. Margaret of Valois (1553–1615, also known as Queen Margot), citing the soldier and chronicler Pierre de Bourdeille (c. 1540–1614), reported that the old Madame de Rendan, having given up her mirror upon the death of her husband, "met her face by chance in someone else's mirror and asked who that woman was."[5] Even before being subjected to any disturbance, the mirror image resists all appropriation and maintains a bit of an odd status.

An "image of the body that might be assimilable to a type of instantaneous photography of objective reality" does not exist either; only vague and subjective approximations. The surrealist writer Pierre Mabille (1904–1952), author of *Mirror of the Marvelous*, said that the first time he went to Paris, he was panic-stricken amid the mirror games created by the department stores and hotels. "Still today, I am disconcerted before the tri-partite mirrors of tailors."[6]

Recent psychological studies have sought to delineate the margin of interpretation each of us has for our own image.[7] In a first group of experiments, individuals were shown artificial distortions of both their mirror image and the mirror image of another person. Subjects of these studies found it easier to articulate the changes in their neighbor's mirror image than in their own. Next, adolescents were invited to look at their reflections in distorting mirrors, and it was noted that only those who felt at ease and secure in their bodies could come to terms with the distortion. These teenagers viewed the hands, nose, face, and shoulders as the most troubling sites of distortion.

A second set of experiments was done with photographs. Adults were presented with truncated images of themselves—seen from the back or sometimes below the neck and the experiment showed how difficult it was for them to identify themselves: thirty-seven percent of the subjects recognized themselves only if their heads were visible, and schizophrenics displayed even greater imprecision in their judgment. Personality disorders appear to give rise to serious deficiencies in the ability to recognize one's mirror image. For some, their image even ceased to appear in the mirror. Such reactions indicate how labored, unsettled, and susceptible to regression an individual's hold on consciousness of his own reflection can be.

No one looks at his mirror image with indifference. Who can admit that this double at the back of the mirror, more or less seductive despite endless touch-ups, is skilled at representing him? "A beautiful woman, looking at herself in the mirror, might believe that she is only that," the philosopher Simone Weil wrote, "but an ugly woman knows that she is not only that." The image we have of our body is neither a reproduction of our anatomical reality nor the product of our social being, but a fluctuating projection, an elaborated concept congealed in the fraction of a moment. "What I want, in short," said Roland Barthes, writing about photographs,

> is that my (mobile) image, buffeted among a thousand shifting photographs, altering with situation and age, should always coincide with my (profound) "self"; but it is the contrary that must be said: "myself" never coincides with my image; for it is the image which is heavy, motionless, stubborn (which is why society sustains it), and "myself" which is light, divided, dispersed.[8]

This reflection invested by society with the power of identification is only a hurtful caricature, a sort of crude packaging of the self, an intolerable obstacle to the omnipotent liberty of consciousness: "The very idea that there is an exteriorized image of myself terrifies me."[9]

Variations on the Theme of the "Same" Thing

To contemplate one's image is to come up against one's limits, to see time work its destruction, to fear painful or disturbing evidence that the subject shelters itself from—his biological and mortal reality. Any mirror is a mirror of vanity and any self-portrait leads to an *automortrait* [self-death portrait], according to critic Philippe Lejeune's clever expression.[10] As both upholder and destroyer of an ideal self, the reflection, unfit for its mission, either cracks or dismisses itself.

In literary history, the Shakespearean hero inaugurates this subjective and disquieting use of the mirror, which captures an unhappy conscience in a negative state. It is at the moment of his forced abdication that King Richard II looks back at himself, trying to recall what he was and no longer is. When the abdication is complete, he demands a mirror from his servant: "Give me that glass, and therein will I read."[11] The clear mirror of the world has lost its intelligibility and the king's specular encounter increases the fracturing because the king doesn't recognize himself in the smooth surface: "No deeper wrinkles yet? Hath sorrow struck so many blows upon this face of mine, And made no deeper wounds? O, flatt'ring glass, Like to my followers in prosperity,

Thou dost beguile me!" The mirror reveals the indecipherable figure of a stranger, the ghost of a past life. And just as the dream of an ideal royalty is shattered, the former king drops the mirror, which breaks into pieces, a sign of the precariousness of glory under the mysterious actions of fate and the fleetingness of terrestrial happiness. Vanity of the world and melancholic thought mutually reflect one another. First the empty mirror, and then the broken one, becomes a sign of the inadequacy of man and the world. Only their fragments can take into account a broken and fallen self.[12]

This mirror of misunderstanding and doubt, in which the king is no longer able to read his identity, is already the mirror of the Romantics, a site of monologue and confession. Aggravated introspection and the exaltation of desires, beginning with Goethe's *The Sorrows of Young Werther*, leads to a maniacal solipsism, which splits the subject into an ideal self with unlimited desires and his skeptical, ironic, and mistrustful spectator. Unable to adapt to the world, the subject clings to his private diary or his mirror in order to protect himself from the anguish of losing himself, and there he discovers his multiple and irreconcilable selves.

But whereas the private journal tames strangeness and orchestrates the plurality of desires in the movement of psychic life, the mirror expels them. Autobiography can take its time with facts and give meaning to questionings. But for its part the mirror refuses all pacts and adjustments: "Coming home, I saw myself in the mirror and almost frightened myself with the wickedness of my features."[13] This note, written by Eugène Delacroix (1798–1863) one evening in June 1824 after a social engagement, is evidence of the sorrowful duality that shines forth in the solitude of the private journal.[14] The monster, this monster he said he had been as a child, appears suddenly in the mirror without his knowing it. The hate that shines in the eyes of the reflection is the always conflictual, inadequate rapport between the imaginary and the real, and art and life. The mirror superimposes its brutal strangeness on the reverie of the private journal that interprets and reconstructs reality.

Facing the mirror, a mute witness of desires or fears and a theater of face-to-face confrontation, the subject hesitates between projection and perception, between the inexhaustible images of the dream and evidence of reality, and is obsessed with distortion. He who observes himself contemplates the man he might have been. It is this mirror that decorates the imaginary salon of Octave de Malivert, the protagonist of Stendhal's *Armance*: with brilliant and somber sides, clear and obscure faces, the mirror attunes itself to the contradictory impulses of the lucid and idealistic man, skeptical and passionate, always a spectator of himself. On the one hand, the clear side is where he sharpens his intelligence and adapts his image; and on the other, dark side, there dwells the dissatisfaction of a tortured soul prone to grandiose outbursts. Octave's profound discontent, an impotence for which Stendhal gives a physiological explanation, more likely arises as a function of his own unconscious insistence, and is thus ill-equipped for joining together the two faces of the mirror. Perhaps Octave might have become a dandy by only contemplating his fractured state and the impossibility of his existence within the confines of the mirror. But through the mirror of Armance's eyes, he is suddenly revealed "as if he had had the appearance of a monster." He is incapable of losing himself in a relationship with an other and, like Narcissus, comes to a bad end.

The man who tries looking at himself in the sole mirror of dreams loses contact with the real. Théophile Gautier confessed that his muse resembled a beautiful young girl who received from her beloved "a mirror of polished steel in which she does not even look, so sure is she that she is always beautiful, always free of wrinkles, without crow's feet or dark freckles"—reality and vulgar sentiments do not reach her.[15] Narcissus no longer even needs to look at himself in the mirror since he is so isolated in his inner world. But as Gautier realizes, his comparison is impossible to sustain since "art in love with itself," standing alone and without context, exposes itself to Narcissus's fate.

Gautier passionately invested his descriptions of the feminine with his aspiration to beauty, making them the image of art's perfection itself. Especially revealing in this regard are the characters of Nyssia or perhaps Spirite, ideal feminine figures, whose beauty the poet savors more as an artist than as a lover.[16] In his novel *Spirite*, the title character, a fantastical projection resulting from a phantom relationship between the self and a dream figure of another, emerges at the precise moment when the hero, Guy de Malivert, abandons the idea of marrying a young—very real—widow and withdraws into himself. He then discovers "in the vague, milky whiteness of the mirror something like a trembling, faraway light" in which he glimpses the ravishing face of a woman. Little by little this reflection comes alive, as though Malivert were hypnotizing himself. In a willing captivity, abandoning all his habitual activities, he finds the face of his beloved each night. The intensity of vision suspends the normal course of life, and death punishes the desertion of the world.

This distance and fusion—this double register—is that of any gaze upon the self. Narcissus dies from not being able to reach his self because the identical cannot grasp itself. The specularity of thought or the splitting of consciousness, a variation of sameness, desperately attempts to articulate opposites by causing a fictitious alterity. But developed to the extreme, the division of the being into a subject and an object, whereby the object then becomes the subject's double, casts doubt on the heart of the real. The mirror no longer reflects anything but reflections of reflections: "Why does no self appear in the mirror when I stand before it? Am I therefore only the thought of a thought, the dream of a dream?"[17] Far from shoring up or anticipating the subject, the proliferation of reflections disperses it and shakes it up. The original takes hold of the double as it would a mirage, and in return, the illusion gradually wins by an endless reflexive reciprocity.

Swiss poet and philosopher Henri Frédéric Amiel (1821–1881), "defeated in active life and victorious in inner life," as the literary scholar Albert Thibaudet put it, whose life was inseperable from ten thousand pages of his journal, incarnates this dreamer who becomes motionless in order to watch himself live and soon perceives himself as disconnected. He sees himself seeing himself. His inner gaze knows of no recourse outside himself capable of guaranteeing his legitimacy, because he is at once judge and litigant, his reason and his critical instrument. He describes himself as "a reflection that contemplates itself (*une réflexion qui se réfléchit*), like two mirrors facing each other, two mirrors that reflect each other and then reflect their reflections, and the reflections of their reflections, as far as the eye can see."[18] The reversibility of reflections foreshadows total unreality: only the vigilance of conscience can assure cohesion.

In a brief short story by Russian Leonid Andreyev (1871–1919), "The Thought," the narcissistic narrator, Doctor Kerzhentsev, goes mad after spurning the weight of reality and entrusting the foundations of his identity to the specularity of the consciousness.[19] What Paul Valèry calls the "delirium of lucidity" of reflexive thought, transmuting desires and objects of the world into mental operations, results in losing all contact with the real. The real, however, exacts its revenge.

Doctor Kerzhentsev contemplates the perfect crime and arrives at such an overestimation of himself, and is so convinced of his own genius, that he believes himself able to feign his reverse side—that is to say, his madness—with impunity. Once his crime is committed, he will never know whether or not he was truly mad. Because his train of thought was suspended for an instant, Kerzhentsev is given over to the omnipotence of his emotions, and when he breaks the mirror—witness of his uncertainty—his ever sharper and stunning mind taunts and then leaves him. Instead of assuring his identity, the mind that considers itself incarnates the strange double of alienation.

The Competition of the Double

The Splitting of the Subject

The gap between man and his reflection, at first a simple crack, generates a malaise that can spread from an unpleasant and furtive experience, described by Delacroix, to the severe schism experienced by Kerzhentsev. Man and his reflection cease to be united. Their divergence is embodied before the mirror, to the extent that the mirror image is emancipated and in the end is no longer perceived as an optical phenomenon but rather as a threatening competitor.

The copy is sometimes the exact replica of the model, sometimes a fragmented projection of the body—Parmigianino's hand, Gogol's story "The Nose," Kerzhentsev's mind—and in both cases, the subject recognizes as his own this image with which he initiates a dialogue. But, by an unsettling of his conscience, the symbolic mediation of the mirror ceases to operate.

For more than a century, psychiatry, following literature's lead, has described these pathological states called heautoscopia or autoscopia, which occur as a result of a variety of causes—cerebral lesions, psychotic disorganization, disturbance of states of waking and sleeping, or even by the voluntary practices tied to artistic creation.[20] Most authors of narratives of the double have lived and researched these visual hallucinations. Poet and playwright Alfred de Musset (1810–1857) was pursued by "a stranger dressed in black who resembled him like a brother." Composer and author of fantastic tales, E. T. A. Hoffmann (1776–1822), studying the effects of lysergic acid upon himself, precisely described this dissociation: "My person, my ego, wandered somewhere in space, whereas I could distinctly see my body lying on the sofa of my room."[21] Symbolist Gérard de Nerval (1808–1855), in his novel *Aurélia*, wrote that each man has a double, and his work is built on these "effusions of the dream in real life."[22]

Stories of the double generally end badly. As the exacerbated expression of a poorly integrated narcissism, the double emerges when the relationship with others is lacking or falsified: the subject locked in a pathological solipsism seeks to create ghosts of those he lacks with the reflection playing this imaginary role. It works as a defense mechanism by which the subject expels an inner part that he censors and projects onto it the responsibility of realizing his shameful aspirations. The double, free from all inhibition and molded to escape various frustrations, wields so much energy that it eclipses its model and absorbs its vitality. Hence these two inseparable traits that writers have described: the reflection is clear, precise, and wicked, and the model loses its substance and becomes blurred. The double imposes a bothersome and menacing character on the model that pursues it until death results and unity is restored.

In a famous book, *Don Juan and His Double* (1914), Otto Rank analyzed the archaic foundations of the belief in the double and remarked that the shadow and the reflection in water, the first means by which man saw his body, also became "the first objectification of the human soul."[23] Born of the division of the self, the double's mission was to protect man from death, for this exact replica of himself was gifted with a real and immortal life, which assured him survival in the future after the disappearance of his body. But at the same time that the double serves as a guarantor of immortality, it reminds man endlessly of his fate, a specter of death that never leaves him. Promise of death and force of life: this ambivalent cachet marks most manifestations of the double, in such a way that it temporarily alleviates the anguish of the subject, but at the same time persecutes him.

In numerous folkloric traditions the double, in the form of a shadow or reflection, indicates vitality, energy, renewal, or even fertility, and the loss of the shadow—a theme largely exploited by the fantastic literature of the nineteenth century—severs the subject from his greatest strengths, provokes anguish, and invites unhappiness. This explains all the unhappy fates associated with the broken mirror. The *Die Frau ohne Schatten* [*The Woman without a Shadow*] (1919) by Richard Strauss (with the libretto by Hugo von Hofmannsthal) incarnates the sterility of the woman who has lost her shadow, this symbol of the creation of life, and with it, all possibility of happiness. The same impotence—whose counterpart is the omnipotence of others—strikes the hero of Adelbert von Chamisso's Faust-like prose work, *Peter Schlemihls wundersame Gesschicte* [*Peter Schlemihl's Wondrous Tale*] (1814), which tells the story of the man who sells his soul to the devil and thus has no shadow. In the *Adventures of Saint Sylvester* by E. T. A. Hoffmann, the shadow is replaced by the reflection. Shadow and reflection make real the aspirations and evil tendencies of their owner, accentuating the splitting of the self. Thus the double takes over on his own and liberates forbidden impulses, relieving the subject of all responsibility. But at the same time, as a helpful safety valve, it becomes the challenged and hostile self that takes revenge.

Sometimes the reflection disappears completely from the mirror in order to affirm its total emancipation. Sight, without desire, leaves the mirror empty. The divided subject looks at itself, but it does not see itself, or no longer recognizes itself. It deserts its body and dismisses its reflection in order to escape a persecuting double.

Guy de Maupassant (1850–1893), who was interested in Charcot's work on the nervous system—he himself was subject to mental disturbances — constructed a fantastic short story on this theme called "The Horla," which has been compared to the tales of Hoffmann. An overexcited insomniac, the hero of "The

Horla," believes he is the pawn of an invisible spirit that torments him at night. One evening after illuminating his bedroom in order to surprise this force, he approaches his mirrored armoire and notices that the mirror remains empty: "My image was not in there and I myself was facing it! Oh, how I was frightened."[24] While the empty mirror contradicts any mental representation of himself, the Horla represents the threatening double onto whom the hero can transfer his madness. It is so intimately linked to him that it feeds on his substance, drinks his glass of milk and "devours the life out of my mouth." The executioner is created by his victim, the terror of the subject maintains the cruelty of the double until death puts an end to this terrifying projection. The Horla, a substitute for identity, designates perhaps the fearsome and symbolic authority of the paternal figure.[25] Various studies have noted, in fact, how often obsessive fictions of filiation, illegitimacy, and the mirror of father-son resemblance recur in Maupassant's work. Empty or untruthful mirrors appear frequently in his tales and short stories, and when there is resemblance, it is always an evil resemblance. They reflect degeneration, self-deprecation, and death.[26]

Rilke's Experience

Aggressive mirrors, empty mirrors, blurred mirrors: these specular disorders always reveal a serious identity crisis. The mirror abandons all symbolic operation and the subject no longer tries to represent himself. The dynamic of the reflection is reversed and, instead of anticipating unity, the reflection returns to an archaic state of psychic disorganization, like an anamorphosis whose perspective would be inaccessible. Among the many examples set forth by literature and cinema over the last century, a few dramatic pages of Rainer Maria Rilke offer a scenario exemplary of a failed mirror encounter, because it lacks the possibility of a reflexive give and take between the other and the self, between projection and perception.[27] Alterity caught unaware in the mirror is not only a strange and unknown double, but an image that, by excluding the subject, strips it forever of all possibility of being the same.

The central scene in the *Die Aufzechnungen des Malte Laurids Brigge* [*The Notebooks of Malte Laurids Brigge*] (1910) occurs at the heart of a submersion in childhood memories and a familial past. The hero, M. L. Brigge, comes from a family of Danish nobility now in decline. His father's death causes the breakup of the clan, and his mother, careless and fickle, makes Brigge assume the role of his dead young sister. These personal memories are projected onto a historical backdrop that accurately recounts the reign of a mad king.

In the course of his investigations, Brigge discovers a pile of old clothes from the past in a trunk. They are tangible witnesses to his family archaeology and, hoping to exorcise secrets of the past, Brigge dons one of the costumes.[28] Thus disguised, he runs to look at himself in an overmantel mirror composed of fragments of green glass. At first lazy and indifferent, the glass does not reflect any image. Then, as Brigge draws nearer, it comes to life and "from the bottom of its troubled water," emerges "a very surprising, unfamiliar thing, different from what had been thought." At the bottom of the mirror as at the bottom of the trunk, Brigge seeks something attached to his origins, but far from reading there a resemblance or foundation, he instead discovers himself duplicated and disguised. The second Brigge does not yet threaten the first. The reflection offers him the burlesque spectacle of a clown, even while imposing a strange reality on him that he is no longer able to govern: "I had hardly donned one of these suits when I had to admit it already held me in its power."

In this way the first flash of anguish suddenly appears. The hand protruding from a lace cuff is independently transformed, and Brigge is not the only one to see it move as if it were someone else's: the hand itself "watched itself move, as exaggerated as that may seem." It is a reminder of the enormous, haunting hand of Parmigianino's self-portrait: the hand gives shape to desire, or to lack. It assumes an independent reality, eclipses the face, and announces the dissociation from the body. Each part is able to represent the entire body, as in cases of schizophrenia. It is precisely in these terms that Freud analyzes the "uncanny": "From scattered members, a decapitated head, a hand detached from the arm as in one of Hoffmann's tales, feet that dance by themselves . . . " And yet, notes Brigge lucidly, "the disguises were not so unbelievable that I felt myself becoming a stranger to myself. On the contrary, the more I was transformed, the more I was immersed in my self." The costume, a metaphor for literary travesty, seems to grant him an identity that responds to his aspirations, and a new security, related to the fantastical security of the dream.

But security is, in fact, a trap laid by the double to make Brigge believe in his perfect mastery. With increasing frenzy, he takes out piles of the gaudy disguises, enjoying the freedom and richness of their inexhaustibility: "I completely forgot what I wanted to represent. It was new and captivating to decide that on the spur of the moment, before the mirror." Enveloped in a yellow cape, a mask stuck to his face, his skull hidden beneath a turban, he returns to the mirror leaning on a cane: the effect is such that Brigge's personality passes from the mask to the reflection. He gauges the omnipotence of the image and turns from actor into spectator of a scene that he no longer directs and that ends in an enigma.

The point of rupture occurs precisely at the moment when the reflection, "the being," as he calls it, prepares to reveal something fundamental to him. Hindered by the clothing to the point of suffocation, Brigge awkwardly overturns the small table, knocking some knickknacks down with it. These objects come to life and become hostile. The costume becomes an absurd yoke that strangles him: "Boiling with anger, I approached the mirror and followed the work of my hands by looking with difficulty through the mask. But that was all he was waiting for.

The moment of revenge had come for him." I and he: the scission is complete and the duel, a fight to the death. The emancipated reflection, now the monstrous other, holds him with its gaze and commands him at will, the reinstatement of a repressive law. "Now he was the stronger and I was the mirror. . . . I very simply ceased to exist. . . . I was running for my life, but he was the one running. He bumped into everything, he did not know the house. . . . I was crying but the mask would not allow my tears to escape." This scene of pursuit evokes the chaotic gestures of madness. In this paroxysm of terror linked to the anguish of childhood and death, Brigge faints in order to escape his persecutor.

This text, of great literary force, describes almost clinically the division of the subject where the "anguish of oppressive strangeness" is united with "daily insignificance," including the insignificance and intimacy of death, and gives way to a moment of madness. In a letter cited by critic Maurice Blanchot, Rilke speaks of Brigge as he would of a young man who made a discovery too great to be accepted, so that "his newly conquered freedom turned against him and, without any defense, tore him apart."[29] The vertigo that takes hold of him before the reflexivity of the self, the vacuity of a freedom without foundation or finality, ends in collapse. After finishing this text, Rilke contemplated abandoning writing.

Other mirrors would present their luminous sides to Rilke. In the mirror of the *Sonnets to Orpheus*, the fatal emptiness returns as promise and a source of poetry. Rilke, said Blanchot once again, makes of poetry "a rapport with absence." The mirror thus offers this suspension of being comparable to absence: "Wasteful mirrors, never yet has what you are been described/You with nothing but riddled holes/Intervals filled with time"[30] Poetry, like the mirror, restores symbolic activity, and far from turning its horn against itself, like the unicorn before the mirror or the subject of the poem, it is nourished by "the possibility of being."

The nothing of the void is also the everything, the always of infinite virtualities.

Mirror Crossing

Wonderland

Our relationship to the mirror may reveal itself to be empty and fatal, but it is initially seductive because it draws its brilliance from elsewhere in the Platonic paradise—the world of symmetry and connections.[31] Its mysterious symmetry leads one to believe that behind it exists an invisible counterpart superior to our daily reality. The dream of crossing through the mirror responds to a need for being reborn on the other side. It makes the fascinating hope of reconciling inside and outside, of living definitively on the side of fantasy, or the imaginary, shimmer in a universe free from the weight of the real and the pressures of guilt. Another logic, the logic of dreams and desires, free of mimetic rivalry, dictates this "other" side. But the crossover is also a transgression, a novel adventure in which the child and the poet believe, a route that is no longer marked by the boundaries of the real.

This is how Lewis Carroll's little Alice begins her passage into wonderland. Just like the young Rétif de la Bretonne discovering a gap in the density of the adult world through the broken mirror, Alice moves about in the freedom of her dream, and from the first sentence, establishes the unlimited power of the imagination and words: "Let's pretend," she says to her little cat, "[that] there's a way of getting through into [the Looking-glass House."[32] And the game begins, the game of "how abouts" and "what ifs" by which Alice, perched on the mantel, invents a universe beyond appearances, more beautiful than the universe of the everyday, yet still resembling it: "Why, it's a Looking-glass book, of course! And, if I hold it up to a glass, the words will all go the right way again."

Even though Alice is delighted to leave everything, her leap into the unknown harbors its share of danger. She has to learn another language and discover other behaviors. She finds herself thrown into the middle of a chess party played according to rules she does not know. A strange party: the bi-dimensional space that has become hers obeys an inverted geometry. The garden she is trying to reach retreats each time she approaches; only detours, indeed regressions, allow her to advance. Alice gets lost in this maze and lives in a mode of discontinuity and instability. She discovers that she herself exists only as a mirror reflection, as a projection of the other, when her two interlocutors, Tweedledum and Tweedledee, question her:

> "[The Red King's] dreaming now . . . about you! And if he left off dreaming about you, where do you suppose you'd be?'
>
> "Where I am now, of course," said Alice.
>
> "Not you!" Tweedledee retorted contemptuously. "You'd be nowhere. Why you're only a sort of thing in his dream!"[33]

On this side of the mirror, identity is most inconsistent, and it takes very little more for slight madness to degenerate into delirium.

The mirror is this "no man's land" between the concrete life of the everyday and the place of dreams. The poet crosses through it when he wants to and, because he is not mad, he continually connects the two sides of the mirror with the magic of words. Jean Cocteau, who conceived of gloves capable of "liquefying" mirrors, suggested that mirrors are "the gates through which death comes and goes," not the death of annihilation, but the promise of an elsewhere, of a luminous night beyond the real, which makes it possible to reach the poetic universe. In Cocteau's *Orphée*, the freedom of the angel Heurtebise, disguised as a glazier, depends on his ability to pass easily from one side to another.[34] But he who settles permanently on the other side risks madness.[35] He loses this separating distance of the gaze that discerns the inner from the exterior, and he is no longer able to form a relationship unless it is within the heart of his fantastical universe. A master of symbols, the mirror is also the labyrinthine space that rejects communication and threatens the ability to distinguish fantasy from reality.

The Empty Mirror of the Twentieth Century

A systematic study of mirror images in the art of the twentieth century would show a recurrence of empty and broken mirrors. In the theme of the dark and melancholic double, inaugurated by German Romanticism, one sees expressed the divisions of subjectivity and the exacerbation of desires in the face of which the real world slowly lost its significance and its credibility. In this divided self, the other, a jealous rival, constituted yet another condition of subjectivity, and the work of art, based on the existence of a symmetrical and brilliant double, assured the possibility of a reflexive shuttling back and forth, of a harmonious or painful synthesis of opposing impulses.

Little by little the exploration of the subconscious, a structuralist game, led to its own dismemberment: both the inflation of images that referred only to themselves and the dislocation of a world deprived of meaning challenged the notion of the subject itself. There are no more autobiographies or self-portraits, but instead randomness, scattered pieces, the anonymity of the impersonal "one," a shattered or cobbled together self. Crossing the mirror leads to nothing. The world of the other side is perhaps, in the final analysis, only a doctored replica that not only highlights the shortcomings of the real, but in addition, it inflicts its own inconsistency on itself. The world represented in the mirror is curiously neutral in that its image depicts only the appearance of an appearance, a dream existing only as a pale and colorless reality that is uncertain of its existence.

This deceptive voyage is that of the surrealist Jacques Rigaut who exclaimed: “And now, reflect, mirrors!”[36] His hero, Lord Patchogue, is unsure of his own existence. Only negation and disinterest can prove to him the reality of a self without desire: the reflection he meets in the mirror is not him, rather it is he who is the reflection of the other, which he realizes as he asks, “Who yawned first?” He hopes to pass to the other side of the mirror as well in order to take on the status of the reflection and escape the weight of his uncertain reality: “My secret: I am on the other side of the mirror. July 20, 1924, at Oyster Bay, in Cecil Stewart’s home, I accomplished this surprising feat—I have my witnesses—I took a slight running jump and, forehead first, I crossed the mirror. It was easy and magical—a mild cut to my forehead, an imperceptible and fatal wound.” The first ironic remark made about this miraculous voyage: “The other side is as good as the right side.”

The crossing is easy for it entails neither transgression nor taboo. There is no wonderland that the creative imagination might bring about. There is no more of the dreamlike self than there is an objective self. Inner and outer are interchangeable, labeling any effort at introspection or desire of evasion nonsense. The subject is the object, the object the subject. Crossing the mirror resembles a gentle suicide, minus the tragedy—the wound is imperceptible and fatal.

While the workers come to replace the mirror that broke under the shock of his passage, Lord Patchogue behind the mirror again sees himself reflected in the new mirror. For the second time, he dashes across the mirror, which breaks once again, and so on. The infinite is nothing other than repetition. This is the story of “the man who watches the man who watches . . . ” and who does not recognize himself anywhere. He is part of a series. He is all the others, or any of the others. And when a woman passes before the mirror, he reproduces, without astonishing her, her gestures, with indifference and a lack of differentiation.

Moreover, "the other side is as good as the right side," observes Patchogue once again.

Faces resemble other faces—they are interchangeable. The loss of identity, the confusion of the same and the other entail the possibility of appropriating all identities. Lord Patchogue's surreal but symmetrical and routine experiment is one that the writer and painter Henri Michaux (1899–1984) conducts in the banality of the street. Michaux tells of being so unfamiliar with his face that he took it for someone else's: "More than once when I turned a streetcorner and came upon a mirror in a store, I took the first man to arrive to be me, provided he wore the same raincoat and hat."[37]

The raincoat and hat are sufficient for establishing resemblance and cobbling together a replacement identity. The uncanny is transformed into a troubling conformity: all the others are me. Dispossessed of his face, Michaux escapes the narcissistic prison and the trap of confinement. He loses his own space and abandons himself to a sort of wandering, making him a victim of conventions. It is this submersion into anonymity that restores a presence. Moreover, there is no "self": "The self is only a position of equilibrium,"[38] or better yet an "average of self." Whereas the nineteenth century based the quest for identity on the quest for the origin, experienced before a hostile mirror, Michaux felt himself shot through, penetrated by the countless tracks of innumerable fathers and mothers who cancel each other out: "What unknown ancestor have I allowed to live in me? From what group? From what sort of ancestors? I was born riddled with holes." The porous self resembles a sieve, whose unity is only a pre-judgment.

The loss of the identifying reflection can be almost the same thing as the sacrifice of the image that Bossuet asked of novices. But being made devoid of its spiritual dimension since Bossuet's era, the reflection is a sign of depersonalization, of the devaluation of the subject. When the painter Francis Bacon stretches, swells, and distorts the faces of his self-portraits, or lets their faces run, a bit like the anamorphoses for which there is no angle that rectifies the image, he does not attempt to penetrate the invisible; instead, he abandons himself to the tragic distraction of flesh with virtuosity. The mirror, often represented on his canvases, constitutes the one stable and clear structure—precisely the one from which the subject is escaping, and if he dares to look at himself from the front, it is his back or a face without a gaze that the reflection reproduces. Sometimes the reflection is clearer than the real, sometimes the image disappears, completely engulfed: "There is nothing behind the mirror, but within it."[39] Bacon himself admits that he relentlessly attempts to attract gazes, even though, under these gazes, his painted face acquires no coherence. He even deliberately erases himself because, at his request, the canvases are placed under glass so that the spectator sees, superimposed on the portrait, his own face. One penetrates the painting—or the mirror—as one does a public and open place, without privacy or secrets. Only then can the painter identify himself, his traits mixed and shaped by fate.

These violations visited upon the mirror image are mutilations that touch man in his artistic endeavors, not only discontinue its role as a privilege place of restructuring, but render it incapable of imparting any symbolic meaning. Contemporary pictorial art is the experience of "there is nothing to understand" made commonplace and reduced by the unlimited processes of mechanical reproduction: "I am sure that I am going to look in the mirror and see nothing," said Andy Warhol. "People won't stop calling me a mirror. And if a mirror looks into another mirror, what will it find when it looks?"[40]

Man exists only in series, facing a mirror that continually resifts through its contents. If the hell of *No Exit* is for Sartre a world without mirrors where each person, reified, is subjected to the gaze of the other, the reproduction of insignificant models removes all landmarks, conceals all identity. The "killing" mirror of surrealist Louis Aragon (1897–1982) and the neutral, mute mirror of Georges Pérec (1936–1982) are so precise that even their excess of information—wrinkles, stretch marks, pores, hairs—repels the imaginary and refuses interpretation:[41] "This rather bovine reflection that experience taught you to identify as the surest image of your face seems to have no sympathy, no gratitude, for you, just as though it did not recognize you—or rather as though, in recognizing you, it took care not to express any surprise . . . There is nothing special to tell you."[42] The eye sees an eye, the empty hole of the pupil. The reflection expresses indifference, and its emptiness contaminates its model. It does not incite any revolt, not even anguish. It creates only ennui.

A forest of mirrors, or a "desert of mirrors," overwhelmed the twentieth century, constantly reminding men of the lesson forged in the seventeenth century: Man is nothing other than reflection and vanity. But the mirror had been stripped of the mystical significance it once had. "Mute surface," is what Borges called the mirror—"uninhabitable, impenetrable, where all is event and nothing is memory."[43] The mirror metaphorically designates the current world of immediacy, of mime, and of forgetting. The other side is only parody, in the same way that the world of the beyond is only a simulacrum that "remains illusorily similar to the one he inhabited on earth." The horror of the mirror, an image of a hated paternity that intensifies and multiplies, haunts Borges, for it provides him with a measure of this labyrinth where man, placed at the center of the interminable trails and inextricable crossroads, always remains far away from an improbable exit.

"What secret do you seek in your cracked mirror?" It is rightly to this secret, this internal knowledge, that man aspires when questioning his reflection. For centuries he has constructed himself, assumed his roles, and integrated the transformations of experience before the mirror. Before his own face, he glimpses the mystery of the face of God. And then his image blurs, and he discovers on the reverse side, the horror of self-consciousness. The mirror cracks or breaks. A whole geography of fantasies is linked to the fragments of the mirror: losses of origin, vacillating identities, phantasms of being engulfed, labyrinthine spaces, and fears of powerlessness and dismemberment.

These same fragments engender the hope of being reborn again on the other side, in the world of dream and imagination that is also that of art. As long as the poet asks that the magic of words and the metaphors of the mirror serve as his vehicle, he recognizes his multiple and changing faces reconstituted in the kaleidoscope of broken shapes. But crossing through the mirror also leads to the incommunicable—to confusion and void. The world loses its intelligibility and, in this chaos, the self perceives its own fragmentation. The unity and independence of the subject are only a momentary and relative illusion.

Indifference and decomposition replace the humanist aim of "Know thyself." The mirror refuses to suggest that there is any correlation between the visible and the invisible and denies itself all symbolic function. Neuropsychiatrists know that the deterioration of the mirror image is one of the most flagrant signs of insanity and that indifference to it is the ultimate symptom: the mirror stage turned inside out, on which *fin-de-siècle* art seems to thrive.

Conclusion

This journey across the centuries, spanning many different fields, has tried to outline the sociohistorical framework within which the gaze upon the self can be understood. The psychological role of the mirror emerges within a conceptual system, established in antiquity, to lay the foundation for analogical reasoning and to aid symbolic thought. The rare, dark, and lustrous image of ancient mirrors, corresponding to that which it mimics through an impalpable bond of resemblance, gives man the first glimpse of a reflection of a supernatural reality.

To the extent that the individual defines himself within his historical and corporeal existence, the mirror offers him the means of drawing his boundaries, of "distinguishing himself." The technical advances in glassmaking in the fifteenth and sixteenth centuries and the greater understanding of the mechanics of vision in the seventeenth century are what led to the "metaphysical decline" of the mirror. By shedding its mystery, the mirror (by then perfectly flawless but ordinary) became an instrument of social conformity and offered man the freedom of a solitary face-to-face encounter. The clarity and distance of the reflection offered a space of performance, a theater lending itself to disguise and show. All games, all illusions are now possible since the transparent mirror makes one forget its physical presence, and the man manipulating space in this fashion delights in his power.

Power and dissatisfaction: for someone who looks at himself can never contemplate himself as pure spectacle. He is at once both subject and object, judge and plaintiff, victim and executioner, torn between what he is and what he knows. He becomes aware of this distance, even as he continues to cling to the image, and his unhappiness stems from this half-acquiescence. The dandy incarnates this ultimate form of self-consciousness through which, as an actor playing himself, he never ceases to contemplate the painful separation of the being and the appearance, identifying with the "specular" self: the dandy has the "beauty of a fading twilight," after which disillusion and boredom sets in, where the subject dissolves into a game of reflections or decomposes into formlessness.[1]

At the same time, the reflection is never quite adequate, veiled by the mist of desire. The process that consists of making an object out of a subject, an exterior of an interior, disfigures the face and distorts resemblance. This deformity is the price of any gaze upon the self. One must see oneself without looking, surprise oneself when least expected, by becoming a stranger to oneself. Truth is captured in the sphere of alterity, but then strangeness becomes a threat.

One must attempt to seduce the mirror, since failing to do so results in seeing one's malevolent double suddenly emerge from it, a grimacing devil, the fantastic projection of inner demons. The authority of the reflection is imposed primarily upon women who, at least at a certain stage of cultural development, construct themselves under the gaze of the other.[2] Civilization can now offer women means of fulfillment outside the beauty-seduction-love paradigm, but the mirror still remains this privileged and vulnerable site of femininity. A tribunal without pity, each morning it summons her to take account of her charms until it is said one day that she is no longer the fairest of them all. No one described better than Colette the ugliness and despair of a body in decline, incapable of reviving desire in the face of this pitiless witness in which the old lover seeks the young girl she once was and discovers only her ghost: "An old breathless woman repeated her gestures in the oblong mirror and Léa wondered what she had in common with this madwoman."[3] The delight in the self is inverted. Literature is full of such agonizing farewells before the mirror.

Before the reflection, other responses are also possible. One can flee, veil, or break the mirror. One can also, like the small child, plant oneself in front of the mirror and stick out one's tongue, roll one's eyes, thumb one's nose, contort oneself, and make oneself look ugly: the grimace wards off the double lurking behind the mirror, by forcing it to expose itself and to come to terms with the subject. Sartre tells us that as a little boy, after a first and particularly painful humiliation, he ran to make faces at the mirror: "Against the searing bouts of shame, I could defend myself by tightening my muscles. The mirror was a great help to me. I gave it the task of teaching me that I was a monster. . . . Through both twisting and bending, I distorted my face, making a caustic expression so as to obliterate my previous smiles."[4] The grimace offers the relief of the anamorphosis, but it is only temporary. The mirror says nothing but the banality of the strange, or the strangeness of the ordinary: "The mirror taught me what I had always known: I was horribly natural."

In today's world filled with mirrors, what can the image, to which we are so accustomed, tell us? One can no longer escape the multitude of observing eyes. At every turn we are reminded of our social status: there is a continuous monitoring of appearances, and even of sentiments and desires, all conforming to an imposed label (youth, health, wealth, and so forth). The individual is transformed into an image, plumbed into his or her deepest depths, to the point that Milan Kundera has proposed an omnipotent science, imagology, with numerous branches and increasingly restrictive laws.[5] The overinvestment of the mirror image goes hand in hand with a devaluation of the subject and a growing and renewed demand for identity.

With modern electronic means of reproduction, capable of showing what was heretofore invisible—movement, depth, the interior within the exterior; the image has acquired new powers.[6] The infinite possibilities of duplication and of the re-creation of synthetic images drains the subject of his alterity and his mystery, but the ingenuity of the machine frees the image from its devalued status as a mere copy, and reproduction thus ceases being the simple tracing of the real. The mirror has been carried along in this vast revolution of the image in which only the visible matters, "in contrast to the previous omnipotent intangibles known as *grands invisibles*."[7] A psychology and a social space that somehow correspond to these innovations have yet to be born, existing only within the realm of science fiction novels.[8]

Too many mirrors? A beautiful painting by René Magritte entitled *La Reproduction interdite* (1937) challenges the mirror's seemingly omnipotent power to turn every image into a cliché. A man, his back to the observer, stands before a mirror, in which he sees not his face but his back. Thus the subject demands the right to turn his back on mass reproduction, on easily consumed images, on the inquisition of an all-seeing society that assigns and enforces rigid identities. In short, he proclaims the right to hide his face and to protect his secret. The more images and reflections there are, the more deeply buried the secret will be. Such scrutiny only makes the invisible retreat further. The mirror will always remain haunted by what is not found within it.

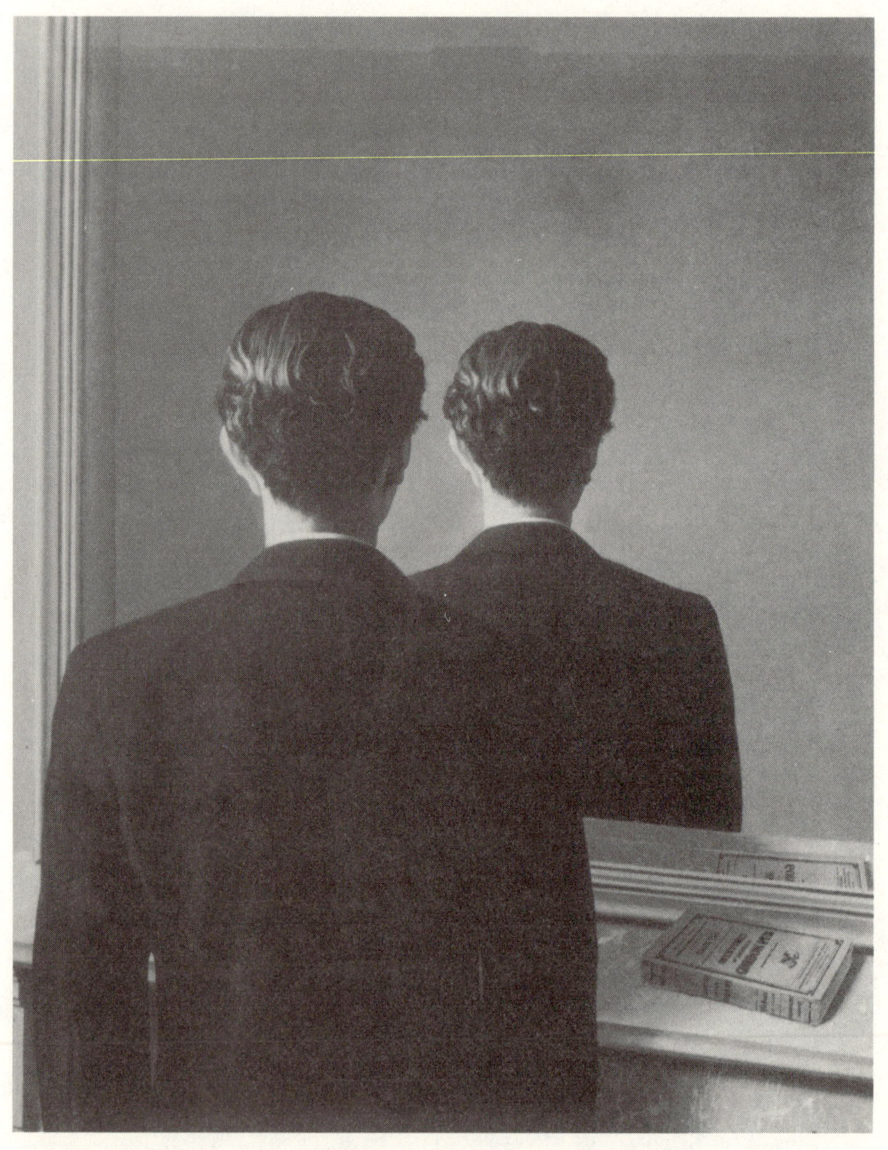

René Magritte, *Portrait of Edward James* (*La Reproduction Interdit*). © Artists Rights Society, New York. Museum Boymans van Beuningen, Rotterdam, The Netherlands.

Notes

Introduction

1. Saint-Simon, *Mémoires* (1699), (Paris: Gallimard [La Pléiade], 1983), I, p. 652.

2. Tallemant des Réaux, *Historiettes*, IV, p. 354, cited by H. Havard, *Dictionnaire de l'ameublement et de la décoration*, 4 vol. (Paris: 1887–1890), III, col. 796.

3. Mme de Chastenay, *Mémoires* (Paris, 1896), p. 226.

4. A. Corbin, *Le Temps, le Désir et l'Horreur* (Paris: Aubier, 1991), p. 231. During a seminar given by Jean Delumeau at the *Collège de France*, Alain Corbin proposed a study of sensitivity and emotions as objects of historical study; his proposal generated this work.

5. J. Lacan, "The mirror stage as formative of the function of the I," *Écrits: A Selection,* trans. Alan Sheridan (New York: W.W. Norton & Co., 1977). Reactions of the child in front of the mirror have been systematically studied in the works of Henri Wallon, Rachel Stutsman (1931), Arnold L. Gesell (1948), and Rene Zazzo (1970–1980). Their results have been presented at various conferences: near the age of five or six months, the child smiles at the mirror image of his father, and when the father speaks, the child turns around in surprise, as though conscious of the difference between the original and the reflection. At around eight months, the child reaches for his mirror image and appears surprised by contact with the surface of the mirror; reactions of avoidance and awkwardness follow. It is only later that the child can reconcile his felt body with his seen body, through the awareness and imitation of others. Self-awareness, according to Gesell's study of five hundred children, occurs between twenty and twenty-four months or, according to others (Zazzo), between twenty-four and twenty-

eight months, when the child can identify and associate his body, his image, and his first name. The age is thus disputable, but all these scholars consider the experience of the mirror to be a valid test for measuring the visible progress of self-consciousness. The mirror stage is important in the construction of the self for it makes the child aware of the unified image of his or her own body, which previously was perceived only piecemeal.

6. M. Coyaud, ed., *La Tortue qui parle, Contes de Corée* [*The Speaking Tortoise, the Stories of Corée*], (Lyon: Federop, 1979), pp. 101–109.

7. In a fable of the eighteenth century by Henri Joseph Du Laurens, *Imirce, ou la fille de la nature* [*Imirce, or the Nature Girl*] (Paris, 1765), a philosopher raises two children in a cave from birth, away from all contact with society, and studies their reactions. One day, they receive a mirror in a basket. Surprised, they are able to identify themselves only by first recognizing each other's faces in the looking glass.

8. Wilhelm Preyer studied the behavior of a duck from Turkey who, at the death of his mate, stood constantly in front of the mirror placed before him; for the duck, its own image appeared as another animal. A dog, according to Henri Wallon, will, when petted by his master in front of the mirror, turn toward the master and ignore or avoid the mirror. The chimpanzee, on the other hand, in studies by Wolfgang Koehler and Gordon Gallup, will pass his hand behind the mirror. If a red spot is applied to his nose, he will inspect himself in the mirror and bring his hand to his nose, thus identifiying his own image. But it is significant that when the same experiment is attempted with a chimpanzee raised in isolation, without any contact with its fellow creatures, the experiment fails; self-recognition thus depends on knowledge of an other and on socialization. Koehler underscores the interest that the chimp takes in his own image, even if he receives no tangible or practical benefit from doing so. Human children raised in the wild are no more conscious of their mirror images. Kasper Hauser and Victor Bonaterre (described by Jean Itard) could not identify their reflections in the mirror. When standing before the mirror they look to see if someone has been placed behind it. Excepting the chimpanzee, there appears to be a natural deficiency in animals, and a cultural one in children raised in isolation, in the ability to recognize oneself in the mirror.

9. Georges Perec, *L'Homme qui dort* [*The Man Asleep*] (Paris: Denoël, 1967), p. 150.

Chapter 1

1. C. Daremberg and E. Saglio, eds., *Dictionnaire des Antiquités* (Paris: Hachette, 1877–1919), art. "Miroir." A. Baudrillart, ed., *Dictionnaire d'his-*

toire et de géographie ecclésiastiques (Paris: Letouzey et Ané, 1912), p. 1415; De Witte, *Les Miroirs des Anciens* (Bruselles, 1872); Petra Oberlander, *Griechische handspiegel* (Hamburg, 1967); Constance Husson, *L'Offrande du miroir dans les temples égyptiens de l'époque gréco-romaine* (Lyon: Audin, 1977). These Egyptian mirrors found in tombs, linked to the cult of the goddess Hathor, were designed to "bring to life" the face of the dead person.

2. Seneca, *Questions naturelles*, I, XVII. The Romans modified the alloy of the bronze mirror, by increasing the amount of tin (65 percent copper, 27 percent tin, and 8 percent lead), which made the mirrors more practical to use but less appropriate for decoration.

3. Apuleius, *Apologie*, XIII; Juvenal, *Satires*, II; Ulpian, *Digeste*, XXXIX, II, 19.

4. Pliny, *Histoire naturelle*, XXXIII, 45.

5. Cited in Diderot's *Encyclopédie*, art. "Miroir."

6. Seneca, *Epistola* 86.

7. Suetonius, *Vies des douze Cesars*, "Domitian," 14; cf. Pliny, *Histoire naturelle*, XXXVI, 163.

8. E. Michon, "Miroirs antiques de verre doublés de plomb," *Bulletin archéologique* (Paris, 1909), pp. 231–250. Glass mirrors were found in Germany in tombs of the Roman garrison from the end of the first century.

9. J. Barrelet, *La Verrerie en France de l'époque gallo-romaine à nos jours* (Paris: Larousse, 1954); P. Piganiol, *Le Verre, son histoire, sa technique*, (Paris: Hachette, 1965).

10. Cited by F. Husson, *Artisans français, étude historique* (Paris, 1903), IV, p. 19.

11. Cited by J. Boulenger, *L'Ameublement français au grand Siècle* (Paris: Arts graphiques, 1913), p. 61.

12. J. Beckmann, *A History of Inventions* (London, 1846), II, p. 76.

13. G. Rose-Villequey, *Verres et verriers de Lorraine* (Nancy: Bialec, 1970), p. 62.

14. L. Fioravanti, *Miroir des arts et des sciences* (Paris, 1602), p. 102 and following.

15. S. Roche, *Miroirs, galeries et cabinets de glaces* (Paris: Hartmann, 1956; republished by the Bibliothèque des Arts, 1988).

16. G. Bechtel, *Gutenberg* (Paris: Fayard, 1992), pp. 237–245.

17. J. de Meung, *Le Roman de la Rose*, vers. 17983 and following.

18. N. Volcyr de Sérouville, *Traitédes Singularitez du Parc d'honneur* (Paris, 1530), ch. IV.

19. Cited by G. Rose-Villequey, *Verres et verriers*, p. 62.

20. Ibid., pp. 62–70.

21. A. Cochin, *La Manufacture des glaces de Saint-Gobain* (Paris, 1865); E. Garnier, *Histoire de la verrerie* (Tours, 1886); A. Gasparetto, *Il vetro di Murano dalle origini ad oggi* (Venice: Neri Pozza, 1958).

22. Cited by A. Cochin, *La Manufacture des glaces,* p. 83.

23. Drawing by G. J. Grelot made at Ispahan in 1674, in *La Relation de voyage de Ambrogio Bembo.* Description of the palace of Lahore in "Voyage de William Finch" (1610) by I. Stchoukine, in *Portraits Moghols, Revue des Arts asiatiques,* VII, 1931.

24. The president of Brosses (*Lettre familières écrites d'Italie,* 1739–1740, Paris, 1858, I, p. 219) described the technique of blowing glass much as his predecessors did when he visited the glass factories of Murano.

25. Claude Mermet, "Farce Joyeuse et Récréative" in *Les Nouveaux Recueils des farces françaises XVe-XVIe siècles* (Geneva: Slatkine, 1968), p. 174.

26. "Les Dits de Maître Aliboron," ibid., p. 207.

27. E. Boileau, *Le Livre des métiers,* (Paris, 1879), p. 37.

28. "Inventaire des meubles d'un marchand d'Auxerre," by E. Drot, in *Bulletin de la Société scientifique de l'Yonne* (1899), pp. 201–202.

29. P. Vidal and L. Duru, *L'Histoire de la corporation des marchands merciers, grossiers et joaillers* (Paris, 1912), p. 76; H. Havard, *Dictionnaire de l'ameublement et de la décoration depuis le XIIIe siècle jusqu'à nos jours* (Paris, 1887–1890), 4 vol., art. "Miroir," IV, column 785 and following.

30. Duplessis-Mornay, *Mémoires* (Paris, 1969), II, p. 210.

31. Viollet-le Duc, *Dictionnaire raisonné du mobilier français* (Paris, 1871), art. "Miroir," pp. 132–137.

32. E. Deschamps, *Ballade* and *La Complainte du trop tost marié,* ed. U. Nystrom (Helin, 1940).

33. Catalogue of the exhibition, *Les Fastes du Gothique,* 1981–1982, pp. 170–171.

34. H. Havard, *Dictionnaire de l'amenblement,* III, col. 795.

35. J. J. Perret, *La Pogonotomie ou l'Art d'apprendre à se raser,* Paris, 1769.

36. S. Roche, *Miroirs galeries et cabinets,* p. 42.

37. H. Havard, *Dictionnaire de l'amenblement,* III, column 803.

38. *Ibid.,* II, column 991.

39. *Description et Inventaire des robbes, bagues, joyaux et meubles que Madame de Saint-Chamond a eus de son père Mgr de Tournon,* February 4, 1610; Sonnet de Courval, *Oeuvres poétiques* (Paris: P. Blanchemain, 1876).

40. La Fontaine, *Fables,* "L'Homme et son image"; Pascal, *Pensées,* VII, 25; Corneille, *La Place royale,* II, 4.

41. *Livre de raison de Marguerite Mercier* (1650–1688), in *La Qualité de la vie au XVII siècle,* 7th Marseille colloquium, no. 109, 1977.

42. P. Le Chaunu, *Objets d'art et objets de piété dans les inventaires après décès, 1580-1630,* master's thesis under the direction of Pierre Chaunu, Paris, 1985.

43. Minutier central, Etudes I, 53, 54, IX, 379, 381, 386, 395, 396, 397, 404, 406, 407, XVI, 22, 457, 458, 459, 460, XVIII, 217, 218, XIX, 314, XX, 306, 307,

308, 309, 310, XXVI, 85, LI, 259, LXVI, 68, 160, LXXII, 300, LXXXIV, 63, LXXXVI, 218, 457, CV, 448, 462, CXII, 287, CXIII, 69.

44. Haudicquer de Blancourt, *De l'Art de la verrerie* (1691) (Paris, 1718), L. 12, p. 233.

45. *Lo Specchio et il Doppio* (Milan: Fabbri, 1987), p. 95.

46. C. Pris, *La Manufacture royale de Saint-Gobain, 1665–1830, Une grande entreprise sous l'Ancien Régime* (Lille: Service de Reproduction des thèses, 1975), p. 75.

47. Ibid., p. 18.

48. E. Frémy, *Histoire de la Manufacture royale des glaces de France* (Paris 1909), annexes.

49. For financial information see J. P. Daviet, *Une Multinationale à la française, Saint-Gobain, 1665–1989* (Paris: Fayard, 1989).

Chapter 2

1. Four major studies trace the rise and growth of the Saint-Gobain mirror manufacture. The first is that of Augustin Cochin, administrator of the company in 1864, *La Manufacture des Glaces de Saint-Gobain* (Paris, 1865). Then that of Elphège Frémy, *Histoire de la Manufacture royale des Glaces de France* (Paris, 1909), with annexes. More recently, two theses have been defended: that of C. Pris, *La Manufacture royale de Saint-Gobain, 1665-1830, Une Grande Entreprise sous l'Ancien Régime* (Lille: Service de Reproduction des thèses, 1975); and that of J. P. Daviet, which focused on the financial aspects of Saint-Gobain: *Une Multinationale à la française, Saint-Gobain, 1665-1989* (Paris: Fayard, 1989). See also L. Zecchin, *Colbert e gli Specchi* (Venice, 1950); the album published by Saint-Gobain on the occasion of its three hundredth anniversary, *Compagnie de Saint-Gobain, 1665-1965*; and H. Hamon, *Du Soleil à la terre, une histoire de Saint-Gobain* (Paris: J. C. Lattès, 1988).

2. On the regulation of glassworks in Venice, see D. Bussolin, *Les Célèbres Verreries de Venise* (Venice, 1847); E. Garnier, who refers to V. Lazari, *Notizia delle opere d'arte e d'antiquita della raccolta correr* (Venice, 1859); P. d'Hondt, *Venise, L'Art de la Verrerie, histoire et fabrication* (Paris, 1893); A. Gasparetto, *Il Vetro di Murano dalle origini ad oggi*; J. Georgelin, *La République de Venise au Siècle des Lumières* (Paris: Mouton, 1978).

3. A. Baschet, *Les Archives de Venise* (Paris, 1870), pp. 650–654; G. B. Depping, *Correspondance administrative sous le règne de Louis XIV* (Paris 1852), III, p. 693; P. Clément, *Lettres, Instructions et Mémoires de Colbert* (Paris, 1863), II, p. 499.

4. E. Frémy, *Histoire de la Manufacture*, pp. 27–51.

5. A. Baschet, *Les Archives de Venise*, p. 653, no. 2.

6. P. Clément, *Lettres, Instructions,* p. 529.

7. A. Baschet, *Les Archives de Venise,* p. 652.

8. Voltaire, *Le Siècle de Louis XIV*, ch. 29.

9. *Le Mercure galant*, December 1682.

10. Madame de Sévigné, *Lettres*, June 13, 1685.

11. J. B. de Monicart, *Versailles immortalisé par les merveilles parlantes des bâtiments, jardins, bosquets, parcs, statues* (Paris, 1720), I, p. 293.

12. J. Guiffrey, *Comptes des bâtiments du roi* (Paris, 1901), 5 vol.

13. According to E. Frémy, *Histoire de la Manufacture,* p. 55, and C. Pris, *La Manufacture royale,* p. 28.

14. A. Cochin, *La Manufacture des Glaces*, pp. 138–139, and E. Frémy, *Histoire de la Manufacture,* p. 74.

15. C. Pris, *La Manufacture royale*, p. 782.

16. P. Clément, *Lettres, Instructions,* p. 499, and G. B. Depping, *Correspondance*, pp. 516 and 830.

17. In a letter dated July 1695. E. Levasseur, *Histoire du commerce* (Paris, 1911), II, p. 530.

18. C. Pris, *La Manufacture royale*, pp. 775–777.

19. Cf. in particular the tales (*Contes*) of Perrault and those of Madame d'Aulnoy.

20. E. Frémy, *Histoire de la Manufacture*, p. 82.

21. Ibid., p. 206.

22. J. P. Daviet, *Une Multinationale*, p. 20.

23. M. Lister, *Voyage à Paris, 1698-1699* (Paris, 1873), p. 129.

24. E. Frémy, *Histoire de la Manufacture*, p. 105.

25. G. Brice, *Description de Paris* (Paris, 1752), II, p. 248.

26. Abbé N.A. Pluche, *Le Spectacle de la nature*, VII, p. 80 and annexes.

27. C. Pris, *La Manufacture royale*, p. 723.

28. Bosc d'Antic, *Oeuvres contenant plusieurs mémoires sur l'art de la verrerie* (Paris, 1780), and C. Pris, *La Manufacture royale*, p. 723.

29. C. Pris, *La Manufacture royale*, p. 730.

30. M. Lister, *Voyage à Paris*, p. 130.

31. *Notice historique de l'Almanach sous verre, 1668-1834*. Citations here from 1781, 1783, and 1785.

32. *Le Livre commode d'Abraham du Pradel* (Paris, 1692), p. 142.

33. *L'Almanach sous verre* (1786 and Year IX).

34. *Bulletin d'encouragement pour l'Industrie nationale* (January 1811), p. 322.

35. *Dictionnaire du Commerce* (Paris, 1844).

36. Cf. E. Frémy, *Histoire de la Manufacture*, p. 328, and J. P. Daviet, *Une Multinationale à la française*, p. 69.

37. L. S. Mercier, *Le Tableau de Paris* (Paris, 1781–1789), 12 vol., IX, ch. 750.

38. In the nineteenth century, this became a ceremonial uniform. N. A. Pluche, *Le Spectacle de la nature*, p. 85.

39. C. Pris, *La Manufacture royale*, p. 708, and E. Creveaux, "La Manufacture des glaces de Saint-Gobain," in *Société historique de Haute Picardie*, vols. 15–16, 1938.

Chapter 3

1. Madame de Sévigné, *Lettres*, June 13, 1680.

2. Ibid., December 28, 1689.

3. Mademoiselle de Scudéry, *Mathilde* (Geneva: Slatkine, 1979), p. 82.

4. Le Laboureur, *La Promenade de Saint-Germain* (Paris, 1669), pp. 53–55.

5. J. Guiffrey, *Les Comptes de bâtiments du roi* (Paris, 1901), 5 vol.

6. C. Pris, *La Manufacture royale de Saint-Gobain* (Lille: Service de Reproduction de thèse, 1975), p. 768.

7. J.-P. Daviet, *Une Multinationale à la française, Saint-Gobain, 1665–1989* (Paris: Fagard, 1989), p. 110. In 1850, one square meter of glass cost 60 F and a worker averaged earnings of 50 F a month.

8. C. Pris, *La Manufacture royale*, pp. 800–810.

9. M. Lister, *Voyage à Paris, 1698–1699* (Paris, 1873), p. 130.

10. C. Pris, *La Manufacture royale*, p. 810.

11. J. Georgelin, *La République de Venise au Siècle des Lumières* (Paris: Monton, 1978), p. 78, and Bosc d'Antic, *Oeuvres contenant plusieurs mémoires sur l'art de la verrerie* (Paris, 1780), p. 58.

12. C. Pris, *La Manufacture royale*, p. 755.

13. F. Husson, *Artisans français, ètude historique*, "Les Miroitiers," (Paris, 1903), IV, p. 2; cf. P. Vidal et L. Duru, *Histoire de la corporation des marchands merciers, grossiers et joaillers* (Paris: Champion, 1912), and E. Fournier, *Le Livre des enseignes de Paris* (Paris, 1884).

14. *Lettre d'un Sicilien* (Chambéry, 1714), p. 2.

15. *Le Mercure galant*, August 1862.

16. P. Verlet, "Le Commerce des objets d'art et marchands merciers à Paris au XVIIIe siècle," *Annales* E.S.C., 1958, no. 1.

17. S. Roche, *Miroirs, galeries et cabinets de glace* (Paris: Hartmann, 1956), p. 23.

18. H. Havard, *Dictionnaire de l'Ameublement*, IV, art. "Toilette"; Lazare Duvaux, *Journal*, Paris, 1751, II, p. 94.

19. A. Pardailhé-Galabrun, *La Naissance de l'intime, Trois mille foyers parisiens XVIIe-XVIIIe siècle* (Paris: PUF, 1978), p. 263.

20. Le Camus de Mézières, *Le Génie de l'architecture* (Paris, 1780), pp. 189 and 146.

21. La Font de Saint-Yenne, *Réflexions sur quelques causes de l'état présent de la peinture en France* (The Hague, 1747), p. 13.

22. J.-F. Blondel, *Cours d'architecture* (Paris, 1774), V, p. 66.

23. Minutier central, Paris, Etudes XX, 400, XXXI, 5, LXVI, 208, CII, 163.

24. G. Brice, *La Description de Paris*, editions consulted: 1684, 1698, 1717.

25. *Annonces, Affiches et Avis divers*, March 22, 1758, June 14, 1758, June 27, 1759.

26. Le Camus de Mézières, *Le Génie de l'architecture*, p. 123.

27. L.-S. Mercier, *Le Tableau de Paris*, I, ch. 89, and IX, ch. 732.

28. A. Young, *Voyage en France* (1787), cited by P. Verlet, *La Maison au XVIIIe siècle* (Paris: Baschet et Cie, 1966), p. 96.

29. J. Eymard, *Le Miroir dans la poésie française* (Université de Lille III, 1975), p. 189.

30. J. Callot, *Mémoires pour servir à l'histoire des moeurs et usages français* (Paris, 1827), II, p. 99.

31. See Vivant Denon, *Point de lendemain,* and Louvet, *Faublas* in *Les Romanciers français du XVIIIe siècle* (Paris: Gallimard [La Pléiade], 1965).

32. J. P. Willebrand, *Ordonnances somptuaires de la République de Genèse* (1765), p. 168.

33. Réstif de la Bretonne, "La Fille du savetier," in *Les Contemporaines.*

34. A. Pardailhé-Galabrun, *La Naissance de l'intime*, pp. 235–241.

35. D. Roche, *Le Peuple de Paris* (Paris: Aubier, 1981), p. 155.

36. Marivaux, *La Vie de Marianne* (Paris: Garnier-Flammarion, 1978), p. 82.

37. H. Havard, *Dictionnaire de l'Ameublement*, II, col. 995.

38. L. S. Mercier, *Le Tableau de Paris*, VIII, ch. 606.

39. Stendhal, *Armance* (Paris: Gallimard Folio, 1975), p. 67.

40. *Bulletin et Mémoire de la Société archéologique d'Ille-et-Vilaine*, 1898. B. de Vismes, *Mobilier et Garde-robe d'une dame bretonne* (1767), (Saint-Brieux, 1906). F. Audran, "La Maison et le Mobilier d'un magistrat breton au XVIIe siècle," and F. Du Bois, "Mobilier d'une bourgeoise de Saint-Malo au XVIIIe siècle" in *Bulletin de la Société archéologique du Finistère*, 1880, VII, and 1959, LXXXV. *Bulletin de la Société archéologique et historique du Limousin*, 1962, XC. R. Muchembled, *L'Invention de l'homme moderne* (Paris: Fayard, 1988), pp. 428–431.

41. M. Garden, *Lyon et les Lyonnais au XVIIIe siècle* (Paris: Flammarion, 1975), p. 407.

42. C. Pris, *La Manufacture royale*, p. 762.

43. Roederer, *Opuscules, an X*, collection of articles published in the *Journal de Paris*, cited by J. Eymard, *Le Miroir dans la poésie française*, p. 189.

44. Florian, *Fables*, "L'Enfant et le Miroir," II, 8.

45. A. Babeau, *La Vie rurale dans l'ancienne France* (Paris, 1882). R. Dauvergne, "Habitation et Mobilier de tisserands beaucerons au XVIIIe siècle," *Chartres, la dépêche d'Eure-et-Loir* (1938).

46. M. Baulant, "Niveaux de vie paysanne autour de Meaux en 1700 et 1750," in *Annales* E.S.C. (1975), pp. 515–518.

47. A. Fillon, *Louis Simon étaminier, 1741–1820* (Université du Haut-Maine, 1986).

48. Ch. Leroy, *Paysans normands au XVIIIe siècle* (Brionne: Gérard Montfort, 1978).

49. O. Perrin, *La Galerie bretonne*, 1835.

50. Maupassant, "Histoire d'une fille de ferme," in *Boule de Suif et autres contes normands*, Garnier, 1971, p. 80.

51. Henry James, *Le Tour d'ecrou [The Turn of the Screw]* (Paris: Stock, 1988), p. 25.

52. S. Tardieu-Dumont, *La Vie domestique dans le Mâconnais rural préindustriel* (Paris: Institut d'Ethnologie, 1964).

53. M. B. Miller, *Au Bon Marché, 1869–1920* (Paris: A. Colin, 1981).

54. H. Havard, *Dictionnaire de l'Ameublement*, I, col. 163.

55. Madame de Graffigny, *L'Art de se mettre en ménage* (Paris, 1910).

56. Jean Baudrillard, *Le Système des objets* (Paris: Gallimard, 1968), pp. 27–28. Available in English as *The System of Objects,* trans. James Benedict (New York: Verso, 1996), p. 22.

57. Comtesse de Gencé, *Le Cabinet de toilette* (Paris, 1870).

58. Gurgan, *Les Grandes Usines* (Paris, 1870), III, p. 2.

59. J. R. Pitte, *La Gastronomie française* (Paris: Fayard, 1991), p. 167.

60. M. Steckel, *Notice sur l'emploi des glaces* (Paris, 1890).

61. E. Zola, *Au Bonhear des dames* (Paris: Fasquelles, 1953), p. 258. Available in English as *The Ladies Paradise* (Berkeley: University of California Press, 1992), p. xvi.

62. D. Hockney, *David Hockney photographe* (Paris: Centre Pompidou, 1982).

Chapter 4

1. P. Hadot, "Le mythe de Narcisse et son interprétation par Plotin," in *Nouvelle Revue de Psychanalyse* (1976), XIII, pp. 81–108.

2. Traces of this belief persisted in the French provinces at the beginning of the twentieth century, when at the time of a death, mirrors were veiled and vessels filled with water were covered, for fear that the soul of the deceased might be captured in the reflection. The evil spell attached to

broken mirrors comes from this tradition as well. L.-S. Mercier, in *Le Tableau de Paris*, recounts that, when the viaticum was brought to a dying person in a home, it was necessary "to veil the mirrors in order that the Holy Sacrament not be multiplied by the mirrors" (L. V, ch. 385). In a number of cultures, the mirror's reflection is a manifestation of the soul or of the mind. Even today certain African tribes refuse to allow themselves to be photographed for fear that the soul might remain imprisoned by the image.

3. V. Ronchi, *L'Optique, science de la vision* (Paris: Masson, 1966), and G. Simon, *Le Regard, l'Etre et l'Apparence, l'Optique dans l'Antiquité* (Paris, Seuil, 1988).

4. Lucretius, *De natura rerum*, L. IV.

5. J.-P. Vernant, "Image et transparence dans la théorie platonicienne de la mimesis," *Journal de psychologie* 2 (1975).

6. A. Delatte, *La Catoptromancie grecque et ses dérivés* (Paris: H. Vaillant-Carmanne, 1932).

7. Plato, *Cratylus* 432c, and *Phaedra*, 235d. The eye is not only a receptive organ: receptor and emitter, it produces light and images.

8. Let us recall how Freud describes the narcissistic stage in the development of the self: "The subject begins by taking himself, his own body, as an object of love before passing to the objectal choice of another person" (*Introduction to Psychoanalysis*). This primary narcissism is a necessary intermediary stage and if it is repressed, it later reverses itself in a double laden with negative affects. This type of narcissism is most often a defense mechanism against a profound devaluation of the subject. Societies condemn Narcissus because he disrupts adaptation into the social milieu.

9. Diogenes, *Vies*, II, 33.

10. Ibid., III, 39. Cf. N. Hugédé, *La métaphore du miroir dans les Epitres de saint Paul aux Corinthiens* (Paris: Delachaux Niestlé, 1957).

11. Seneca, *De Ira*, II, 36.

12. Plautus, *Epidicus*, vv. 382–389.

13. Fr. Garnier, *Le Langage de l'image au Moyen Age* (Paris: Le Léopard d'or, 1989), II, p. 223.

14. P. Hadot, "Le mythe de Narcisse et son interprétation par Plotin."

15. H. Grabes, *Speculum, mirror and looking glass* (Cambridge: Cambridge University Press, 1982), p. 240. Cf. *Dictionnaire de Spiritualité*, art. "Miroir," and R. M. Bradley, "Backgrounds of the title Speculum in Medieval Literature," in *Speculum* 29, 1954.

16. R. Javelet, *Image et Ressemblance au XIIe siècle, de saint Anselme à Alain de Lille* (Paris: Letouzé, 1967).

17. *Cantique des Cantiques* (Paris: Vrin, 1959), pp. 49 and 81.

18. L. Vinge, *The Narcissus Theme in Western European Literature up to the Early 19th Century* (Mälmo: Gleerups, 1967).

19. Hildegarde von Bingen, *Liber divinorum operum*, Patr. Latine, 197, col. 674.

20. On the origin of these book-mirrors linked to the Cistercian and Benedictine movements, cf. *Cahier d'Etudes médiévales, Jean de Beauvais* (cahier spécial no. 4), Vrin 1990, and especially Einar Mar Jonsson's article "Le Sens du titre *Speculum*," pp. 11 and following.

21. Saint Thomas, *Somme*, II, 2, q. 180 a. 3. Cited by H. Leisegang, "Dieu miroir de l'âme et de la nature," in *Revue d'histoire et de philosophie religieuse*, 17 (1937).

22. Crombie, *Robert Grosseteste and the Origins of Experimental Sciences* (Oxford: Clarendon Press, 1953).

23. G. de Bruyne, *Etude d'esthétique médiévale* (Geneva: Slatkine, 1975), III, p. 239 and following.

24. J. Eberley, "The Lover's Glass: Nature's Discourse on Optics and the Optical Design of the Romance of the Rose," *University of Toronto Quarterly* (1977).

25. G. de Bruyne, *Etude d'esthétique médiévale*, III, p. 151.

26. Marguerite de Porete, *Le Miroir des âmes simples et anéanties* (Paris: Albin Michel, 1984). Cf. on this theme the *Dictionnaire de Spiritualité*, art. "Miroir."

27. Cf. for example Nicolas Froment, *Le Buisson ardent* (1476), and Konrad Witz, *La Vierge et l'Enfant se mirant dans un bassin* (line 1445).

28. A. Tripet, "Aspects de l'analogie à la Renaissance," *Bibliothèque d'Humanisme et Renaissance* (1977), XXXIX, pp. 6–21.

29. M. de Certeau, "Le Secret d'un regard," *Traverse* 30–31 (1984). Cf. also A. Minazzoli, *La Première ombre* (Paris: De Minuit, 1990).

30. N. de Cusa, *Le Tableau ou la Vision de Dieu*, trans. A. Minazzoli (Paris: Cerf, 1986), ch. IV, p. 36.

31. P. Magnard, "Imago Dei, Imago mundi," in *Miroirs et Reflets, Cahier du Centre de Recherche sur l'Image, le Symbole, le Mythe* (Presses universitaires de Dijon, 1989).

32. J. Vilain, "L'Autoportrait caché," *Revue d'art* 8 (1979), p. 53.

33. G. Didi-Huberman, "Le Visage entre les draps," *Nouvelle Revue de Psychanalyse* 41 (1990), pp. 21–54.

34. The bishop Briçonnet writes to Marguerite to invite her to look at herself ceaselessly in this "mirror without a smudge, purging, illuminating and perfecting all other mirrors," and she responds by writing her *Miroir de Jhesus crucifié* (Alessandria: Dell'Orso, 1984), p. XXII.

35. Ibid., line 6.

36. Ibid., line 833.

37. Thérèse d'Avila, *Autobiographie* (Paris: Cerf, 1982), ch. 49, p. 385. The sin of the heretics, she adds, broke the mirror.

38. Ch. Bovelles, *De la Sagesse*, ed. P. Magnard (Paris: Vrin, 1982).

39. Manetti, *De Dignitate et Excellentia Hominis* (Basel, 1582), L1, p. 121.

40. J. de Chesnes, *Miroir du Monde* (Paris, 1587), Prefaces.

41. Cited by Mario Praz, *Studies in XVIIth century imagery* (Rome: Storia e Letteratura, 1964).

42. G. Simon, *Structures de pensée et objets du savoir chez Kepler* (Lille: Service de Reproduction des thèses, 1979), pp. 518–589.

43. Merleau-Ponty, *L'Oeil et l'Esprit* (Paris: Gallimard, 1964), p. 38.

44. Apocryphal article from the *Leipziger Stadtanzeiger* of 1839, cited by Walter Benjamin in *Petite Histoire de la Photographie, Essais*, I (Paris: Denoel-Gonthier, 1983), p. 150.

45. On this theme of substituting the powers of the image for the original model thanks to techniques of photography and cinema, cf. the science fiction novel by the friend of Jorge Luis Borges, Adolfo Bioy Casares, *L'Invention de Morel* (Paris: R. Laffont, 1973).

Chapter 5

1. Cited by J. Cabanis, *Saint-Simon l'admirable* (Paris: Gallimard, 1974), p. 57.

2. François, duc de La Rochefoucauld, *Maxime* (Paris: Larousse, n.d.), p. 206.

3. Mademoiselle de Scudéry, *Histoire de Célamire* (Geneva: Slatkine, 1979), p. 602.

4. *Lo Specchio e il doppio* (Milan: Fabbri ed., 1987). Cf. A. Zucchari, "La Prudenza," pp. 152–156, "La Conoscenza," and "La Vista," pp. 168–175.

5. Cornelius Agrippa, *Sur la Noblesse et l'Excellence du sexe féminin* (Paris: Côté femmes, 1990), p. 44.

6. Fr. Filelfe, *Le Guidon des parens en instruction et direction des enfans* (Paris, 1518), ch. 4, n.p.

7. Bérenger de la Tour d'Albenas, "Le Miroir" in Poèmes du XVIe siècle (Paris: Gallimard [La Pléiade], 1953), p. 353.

8. J. Liébault, *Trois livres de l'embellissement et ornement du corps humain*, (Paris, 1582), preface.

9. B. Castiglione, *Le Livre du courtisan* (Paris: G. Lebovici, 1987), p. 85.

10. Bérenger de la Tour, "Le Miroir," p. 355.

11. G. Cardano, *La Physionomie humaine* (Paris, 1808 edition), p. 8.

12. Lemnius, *Les Occultes Merveilles et Secretz* (Orléans, 1568), L. 2, p. 203.

13. J. J. Courtine and Cl. Haroche, *Histoire du visage* (Paris: Rivages, 1988).

14. B. Gracian, *L'Homme détrompé* (*El Criticon*) (Paris: Stock, 1931), p. 102.

15. A. Torche, *Le Chien de Boulogne*, (1668) (Geneva: Slatkine, 1979), pp. 4–5.

16. Tristan l'Hermite, *Le Page disgracié*, (1643), (1898 edition), p. 124.

17. Somaize, *Le Grand Dictionnaire des Précieuses* (1660), (1856 edition), I, p. 51. The mirror is the "advisor of manners, the painter of greatest fidelity, the mimic of nature, the chameleon." The mirror belongs to the vocabulary of gallantry:

O but a beautiful woman is happy and O what sweet moments
Accompany her life when she knows how to make use of
On the one hand, the mirror, on the other, her lovers
All praise her: is there nothing more deserving of envy?"

La Fontaine, *Clymène* (1893 edition), VII, p. 168.

18. A. Torche, *Le Chien de Boulogne*, p. 5.

19. P. Nicole, *Premier Traité de la connaissance de soy-mesme* (1669), XIII, p. 27.

20. *Recueil de portraits et éloges,* dedicated to La Grande Mademoiselle (1659), p. 89.

21. Madame de Staal-Delaunay, *Mémoires*, (1755), (Paris: Mercure de France, 1970), p. 40.

22. Les "Miroirs" de Cotin, in particular, are teeming with riddles.

23. *Les Entretiens galans d'Aristipe et d'Axiane* (Paris, 1664), "Dialogue du grand miroir et du miroir de poche," pp. 145–215.

24. La Fontaine, *Psyché*, *Oeuvres* (Paris, 1892), VIII. L. 2, p. 155.

25. N. Faret, *L'Honneste Homme ou l'Art de paraître à la cour* (Paris, 1630), p. 21.

26. J. de Courtin, *Traité de civilité*: "It's a great incivility to look at ourselves in the mirror and to comb our hair in the presence of a person that we hold in high esteem." (Paris: 1766 edition), p. 151.

27. *Le Mercure galant* (March 1672), p. 189.

28. Bussy-Rabutin, *Histoire amoureuse des Gaules* (Paris: Garnier-Flammarion, 1967), p. 87.

29. B. Gracian, *L'Homme universel (El Discreto)* (Paris: G. Lebovici, 1980), p. 79.

30. N. Faret, *L'Honneste Homme,* p. 29.

31. *Lettre d'un Sicilien à un de ses amis* (Paris: Chambéry, 1714), p. 32.

32. *Les Lois de la galanterie* (1644) (Paris: 1835 edition), p. 17.

33. Duc de Saint-Aignan, lines dedicated to Madame de Maintenon, cited by E. Delerot, *Ce que les poètes ont dit de Versailles* (Versailles, 1910), p. 27.

34. Nicole, *Premier Traité,* XIII, p. 11.

35. Enigma of the mirror offered by Mademoiselle de Scudéry, *Le grand Cyrus*, 1653, IX (Geneva: Slatkine, 1972), p. 363.

36. Mademoiselle de Scudéry, *Conversations morales* (Paris, 1686), p. 134.

37. Ch. Sorel, *L'Isle de portraiture, Voyages imaginaires* (Amsterdam, 1788), p. 345.

38. D. Arasse, "Les miroirs de la peinture," in *L'Imitation, aliénation ou source de vérité* (Paris: Documentation française, 1982), pp. 63–85.

39. L. S. Mercier, *Le Tableau de Paris,* VI, ch. 498. La Font de Saint-Yenne, *Réflexions sur quelques causes de l'état présent de la peinture* (Paris, 1747), pp. 132.

40. La Font de Saint-Yenne, *Réflexions sur quelques ouvrages de peinture* (Paris, 1754), pp. 7 and 24.

41. L.-S. Mercier, *Le Tableau de Paris*, VI, ch. 457.

42. Ch. Mermet, *Maximes pour vivre heureux* (Paris, 1662), p. 51.

43. J. J. Rousseau, *Les Confessions* (Paris: Gallimard [La Pléiade], 1959), pp. 446 and 510.

Chapter 6

1. Sainte-Beuve, *Port-Royal* (Paris: Gallimard [La Pléiade], 1953), III, p. 830.

2. "Portrait d'une abbesse" in *Recueil de portraits et éloges*, dedicated to La Grande Mademoiselle (1659), p. 653.

3. Lemnius, *Les Occultes Merveilles et Secretz* (Orléans, 1568), p. 203.

4. Bérenger de la Tour, "Le Miroir," in *Poèmes du XVI siecle,* (Paris: Gallimard [La Pléiade], 1953), p. 353.

5. J. Liébault, *Trois Livres de l'embellissement et ornement du corps humain* (Paris, 1582), p. 11.

6. J. L. Vivès, *Trois Livres de l'instruction de la femme chrétienne* (Paris, 1587), p. 75.

7. J. Liébault, *Trois Livres de l'embellissement,* preface.

8. C. Ginzburg, *Mythes, Emblèmes, Traces* (Paris: Flammarion, 1989), p. 133.

9. "He who imagines, prepares or keeps lascivious and dishonest images sins mortally," Azpilcueta, *Manuel des Confesseurs* (Rouen, 1626), p. 69.

10. N. Comes, *Mythologiae sive explicationes fabularum* (Paris, 1583), p. 1006. Leo the Hebrew, *Philosophie d'amour* (Lyon, 1551), p. 175. Cited by J. Eymard, *Le Miroir dans la poésie française* (Université de Lille III, 1975), p. 443.

11. B. de Sainte-Maure, *Le Roman de Troie*, line 14630 and following. Utopian cities and paradises are frequently represented having crystal walls and mirrors; the Jerusalem of the Apocalypse serves as a prototype for these imaginary palaces, as does the palace of John the priest, paved with

crystal and topped with a mirror that allows one to see as far as the horizon ahead; this theme was revisited in the Renaissance in *Le Songe de Poliphile,* by Rabelais with the abbey of Thélème, and in the works of Bernard Palissy.

12. René d'Anjou, *Le Livre du Cuer d'amour espris* (1457) (coll. 10/18, 1980), p. 160.

13. Fr. Colonna, *L'Hypnerotomachie ou Songe de Poliphile* (Paris: Club des Libraires de France, 1963), folio 9.

14. Rabelais, *Gargantua*, LV.

15. Montaigne, *Essais*, III, p. 13. Available in English as *The Complete Essays,* trans. M. A. Screech (New York: Penguin, 1991), p. 1208.

16. The mirror remains a privileged religious metaphor. In a long treatise, *Duodecim Specula* (Anvers, 1610), the Jesuit J. David analyzes all the forms of mirrors in order to bring them back to the mirror of the Creator, whereas Father Claude Maillard develops a comparison between marriage and the mirror in a long preface in which he brings together the various metaphors of reflection (*Le Bon Mariage*, Douai, 1643).

17. R. de Piles, *Cours de peinture* (1708) (Paris: Gallimard, 1989), p. 93.

18. Nicole, *Premier Traité,* p. 6.

19. Ibid., p. 142.

20. M.-Cl. Lambotte, "La Destinée en miroir," in *Les Vanités dans la peinture au XVIIe siècle*, exhibition catalog (Paris: Musée du Petit-Palais, 1990–1991), pp. 31–41.

21. Puget de la Serre, *Les Amours des déesses* (Paris, 1626). This image is common among moralists until the eighteenth century.

22. J. J. Du Guet, *Traité des Scrupules* (Paris: 1718), p. 34.

23. La Fontaine, *Fables*, "L'Homme et son image," I, p. 11.

24. D. Arasse, "Les Miroirs de la peinture," *L'Imitation, aliénation ou source de vérité* (Paris: Documentation Française, 1982), p. 83.

25. S. Alpers, *L'Art de dépeindre, la peinture hollandaise au XVIIe siècle* (Paris: Gallimard, 1990), p. 135.

26. Among the many analyses of Velasquez's work are those of Michel Foucault, *Les Mots et les Choses* (Paris: Gallimard, 1966), pp. 19–31; S. Sarduy, *Barroco* (Paris: Gallimard Folio, 1975), pp. 125–131; and S. Alpers, *L'Art de dépeindre,* pp. 126–127.

27. This theme is addressed several times by Vermeer and, in a more narrative fashion, by G. Metsu, *Woman Reading a Letter*: the empty mirror clearly indicates the practice and power of the painter.

28. It is not clear whether Vermeer used a model to stand in for him; doing so would have eliminated the need for mirrors. Cf. D. Arasse, *Ambition de Vermeer* (Paris: Adam Biron, 1993), pp. 76–140.

29. S. Alpers, *L'Art de dépeindre*, p. 48.

30. This theme is present in Rotrou's *Les Sosies*: the actor's craft engenders another truth which transforms it. It continues throughout the eighteenth century and culminates with the diffusion of large full-length mirrors in the nineteenth century. Maupassant frames the story "Bel Ami" with two scenes in which the hero looks at his image in the mirror and measures his social ascent; in seeing himself for the first time in a full-length mirror of a bourgeois house, he can anticipate his success and become an other.

31. V. Nahoum, "La Belle Femme ou le stade du miroir en histoire," *Communication* 31 (1979): 22–32. Cf. Ph. Perrot, *Le Travail des apparences* (Paris: Seuil), 1984, p. 101, and D. Roche, *La Culture des apparences* (Paris: Fayard, 1991).

32. A. Leroy, *Recherche sur l'habillement des femmes et des enfants* (Paris, 1772), p. 239.

33. P. de Marivaux, *Le Paysan parvenu* (Paris: Gallimard [La Pléiade], 1957), p. 574. Cf. M. Deguy, *La Machine matrimoniale* (Paris: Gallimard, 1981), and R. Demoris, *Le Roman à la première personne* (Paris: A. Colin, 1975).

34. P. de Marivaux, *Télémaque travesti*, in *Oeuvres de jeunesse* (Paris: Gallimard [La Pléiade], 1972), p. 772.

35. P. de Marivaux, *Le Spectateur français*, in *Journaux et Oeuvres diverses* (Paris: Garnier, 1969), p. 118.

36. Crébillon, *Les Egarements du coeur et de l'esprit* (1736) (Paris: Gallimard Folio, 1988), p. 244.

37. L.-A. de Caraccioli, *Dictionnaire critique et pittoresque* (Lyon, 1768).

38. J. Starobinski, "Brève Histoire de la conscience du corps," *Genèse de la conscience moderne* (Paris: PUF, 1983), pp. 215–229.

39. Bachelard, *L'Eau et les Rêves* (Paris: José Corti, 1942), p. 35.

40. Stendhal, *Le Rouge et le Noir* (Paris: Garnier, 1973), p. 99.

41. Baudelaire, *Mon Coeur mis à nu*, in *Oeuvres* (Paris: Gallimard [La Pléiade], 1987), I, p. 678.

42. Baudelaire, *La Fanfarlo,* trans. Greg Boyd, (Berkeley: Creative Arts Book Company, 1986), p. 28.

43. Théophile Gautier, *Mademoiselle de Maupin* (Paris: Garnier-Flammarion, 1966), p. 152.

44. L.-S. Mercier, *Le Tableau de Paris*, t. IX, ch. 750.

45. Barbey d'Aurevilly, *Du Dandysme et de G. Brummell, Oeuvres* (Paris: Gallimard [La Pléiade], 1964), II, p. 703.

46. Edgar Allen Poe, "The Philosophy of Furniture," *The Complete Works of Edgar Allan Poe*, ed. James Harrison, Vol. XIV (New York: AMS Press, 1965), p. 105.

47. Barbey d'Aurevilly, *Du Dandysme*, p. 692.

48. G. Peylet, "Le Moi spéculaire dans la littérature fin de siècle," in *Miroirs et Reflets, Cahier du Centre de Rocherche sur l'Image, le Symbole, le Mythe* (Presse universitaires de Dijon, 1989).

49. Flaubert, *Correspondance*, cited by J. Rousset, *Forme et Signification* (Paris: José Corti, 1962), p. 127.

50. Théophile Gautier, *Le Capitaine Fracasse* (Paris: Gallimard Folio, 1972), p. 124.

51. Ibid., preface, p. 18.

52. Oscar Wilde, *Le Portrait de Dorian Gray* [*Portrait of Dorian Gray*], in Oeuvres (Paris: Stock, 1977), I, p. 38.

Chapter 7

1. Cited by J. Duvernoy, *Le Registre d'inquisition de Jacques Fournier* (Paris: Mouton, 1978), p. 283.

2. Cited by J. Baltrusaïtis, *Le Miroir* (Paris: Elmayan-Seuil, 1978), p. 194.

3. A. Delatte, *La Catoptromancie grecque* (Liège: H. Vaillant-Carmanne, 1932), p. 28.

4. Ibid., p. 41.

5. *Bullarium romanorum pontificorum* (Turin, 1860), III, p. 2.

6. J.-B. Thiers, *Traité des superstitions* (1702 edition), I, p. 127.

7. P. de Ronsard, *Hymnes*, "Les Daimons" (Paris: Gallimard [La Pléiade], 1950), II, p. 174.

8. G. Cardano, *De la Subtilité* (Paris, 1556), folio 89.

9. A. d'Aubigné, *Lettres touchant quelques points de diverses sciences* (Paris: Gallimard [La Pléiade], 1969), p. 855.

10. G. B. Della Porta, *La Magie naturelle*, L. IV, ch. 4, p. 348.

11. J. Baltrusaïtis, *Le Miroir*, ch. 8.

12. Collin de Plancy, *Dictionnaire infernal* (1865 edition), p. 145.

13. J. Bertaut, *Oeuvres poétiques*, "Timandre" (1601) (1891 edition), p. 217.

14. H. Martin, *Le Métier de prédicateur* (Paris: Cerf, 1989), p. 445.

15. V. de Beauvais, *Speculum doctrinale*, ch. 176.

16. J. Dupin (1302–1374), *Le Roman de Mandevie*, n.d. folio 53.

17. J. Gerson, *Oeuvres* (Paris: Desclée, 1973), IX, p. 158.

18. R. Van Marle, *Iconographie de l'art profane* 2 vols. (The Hague: M. Nijhoff, 1931–1932), II, p. 54. Cf. also *Lo specchio e il doppio* (Milan: Fabbri, 1987), pp. 157–167.

19. Comenius, *Janua linguarum* (Geneva, 1638), no. 158.

20. On the engravings of the woman at the mirror, see S. Matthews-Grieco, *Ange ou Diablesse, la représentation de la femme au XVIe siècle* (Paris: Flammarion, 1991).

21. J. de Sponde, "Méditation sur le Psaume 48," *Méditations* (1588) (Paris: J. Carti, 1954), p. 130.

22. Puttenham, *The Arte of English Poesie*, 1589, p. 19. The mirror-imagination association was widespread in the sixteenth century; both engendered monsters and chimera. Cf. also Dampmartin, *De la Connaissance des merveilles du monde et de l'homme* (1585), folio 126.

23. M. M. Martinet, *Le Miroir de l'esprit dans le théâtre élisabéthain* (Paris: Didier, 1981), p. 82 and following.

24. A. Du Laurens, *Discours sur la conservation de la veue, des maladies melancholiques, des catharres, de la vieillesse* (Paris, 1597), p. 110; and M. Scève, La Délie, emblem 26. Cf. J. Starobinski, *La Mélancolie au miroir* (Paris: Julliard, 1989).

25. M. Psellus, *Traité par dialogue de l'énergie ou opération des diables*, tran. P. Morineau (1576), pp. 26–27.

26. J. Molinet, "Le Miroir de vie," in *Faicts et dictz de Jean Molinet* (Paris: Société des anciens textes français, 1937), II, p. 673.

27. J. Le Loyer, *Discours sur les spectres* (Paris, 1608), p. 47.

28. Josse Bade, *La Nef des folles* (n. d.), folio 7.

29. *Eulenspiegel*, stories 40 and 95. Cf. J. Lefebvre, *Les Fols et la Folie* (Paris: Klincksieck, 1968), p. 283.

30. Cf. S. Matthews-Grieco, *Ange ou Diablesse la représentation de la femme au XVIe siecle* (Paris: Flammarion, 1991).

31. L. Mâle, *L'Art religieux au XIIIe siècle* (Paris: A. Colin, 1931), p. 121. Cf. also "L'Iconographie de Vénus et de son miroir à la fin du Moyen Age," in *L'Erotisme au Moyen Age*, 3e Colloque de l'Institut d'Etudes médiévales (Montréal, 1977).

32. G. de Tervarent, *Attributs et Symboles dans l'art profane* (Geneva: Droz, 1959), II, p. 354.

33. P. de Ronsard, *Les Amours*, "La Quenoille" (Paris: Gallimard [La Pléiade], 1974), I, p. 168.

34. G. de Lorris, *Le Roman de la Rose*, I, v. 550 and following.

35. "La Complainte du trop tost marié," in P. U. Nystrom, *Poèmes français sur les biens d'un ménage* (Helin, 1940), p. 23.

36. Jean de Caures, *Oeuvres morales* (1584), VI, 11, folio 305. Cf. also Jean de Marconville, *De la Bonté et Mauvaiseté des femmes* (Paris: Côté femmes, 1991), p. 63.

37. S. Matthews-Grieco, *Ange ou Diablesse*, p. 275.

38. Clément d'Alexandrie, *Le Pédagogue* (Sources chrétiennes no. 158), III, 2, p. 31.

39. Tertullian, *La Toilette des femmes* (Sources chrétiennes no. 173), I, 1, p. 47.

40. Cited by J. Wirth, *La Jeune Fille et la Mort* (Geneva: Droz, 1979), p. 64.

41. S. Brant, *La Nef des fous* (Strasbourg, 1977), p. 360.

42. G. de Deguilleville, *Le Pèlerinage de l'âme humaine*, folio 49. Dante, "Purgatorio," XIII, v. 22–154.

43. J. Clair, *Méduse* (Paris: Gallimard, 1989); illustr. 32.

44. H. Martin, *Le Métier de prédicateur*, p. 368.

45. C. de La Tour-Landry, *De L'Education des filles* (Paris, 1866), p. 70.

46. R. Brusegan, "Femmes au miroir," in *Diables et Diableries* (Geneva: Musée d'Art et d'Histoire, 1977).

47. *Acta Sanctorum*, VIII, p. 813.

48. Otto Rank, *Le Double* (Paris: Payot, 1975), p. 85, note 2.

49. Hélinant de Froidmont, *Ver de la Mort*, verse II. On the theme of the mirror and death, Jean Delumeau (*Le Péché et la Peur* [Paris: Fayard, 1983]) cites a canticle still sung in the eighteenth century and directly inspired by the *Contemptus mundi*: "Contemplate this lugubrious object (the cadaver)/Look at yourself—you see ashes and dust reflected there/. . . You will never know how to see yourself/In a more loyal mirror," p. 405. Cf. also pp. 94 and 375.

50. J. Wirth, *La Jeune Fille et la Mort*, p. 83.

51. Shakespeare, Sonnet 77, ed. C. J. Sisson, Riverside edition.

52. J. Wirth, *La Jeune Fille et la Mort*.

53. Cited by E. Panofsky, *Les Primitifs flamands* (Paris: Hazan, 1992), p. 17.

54. Cf. G.F. Hartlaub, *Zauber der spiegel* (Munich: R. Piper, 1951).

55. On this theme, cf. the fifteenth story of the *Heptameron* by Marguerite de Navarre.

56. S. Melchior-Bonnet: "Narcisse au féminin, une fiction de la Renaissance," in *Miroirs et Reflets, Cahier du Centre de recherche sur l'Image, le Symbole, le Mythe* (Dijon: Press Universitaires de Dijon, 1989).

57. Marin, *Madrigaux*, "Dame qui se mire," LXXII.

58. G. Corrozet, *Les Blasons domestiques*; Fr. Bérenger de la Tour d'Albenas, "Le miroir."

59. Aguolo Firenzuola, *Discours de la Beauté des Dames*, trans. J. Pallet (Paris, 1578), folio 31.

60. Cervantès, *Don Quichotte de la Manche* (Paris: Gallimard [La Pléiade], 1956), part 1, ch. 33, p. 322.

61. L. Beyerlinck, *Magnum Theatrum vitae humanae* (Anvers, 1631), art. "Speculum," VI, p. 299.

62. F. Sénault, *L'Homme criminel* (Paris, 1663), p. 63.

63. Dom Vincent, "Conférence pour une profession monastique," *Les Orateurs sacrés, Encycl. Migne,* CVIII, col. 796.

64. V. Houdry, "Sermons," *La Bibliothèque des prédicateurs* (1715), II, p. 708.

65. Mme. Guyon, *Vie* (Paris: Mercure de France, 1988), p. 64.

66. P. Tronson, *Examens particuliers* (Paris 1927), ch. 97, p. 226.

67. Odile Arnold, *Le Corps et l'Ame* (Paris: Seuil, 1984).

68. Cf. the rules of the communities studied by Martine Sonnet, *L'Education des filles à Paris au XVIIIe siècle* (Paris: Cerf, 1986). Warnings were reiterated in the nineteenth century. A famous manual offers this advice to the woman taking her bath: "Since the involuntary embarrassment of modesty prevents the easy completion of these important tasks, without which the bath is more harmful than healthy, wrap yourself well in your robe and, if necessary, close your eyes until you have finished this operation" (Madame Cénart, *Manuel des Dames*, 2nd edition [1833], p. 37). Up until the middle of the twentieth century, former schoolgirls educated in convents confirm that they could not take a bath without being wrapped in a blouse.

69. D. Roche, "Education et Société dans la France du XVIIIe siècle, l'exemple de la maison royale de Saint-Cyr," in *Cahiers d'histoire* (1978), no. 1, pp. 3–24.

70. *Instruction chrétienne des jeunes filles* (1715), p. 273.

71. *Geistliche weihranchkorner oder andacht lieder* (Nuremberg, 1652), I, 12: "I certainly see an image, but it is not Thine, O God, that Thou hast given me. The sin is that within me that breaks Thy mirror. Thou shall, however, reassemble the pieces."

72. N. Pasquier, *Lettres* (Paris, 1632), L. 1, p. 280.

73. E. Gauthier, *Traité contre l'amour des parures*, 2nd edition (1780), p. 122.

74. P. Caussin, *La Femme, ses vertus, ses défauts* (1864 edition), III, p. 211.

75. A. Petit, *Le Miroir* (Paris, 1747).

76. P. Le Moyne, *Les Femmes, la Modestie et la Bienséance chrétienne* (1667), (Paris, 1868 edition), p. 75.

77. B. Lamy, *De la connaissance de soy-mesme* (Paris, 1669), p. 57.

78. J. Delumeau, *Le Péché et la Peur*, p. 477.

79. J. Ancelin, *L'Amant ressuscité*, (1658) (Geneva: Slatkine, 1980), p. 14.

80. A. Ferrand, *Histoire des amours de Cléante et Bélise* (1687) (Geneva: Slatkine, 1979), p. 36.

81. Mademoiselle de Scudéry, *Conversations morales* (Paris, 1686), pp. 85–148.

Chapter 8

1. E. Tabourot, *Les Apophtegmes du Sieur Gaulard* (Rouen, 1626), p. 9.

2. M. Proust, *A la Recherche du temps perdu* (Paris: Gallimard, 1987), I, 8.

3. S. Freud, "L'inquiétante étrangeté," *Essais de psychanalyse appliquée* (Paris: Gallimard, 1952), p. 205.

4. L. B. Alberti, *Traité de la peinture* (Paris: Macula, 1992), p. 193.

5. Montaigne, *The Complete Essays*, trans. M. A. Screech (New York: Penguin Classics, 1991), p. 1208.

6. Ibid., p. 40.

7. Ibid., p. 995.

8. Svetlana Alpers, *L'Art de dépeindre, la peinture hollandaise au XVIIe siecle* (Paris: Gallimard, 1990), p. 117. She compares this famous nude to a painting by Goltzius representing Venus as seen from three juxtaposed perspectives: a live woman, a painted representation, and a reflection.

9. J.-B. Chassignet, "Retourne le miroir," *Le Mespris de la vie*, CCLXXIV.

10. Mirami, cited by Baltrusaïtis, *Le Miroir* (Paris: Elmayan-Seuil, 1978), p. 241.

11. L. Van Delft, *La Morale classique* (Geneva: Droz, 1982), p. 145.

12. Sonnet d'Etelan, "Le Miroir," cited by Jean Rousset, *Anthologie de la poésie baroque*, 2nd edition (Paris: A. Colin, 1968), p. 255. Cf. also Cecilia Rizza, "L'Image dans le miroir," in *Baroque* 3 (Montauban, 1969).

13. Puget de la Serre, *Le Miroir qui ne flatte point* (Paris, 1668), p. 11.

14. Le Moyne, *Les Peintures morales* (Paris, 1645), l. 5, p. 499.

15. Cf. G. R. Hocke, *Le Labyrinthe de l'art fantastique* (Paris: Gonthier, 1967), p. 110.

16. Comenius, *Le Labyrinthe de l'âme*; B. Gracian, *El Criticon*.

17. Plato, *Phèdre*, 255, and *Le Premier Alcibiade*, 132d.

18. M. Scève, *Microcosme*, I, lines 213–218.

19. Cl. de Taillemont, *Champ a plesir*, cited by J. Eymard, *Le Miroir dans la poésie française* (Lille: Université de Lille III, 1975), p. 475.

20. Cited by J. Frappier, "Variations sur le thème du miroir de Bernard de Ventadour à Maurice Scève," *CAIEF* (1959):134–158.

21. R. Belleau, "Amours et Nouveaux Eschanges," in *Poèmes du XVIe siècle* (Paris: Gallimard [La Pléiade], 1953), p. 543.

22. M. Scève, *La Délie*, stanza 307.

23. Aragon, *Le fou d'Elsa*, cf. J. Lacan, *Séminaire XI* (1975).

24. M. Tetel, *Lectures scèviennes* (Paris: Klincksieck, 1983), "Poésie et spécularité," p. 100 and following.

25. J. Froissart, *Poésies*, "L'Espinette amoureuse." These magical mirrors are innumerable in literature. There is the magic fountain of *L'Astrée*, which has the unusual quality of revealing not only the face of one's beloved, but also of discovering the true face of the lover. Goethe, Lewis, and Gautier make the ideal woman appear in the mirror. Germaine de Staël literally transcribes these scenes by making Corinne see the reflection of the man she loves in the Trevi fountain.

26. J. Starobinski, *L'Oeil vivant* (Paris: Gallimard, 1961), p. 218.

27. Stendhal, *Le Rose et le Vert* (Gallimard Folio, 1982), p. 249.

28. Flaubert employs this method on several occasions.

29. Goethe, *Voyage de Wilhelm Meister* (Paris: Gallimard [La Pléiade], 1954), p. 1057.

30. L. Fioravanti, *Miroir des arts et des sciences* (Paris, 1602), p. 104.

31. G. B. Della Porta, *La Magie naturelle,* p. 348.

32. J. Baltrusaïtis, *Anamorphoses ou Perspectives curieuses*, O. Perrin, 1st edition, 1955, 2nd edition, 1985. Cf. also J.-Cl. Margolin, "Aspects du surréalisme au XVIe siècle," *Bibliothèque d'Humanisme et Renaissance*, 1977.

33. C. Chevalley de Buson, "La Rationalité de l'anamorphose," *XVIIe Siècle* (24 July 1979):296.

34. J.-F. Nicéron, *La Perspective curieuse* (Paris, 1638), p. 71.

35. Athanasius Kircher, *Physiologia* (Amstel, 1680), p. 125.

36. *Le Temple de la paresse. Recueil de pièces nouvelles et galantes* (Cologne, 1667), p. 100.

37. J. Starobinski, *L'Invention de la liberté* (Geneva: Albert Skira, 1965), p. 14.

38. P. Scuri, "Lo Specchio Rococo," *Rassegna: Attraverso lo specchio*, March 1983.

39. Le Camus de Mézières, *Le Génie de l'architecture* (Paris, 1780), p. 119 and following.

40. La Mettrie, *L'Art de jouir, Oeuvres*, t. 3, 1796, p. 210.

41. D.-V. Denon, *Point de lendemain*, in *Les Romanciers français du XVIIe siècle* (Paris: Gallimard [La Pléiade], 1965), p. 397.

42. Cited by J. Rousset, *L'Intérieur et l'Extérieur* (Paris: José Corti, 1969), p. 203. Many boudoirs and houses of assignation decorated with mirrors can be found in literature from the eighteenth century on: for example, in Louvet's *Une Année de la vie de Faublas* and in Sade's *Zoloe*. In *Ferragus,* Balzac describes the ideal bedroom for lovers as one decorated with mirrors.

43. "In perverse voyeurism, everything is set in motion by the subject to assure that he is seen seeing and thus captured by censure, as though he expected from it the cohesion he lacks," writes Gérard Bonnet (*Voir, être vu* [Paris: PUF, 1983], II, p. 67).

Chapter 9

1. Rétif de la Bretonne, *Monsieur Nicolas, Oeuvres* (Paris: Gallimard [La Pléiade], 1989), p. 21.

2. D. W. Winnicot, *Jeu et Réalité* (Paris: Gallimard, 1971), p. 156.

3. In certain cosmogonies of late antiquity in Greece, it is Dionysus's murder by the Titans that explained the state of man tossed into the world: in order to attract his attention, the Titans (or jealous Hera, according to another version) offered different toys, including a mirror to the child Dionysus, born of Zeus and a mortal woman, and they took advantage of

his fascination with his reflection to strike and slaughter him. For the Neoplatonic commentator, the soul inserted into the visible world, preoccupied with its reflection and therefore with its body, allows itself to be torn apart and dispersed by passions as was Dionysus by the Titans.

4. Pär Lagerkvist, *Le Nain* [*The Dwarf*] (Paris: Stock, 1946), p. 50: "When one moves away from the mirror, it is preferable that the image not remain frozen and that noone be able to capture it; I understand why one might refuse to have his portrait made." Available in the English translation by Alexandra Dick, *The Dwarf* (New York: Noonday Press, 1998).

5. Marguerite de Valois, *Mémoires* (Paris: Société de l'Histoire de France, 1824), p. 2.

6. P. Mabille, "Miroirs," *Le Minotaure* 11 (1938). François Mauriac, who was shown a film of himself from a news report, confessed his utter dismay and astonishment: "We think we see ourselves in the mirror, but this is not true. When I saw the old man come into my living room, I thought that it was an older person. I was dismayed. We are no more familiar with our physical aspect than with the sound of our voice." Cited by G. Gusdorf, *Les Ecritures du moi* (Paris: Odile Jacob, 1990), p. 130. Studies addressing the perception of one's own voice have demonstrated the frequency of negative judgments, or our general lack of recognition of this voice.

7. Cf. the very rich articles collected by J. Corraze, *Image spéculaire du corps* (Toulouse: Privat, 1980).

8. R. Barthes, *Camera Lucida,* trans. Richard Howard (New York, Hill and Wang, 1981), p. 12.

9. G. Edvards, cited by G. Gusdorf, *Les Ecritures du moi*, p. 130.

10. Ph. Lejeune, *Moi aussi* (Paris: Seuil, 1986).

11. Shakespeare, *Richard II*, IV, 1, in *The Works of Shakespeare*, ed. John Dover Wilson (London: Cambridge University Press, 1939), pp. 76–77.

12. The psychoanalyst René Major mentions a young female patient who no longer recognized her image in the mirror. It was when she shattered the mirror that she could identify herself. The broken piece caused an appropriate representation of herself to symbolically appear.

13. E. Delacroix, *Journal* (Paris: Plon, 1932), I, p. 107.

14. Andre Gide wrote his *Journal* in front of a mirror.

15. Th. Gautier in *Salon de 1859* (Paris, 1859). This book is a collection of art reviews by Gautier, Baudelaire, and others.

16. Th. Gautier, *Le Roi Candaule, Spirite*, in *Oeuvres* (Geneva: Slatkine, 1978). Spirite, the ideal young girl, is the substitute for the castrating mother, whose real presence in the widow reactivates the threat.

17. *Les Veilles de Bonaventura* (1801), cited by A. Montandon in "Le Double dans le romantisme allemand," *Le Double dans la littérature anglo-américaine*, publication of the Faculté des Lettres de Clermont-Ferrand, 1984.

18. H. F. Amiel, *Journal* (Paris: Stock, 1927), II, p. 137, April 19, 1876. He later adds: "Inconsistent, vaporous, illusory, my wakefulness is known as the dream of a dream."

19. L. Andreyev, *La Pensée* (Paris: Ed. Ombres, 1989).

20. J. Lhermitte, "L'Image de notre corps," *Nouvelle Revue critique*, 1939. E. Blumel, "L'Hallucination du double," *Ornicar Analytica* 22. The subjects prey to this sort of hallucination describe their double as a gray and amorphous shape.

21. Cited by H. Faure, *Les Objets de la folie* (Paris: PUF, 1966), II, p. 50.

22. G. de Nerval, *Aurélia* (Paris: Gallimard Folio), p. 296.

23. Otto Rank, *Don Juan et son Double* (Paris: Denoël, 1932).

24. Maupassant "Le Horla," in *Contes et Nouvelles* (Paris: Albin Michel, 1956), pp. 1120–1121. J. Postel describes this phenomenon as "confused-dreamlike episodes at the beginning of a general paralysis" (*Image spéculaire du corps*). Charcot had specifically referred to a case of prosopoagnosia.

25. Ph. de Bonnefils, "Maupassant," in *Naturalisme*, 10.18 (1978), 287.

26. Cf. for example "La Morte," in the collection *La Main gauche*, ed. Rencontre, p. 160.

27. With *The Student of Prague*, the cinema of the 1930s created a spectacular image of the mirrored double.

28. R. M. Rilke, *Les Cahiers de Malte Laurids Brigge, Oeuvres* (Paris: Seuil, 1966), I, pp. 598–600.

29. M. Blanchot, *L'Espace littéraire* (Paris: Gallimard Folio, 1955), p. 166.

30. R. M. Rilke, *Sonnets à Orphée, Oeuvres,* II, p. 395. These pages are comparable to those of Mallarmé where Igitur sees "the phantom of horror gradually absorbing what was left of sentiment and pain in the mirror." The transparency of the mirror is linked with death, the "beautiful diamond of emptiness," which leads one to feel the suffocating weight of eternity. *Igitur* (Paris: Gallimard [La Pléiade], 1945), p. 441.

31. On the symbolism of the mirror, cf. J. Michaud, "Le Thème du miroir dans le symbolisme français," *CAIEF*, p. 199.

32. Lewis Carroll. *Through the Looking-Glass* (New York: Horace Liveright, 1925), p. 171.

33. Ibid., p. 218.

34. J. Cocteau, *Orphée*, scene 7.

35. The Belgian poet G. Rodenbach presents just such a pathetic experience. He writes: "the friend of mirrors," leans tirelessly over "their fluid mystery," but then one day, they reject reciprocity and become greedy and voracious. Mirror images, which connect like roads and form a labyrinth through which seductive women constantly pass back and forth, invite the poet to enter: "It must be really pleasant in the mirror." The dreamer projects himself into the irreal world of his hallucinations. At dawn he is

found, delirious and covered with blood, at the foot of the mirror. *Le Rouet de brumes* (Paris: Flammarion, n.d.), pp. 32–38.

36. J. Rigaut, *Ecrits* (Paris: Gallimard, 1979), pp. 51–66.

37. Cited by Sami Ali, *Corps réel, corps imaginaire* (Paris: Bordas, 1977), p. 119.

38. Henri Michaux, *Plume, précéde de Lointain Intérieur* (Paris: Gallimard, 1963), p. 215.

39. Michel Leiris, *Francis Bacon* (Paris: Albin Michel, 1987).

40. Cited by Sami Ali, *Le Banal* (Paris: Gallimard 1980), p. 71.

41. In *La Mise à mort* by L. Aragon (Paris: Gallimard, 1965), the act of putting to death the subject and a *mise-en-abîme* of the narrative illustrates the end of an illusory plenitude of the narrator. The multilayered story is read in juxtaposed sections, in exactly the same way that the three-way mirror offers its owner, Christian, long, varying lines of reflections, "the regiment of Christians and Company." Man exists only in a series, "angel series, demon series, calico series," in repeated and devalued images, "dizzyingly similar and dissimilar." The book ends with a broken mirror.

42. G. Perec, *L'Homme qui dort* (Paris: Denoël, 1967), p. 150.

43. J. L. Borgès, "Les Miroirs," *L'Auteur et Autres textes* (Paris: Gallimard, 1953), p. 121; also "La Rose profonde," in the same book, p. 162.

Conclusion

1. J. Starobinski, *La Mélancolie au miroir* (Paris: Julliard, 1989), p. 25.

2. Simone de Beauvoir writes at length on feminine narcissism: "The woman, knowing herself, making an object of herself, believes that she is really able to see herself in the mirror. . . . Bored with household chores, she has the spare time to dream up her own face." *Le Deuxième Sexe* [*The Second Sex*] (Paris: Gallimard, 1949), II, pp. 459–465.

3. Chéri Colette, *Oeuvres complètes* (Paris: Flammarion, 1959), VI, p. 158.

4. J.-P. Sartre, *Les Mots* (Paris: Gallimard, 1968), p. 52.

5. M. Kundera, *L'Immortalité* (Paris: Gallimard, 1990). Available in English translation by Peter Kussi, *Immortality* (New York: HarperCollins), 1999.

6. Fr. Dagognet, *Corps réfléchis* (Paris: Odile Jacob, 1991), pp. 256–257.

7. Régis Debray, *Cours de médiologie générale* (Paris: Gallimard, 1991), p. 387.

8. For example, *L'Eve nouvelle* by Barbey d'Aurevilly or *L'Invention de Morel* by Bioy Casares.

Index

Index

Index

Index

Index

Index